HISTORICAL
METHODS
IN MASS COMMUNICATION

COMMUNICATION TEXTBOOK SERIES

Jennings Bryant — Editor

General Communication Theory and Methodology

Jennings Bryant — Advisor

STARTT/SLOAN • Historical
Methods in Mass
Communication

HISTORICAL
METHODS
IN MASS COMMUNICATION

James D. Startt
Wm. David Sloan

LAWRENCE ERLBAUM ASSOCIATES, PUBLISHERS

1989   Hillsdale, New Jersey   Hove and London

Lawrence Erlbaum Associates, Inc., Publishers
365 Broadway
Hillsdale, New Jersey 07642

Library of Congress Cataloging-in-Publication Data

Startt, James D., 1932–
    Historical methods in mass communication / by James D. Startt and
Wm. David Sloan.
       p.   cm.
    Bibliography: p.
    Includes index.
    ISBN 0-8058-0433-1:
    1. Mass media—Methodology. 2. Mass meda—Historiography.
I. Sloan, W. David (William David), 1947–   . II. Title.
P91.S72 1989
001.51—dc19   888-26033
                                                               CIP

Printed in the United States of America
10 9 8 7 6 54 3 2

Contents

Acknowledgments

We appreciate the contributions of several colleagues and assistants in the preparation of this book. Two librarians at Valparaiso University, Ellen B. Meyer and Judith K. Miller, contributed their advice and assistance to Chapter 5. Dr. William Horne of the Broadcasting and Film Communication Department at the University of Alabama offered valuable suggestions and criticism for our discussion of mass communication sources in Chapter 6. We appreciate their enthusiasm for this book and have benefited from their counsel and expertise. Dai Minxiang, Chris Roberts, Penny Poole, and Christine Thompson, University of Alabama students, spent innumerable hours helping in the mechanical preparation of the manuscript.

Preface

An interest in history permeates Western civilization. The past find its way occasionally into the thoughts of most people; it fascinates others. For some, the study of history becomes a life's work. Of those, some are drawn especially to communication history. They have selected for study a subject that has played an integral part in mankind's and in this nation's past. For almost two centuries American historians have been studying communication; and all signs indicate that, rather than declining, the interest in communication history is on the rise. That interest raises the question of why study history, and, more specifically, communication history.

Besides the simple enjoyment they derive from studying history, historians, and students as well, give various answers. Coming from professional backgrounds in such areas as journalism and advertising, some want to learn from the past so that they may be better practitioners in their professions. Oriented primarily toward the present rather than the past, some examine the past to help them find the roots of present practices. Others pragmatically believe they can learn mistakes of the past so that they can avoid repeating the errors, while others think they can use the past to help prepare for the future.

All these views may have some validity -- some, more than others -- but the serious historian finds that the study of history is valuable primarily in other ways. First, it helps us to understand the past. Although historians may first approach the past for some other reason, with continued study they find that it has intrinsic value in itself. They wish to study the past for its own sake. Second, the study of history can help us understand people. Conditions and times may change, communication technologies and publishing and broadcasting enterprises come and go, but human nature, the human character, human relationships, and the human spirit endure. Third, it can help us understand the present. Its value, however, is not simply in helping discover the paths by which the present emerged, but in revealing particulars from the past which may serve as comparisons with the present, as lenses through which to consider our own times. Fourth, the study of history is valuable for the intellectual stimulation it provides. Professional communication schools today emphasize courses of study to prepare students for careers, but the true value of education lies in developing a critical intellect in the student. The study of history, requiring as it does rigorous and mature thinking, helps nurture the intellect as few other disciplines can do.

For the study of history to provide its benefits, however, it must be done properly. The purpose of this book is to guide communication historians and history students in the methods of proper research. It is structured in such a way as to assist both the beginning researcher and the experienced historian. The student doing his or her first historical study will find instruction in the fundamentals of sound research necessary for all projects beginning with the most elementary, while the established historian will find material and discussion of matters that must be considered by the mature researcher. It also is intended to assist historians who come to communication from other fields by providing reference material and assistance on problems specific to communication history. Communication researchers who are not historians also will find, we hope, the advice offered here of value as they attempt to expand their knowledge of various methods that can be used fruitfully in their own studies.

Historical research, the oldest form in communication, also is the most modern. Other methods of research from the social and behavioral sciences became popular in communication studies in the second half of the twentieth century. At first, researchers greeted them confidently as the ways to answer all questions. But as researchers matured and the methods lost their newness, scholars began to subject the methods to more critical scrutiny. The methods lost some of their sheen, but the scrutiny also refined them. Researchers are now more aware of the limitations of behavioral and social science methods, and they recognize that much refinement still is needed. Historical methods, being as old as they are, for generations have been subjected to similar scrutiny and refinement. But they, unlike soft-science methods, are long past their infancy, and historians through long practice have tested them. Those that were usable, they refined. The useless, they discarded. The result is that historical research now is based on an assorted but cohesive set of tested and proven methods. While mature compared with many other methods, historical methods at the same time are in many ways the most modern. Historians have not been oblivious to the methods used by other researchers and have readily adopted those refined, proven methods as they have shown themselves useful to the study of the past. Incorporating the most recent research devices, historical study therefore has remained at the forefront of contemporary methodology.

Historical research also possesses an intrinsic ability, unlike other methods used in communication research, to study almost the total range of the human experience. It is not so esoteric as other fields of theoretical, behavioral communication research. The methods of social and behavioral sciences cannot fully study the life of man, but historical research can incorporate most other communication research methods. Combining them with methods unique to the study of history, it is not as limited or as limiting as other communication research methods and therefore can come closest to helping us understand mankind in its full dimensions. History therefore is the preeminent study among the various fields of communication research, for it brings together the methods, findings, and insights of the others and shapes them into a coherent explanation of mankind.

As one recognizes the vast range of methods used in history and the broad expanse of the fields it covers, one comes to realize that historical study is neither simple nor easy. It requires much from the historian, considerably more than is normally expected from other communication researchers. The rigor of method and amount of work necessary cannot be overstated. Foremost, historical study demands an absolute desire to find the truth. Commitment to a philosophy, an ideology, a theoretical framework must take a backseat. Commitment to anything other than truth cannot be tolerated.

Furthermore, history requires unsurpassed rigor. Historians must bring thoroughness and tirelessness to the effort of collecting and analyzing source material. The task may sometimes require hour upon hour of research to find the minutest detail. Historians also must have or must develop an acute thinking ability. Unlike communication researchers who use social and behavioral research methods, historians rarely have mathematical formulae and statistical systems on which to rely. In judging and analyzing research material, they must depend on their own mature judgment, critical mind, and incisive analytical ability. While harshly analytical, they also must be judicious in their treatment of the material and the people whom they study. The search for historical truth requires that they deal openly and fairly with their subjects.

Finally, historians, must have a power of imagination. The cold facts of history alone are nothing more than cold facts. They remain dead unless subjected to the thoughtful, imaginative mind of the historian who can perceive relationships among the materials and meaning in them. It is the duty of the historian to breathe life into them. Piling data upon data is not enough. As the historian Page Smith, winner of the Bancroft prize for his biography *John Adams*, has commented in regard to researchers who amass research but never bring life to it, "Research is too often a substitute for thought, for bold speculation, for enlightening generalization."[1] In summary, historical research cannot be based on vague, haphazard, lackadaisical method. It must be founded on rigorous, proven methodological procedures and an incisive mind.

Finally, a word about what this book does and what it does not do. It is based on the fundamentals of historical research. It eschews the vague "philosophical" and "theoretical" and "grand theory" recommendations that are faddish among some communication historians today. Likewise, while taking account of the usually quantitative methods drilled into graduate students in theoretical communication programs, it attempts to keep those methods in perspective as only one limited part of research necessary in history.

The concept underlying this book is that historians and students must have a knowledge of the well-prescribed methods which have proven themselves. It therefore is offered as guidance for communication historians who wish to improve their skills and for students who wish to learn the fundamentals of historical research.

Let the authors be permitted one final observation. We have approached the study of communication history as primarily history rather than primarily communication. It is our belief that the broader perspective brings to communication historians a greater recognition of the potential value of their research. To reach its broader potential, however, communication history must move beyond the generally poor standards of scholarship now present in that field of study. By associating themselves with the broad study of history, we believe, they will become more aware that their research must meet the high standards required of historical study. No less should be acceptable or expected.

---

[1]Page Smith, *The Historian and History* (New York: Alfred A. Knopf, 1964), 145.

1

The Nature of History

Everyone thinks about the past. The habit is a human indulgence. In fact, the reasons an individual contemplates the past are endless. To some, interest in history is a matter of genealogical curiosity about their own family; to others, a matter of civic pride or patriotism. For yet others, it is a matter of interest stimulated in a person or aspect of the past by film, fiction, or some experience of life. Perhaps those courses in history, taken by choice or by compulsion in school, can claim some responsibility for stimulating an historical interest. Let us hope at least that they did not dull interest, for history is a natural form of thought for modern man. As such, it can be a burden or an inspiration, a curse or a blessing, a source of confidence or a source of confusion. History lends itself to both use and abuse. The past is also the object of attention for those men and women who call themselves historians, people who devote their professional lives to a serious study of its many facets. These scholars believe their labor is as important as truth and hope that it will set a standard for others in their treatment of historical knowledge.

History as a Form of Knowledge

The essence of history lies in present thought about particular things in the past. The Hebrews were the first to think of historical time as linear rather than cyclical (that is, as moving from beginning to end rather than as repeating itself). We normally, however, credit ancient Greeks, despite their cyclical concept, with inventing the study of history. In a sense, historians today still work under the timeless shadow of Herodotus and Thucydides, those two Greek writers who gave birth to history as a literary form. It has survived as a subject of commanding importance to this day, although it had to endure inhospitable medieval centuries before emerging in its modern form.

What do these two founders have to do with the study of communication history today? The answer is: quite a bit. Herodotus, "the Father of History," opened *The Persian Wars* by explaining that he was publishing his "researches...in the hope of...preserving from decay the remembrance of what men have done...."[1] Few historians have written better or told a better story or conveyed more of a sense of humanity than he. Herodotus, curious about the Persians as well as the Greeks, conducted a careful inquiry into the people and cultures involved in the famous war of which he wrote. Although he intended his history to be humanistic rather than mythical or theistic, his interest in cultures led him to include myths and tales in his writing when he believed them to be part of the whole culture he was describing. His subject, however, was the deeds of men. Thucydides, on the other hand, seems even more modern. He turned to man's records for his classic study, *The Peloponnesian War*. As he tells us early in that masterpiece, he measured the accuracy of his evidence against the "most severe and detailed tests possible."[2] Both men sought to produce an account of a singular event worthy, they thought, of contemplation then and in the future.

These two ancient historians provide many clues regarding the nature of history. From its inception in their hands, history has been neither theistic nor mythological. Although religion has been a central idea in the works of many Western historians, history has been primarily a humanistic study, an exploration into what people have done. It is a form of inquiry into the past that asks questions about the things people have done and elicits answers based on evidence. In that process there is a story to be told and truth to be found. Most of all, Herodotus and Thucydides alert us to the fact that when historians deal with the study of the past, they assume that it possesses certain characteristics. What are these characteristics? That short question can produce a long answer. Nevertheless, it is possible to offer a brief response to it, however tentative it might be, by suggesting that historical study contains at least three elements: (a) evidence, (b) interpretation, and (c) narrative. Let us consider each

---

[1]Herodotus, *The Persian Wars,* trans. George Rawlinson (New York: Random House, The Modern Library, 1942), 3.

[2]Thucydides, *The Peloponnesian War*, trans. R. Crawley (New York: Random House, The Modern Library, 1934), 14.

for a moment.

First, take the matter of evidence. Since the time of Herodotus, evidence has been the basis for history. Without it one does not have history. Beyond that, it should be appreciated that when modern historians speak of evidence they have a certain kind of evidence in mind. This evidence, collectively called "the record," can be described first as a record of reality. It is an account of what real people in the past did or failed to do. Thus history is restricted to the study of the human past and accordingly is viewed as an investigation apart from the natural past, the mythological past, or the theistic past. Beyond that, the evidence historians use is that which has been screened and tested to assure as much accuracy as possible. A major portion of the historian's effort must be devoted to proper use of evidence.

Regarding the matter of interpretation, it stands to reason that references to history as the reconstruction of the past actually refer to reconstruction as an interpretive act. When the historian reconstructs something from the past, think of the material that is never available for the process. How much of the past has been lost forever? How little we know even about great events, figures, and movements that occurred in times past!

Ask yourself, how much do we actually know about many of the famous publicists of the last several centuries, and how much of that does the record prove beyond doubt? Complete sources providing answers to all one might wish to know about some past figure or event are seldom, if ever, available. Sometimes governments, institutions, or individuals place restrictions on records. In other instances, the desired record may never have been made in the first place. Consequently, historians cannot find all the source information they might wish to know about human motive and opinion and many other things. Sometimes historical records have been lost or destroyed. Communication historians encounter this problem frequently. Records needed for their studies may have been too bulky or too expensive to keep.

The problem of incomplete records hinders even probes into the recent past. In his book *So It Was True: The American Protestant Press and the Nazi Persecution of the Jews*, a study for which one might suppose a full record of publications would exist, Robert W. Ross warns that this was not the case. "All of the periodicals were not available for all of the years between 1933 and 1945," he explains. "Some published in 1933 became victims of the Great Depression and either went out of business or merged with other existing periodicals."[3] On the other hand, think of the amount of published material that he had to distill in order to write that book.

Consider the vastness of the limited, or even small, piece of the total past that remains in the historical record as it is left, collected, and passed from generation to generation. One cannot know it all equally; nor can one make it all a part of historical explanation. Historians select information from the record to include in their studies. Communication historians, because of the extent of records they use, face problems of selection all the time. Consequently, one only has to reflect upon how historians make conscious decisions about the use of evidence to understand that problems of its availability and selectivity guarantee the interpretive nature of their inquiries.

Anyone who has tried to write a serious account of some past occurrence can appreciate the interpretive nature of history. One can understand that the writing of history involves constant decisions about finding meaning in the record of the past and explaining that significant part of the total, available record to an audience. The "facts" of history have explanations attached to them. Take President Woodrow Wilson's first presidential press conference as an example. He held it on March 15, 1913, just eleven days after his inauguration. The simple fact of that conference tells us little. Historians ask and answer a number of questions about such "facts" before employing them as part of their explanations. In this case they might ask: How and why did this meeting originate? Was it intended to serve the interest of the president, the press, or the public? What did it accomplish? Was it a success or failure? How does it fit into larger historical themes such as the nature of the relationship between the presidents, or the presidency, and the press? As one observes historians such as James E. Pollard and George Juergens address these questions in their inquiries, it becomes clear that the simple "facts" of history, in this case that of the first regularly instituted presidential press conference, do not stand alone. They are loaded with explanation.

Thus fact and interpretation, however scrupulous and honest the historian may be in the search for the truth, go together. The early twentieth-century British journalist C.P. Scott used to say, "Comment is free, but facts are sacred."[4] Whether or not one agrees

---

[3]Robert W. Ross, *So It Was True: The American Protestant Press and the Nazi Persecution of the Jews* (Minneapolis: University of Minnesota Press, 1980), 305.

[4]Quoted in Sir Linton Andrews and H.A. Taylor, *Lords and Laborers of the Press: Men Who Fashioned the Modern British Newspaper* (Carbondale:

with Scott's statement, it cannot be applied to history, a study in which fact and opinion are bound together in more ways than one might suppose. Historians select the evidence as they assemble it into their accounts, and finally offer a general interpretation by way of shaping an overall understanding of the subject.

Finally there is the element of narration to consider. By speaking of the narrative element in history, one is not referring to those majestic narrative histories produced by nineteenth-century historians but rather to the narrative element that is bound up in the writing of history. Since the time of Herodotus, who was a master of narration, the element of "story" and its telling have been an integral part of history. They remain central to historical writing today and help to give history a distinguishable form. As G.R. Elton, one of the most influential of contemporary historians, reminds us, "...if it cannot be told as a story it can no longer be called history....The story may be short or long, simple or complex, but the element of story has to be there if what he [the historian] is producing is to be history."[5]

These characteristics will be covered at greater length later. But even this brief introduction suggests that history is a distinctive study. Yet it shares a common body of information with other subjects, and courses in history are sometimes found in various other academic departments. To make matters even more confusing, a number of courses other than history contain an historical component. The problem stems from perceptions of how knowledge should be divided and from considerations regarding curricular design and structure. Before undertaking serious historical inquiry, students of communication history should understand the reasons for the varied placement of history in a university curriculum as well as the qualities that characterize historical study. Accordingly, let us review a few fundamental considerations.

Most American colleges base their curriculum on fields of knowledge known as disciplines; each has its own type of information and regimen of inquiry. For example, history and geography are disciplines. The various disciplines are accommodated by departments for purposes of teaching, scholarship, research, and administration. Beyond that, disciplines are grouped together into larger subject fields or divisions. These aggregate subject fields normally are designated the humanities, the social sciences, the

Southern Illinois University Press, 1970), 13.

[5] G.R. Elton, *Political History: Principles and Practice* (New York: Basic Books, 1970), 176.

arts, the physical sciences, the biological sciences, and the professional programs. There is usually a methodological similarity among the disciplines in each division, but that is not always the case. Some disciplines pose no difficulties regarding where they fit into the larger aggregate groups. Political science, for instance, readily can be designated a social science. History, however, defies such clear classification, as does communication.

The difficulty regarding the placement of history is twofold. First, it involves not only those courses traditionally classified as "history" but also various types of other courses that are difficult to place because of problems of staff, program continuity, and sometimes competition between departments. Communication history is an example of the latter type of course. Should it be placed in a history or communication department, and how should it be taught? Second, what is the proper classification of history itself? Does it belong among the humanities or the social sciences? In order for students to understand the nature of the content and method of a course like communication history, they need answers to these questions.

Should a course in communication history be taught in a history or communication department, and how should it be taught? The answer to the first part of that question is simple. It can be placed in either department; it might even be cross-listed as a course for which one might receive credit in either department. The important thing is not where it resides as a course but how it is perceived and taught. If it is called history, one might reason, then it should be taught as history, though some exceptions to that rule exist. Remember, scholars other than historians deal with the past, but only historians deal with the past as history. Political scientists, for instance, who are studying presidential elections, might extend their investigations to past presidential elections, a topic that interests historians too. When studying such material, political scientists proceed in their own way. They use their own methods, and their work is judged by the accepted standards of political science. Their work is significant and stands on its own merits as political science. It is not history, nor is it judged as history. So it is with the field of communication. Many aspects of the work of scholars in that field lead them to make probes into the past. Valuable as that work may be, one should realize that it is not history if it fails to manifest the distinguishing characteristics of history. If not, then another name should be found for it, for names convey substantive meaning.

There are other considerations that underscore the need to classify communication history as part of history. Its subject content is so integrated into the context of modern society that it is impossible to isolate one from the other. Mass communication, journalism, the press, and such other topics that are a part of communication cannot be separated from the broader society without becoming at best narrow and at worst trivial. Indeed, communication history engages the larger history of the past at so many points that it would appear artificial to classify it as anything other than history. In the first volume of *The Information Process*, Robert W. Desmond claimed that "the history of the press itself is a part of the social history of mankind in his search for information and understanding." Desmond's purpose in compiling his comprehensive survey of world news was to "repair...[an] omission in the social history of man, and to establish its relation to political history."[6] His purpose was as suggestive as it was laudatory, for the story of how people have communicated by the various vehicles of mass media throughout time cannot be removed from history without damaging its integrity. But for communication history to reach its potential as history it should have the hallmarks of history.

Before proceeding farther, several qualifications should be made about whatever designation we choose for a subject such as communication history. First, to some extent the distinction made is artificial. Sometimes it is simply the result of the academic curriculum design. Subjects have to fit somewhere; compromises are made in the process. Second, since all of the humanities and social sciences are worthy studies and all frequently borrow from and contribute to the others, it little behooves practitioners of one field to indulge in scoffing and derogatory comments about areas of study other than their own. Human nature being what it is, such comments are common enough, but they only impair the effort to understand a particular discipline. In a sense, every major discipline can think of many other closely associated ones as auxiliary fields. These qualifications should be kept in mind as one attempts to distinguish between the various disciplines.

Now let us return to the matter of the positioning of history. Should it be considered as part of the humanities? It can be if the term *humanities is* broadly defined. If it is used in reference to the study of mankind in its many dimensions, then history qualifies as a humanities. Moreover, since history contains a definite artistic element and since it deals with some of the great statements of people's achievements, it can always qualify on those grounds as a humanities. But if the definition of humanities is narrowed to mean only an organized study of great achievements in literature, philosophy, and perhaps the fine arts, then history fits less well.

---

[6]Robert W. Desmond, *The Information Process: World News Reporting To the Twentieth Century* (Iowa City: University of Iowa Press, 1978), XII.

Although the works of historians such as Herodotus, Macaulay, Trevelyan, and Parkman are themselves considered great literary achievements, the study of history usually encompasses more than a consideration of only such masterpieces. It pushes out into a vast area of people's actions in social, economic, cultural, and political realms. Nevertheless, the relationship between history and what might be called the pure humanities is close and compatible.

Is there a similar compatible relationship between history and the social sciences (more recently the behavioral sciences)? They share a number of common interests. Both historians and social scientists study the past, or, more precisely, they study things in the past. They both deal with analysis, explanation, and generalization. Both employ method in their work, aim for precision, and are concerned with the verification of conclusions reached. To be sure, they tend to go about these tasks in different ways, and the tasks themselves do not necessarily mean the same thing to the one group as to the other. By methodology, for instance, historians usually have something quite different in mind than the social scientist. Consequently, distinctions between them can be blurred. To make matters more confusing, some historians think of themselves as social scientists, particularly, but by no means exclusively, those interested in social history. On the other hand, many social scientists think of themselves as behavioralists. Social scientists, however, do not compose a monolithic group. Some of their scholarly interests are more traditional than they are behavioralist. The various disciplines of the social sciences continue to define and redefine themselves. So does history.

What then are the differences? In answering that question one must keep in mind the variety of interest found among social scientists and the diversity of the definitions of their individual disciplines. It is, consequently, only fair to speak of tendencies in much of their work and how they differ from those found among historians -- who are by no means of one mind regarding the nature of history. Social scientists, for instance, tend to think of themselves as scientists. The tendency is most pronounced among behavioralists.

Do historians think of history as a science? The question is, of course, an old one that carries one back to nineteenth-century debates about the nature of history. It is correct enough to think of history as a science if *science* is loosely construed to mean a rational investigation in which generalizations will be advanced based on evidence, and if it is thought of as a study that is concerned with establishing truth. The scientist, however, can experiment in the laboratory and subject the experiment to a type of verification impossible for historians to use. The scientist seeks laws; the historian hopes to generalize, and the generalizations are usually qualified. The scientist can measure, but measurement is not always within the province of the historian. Can the historian measure the impact that a war, revolution, or an idea made upon the mind of someone or some group of people who lived in times past? The scientist deals with prediction, but history is not predictive in nature. Historians do not claim that their study of the past allows them to predict the future. They study what people have done, thus helping one to understand what people can do, but they do not predict what people will do. A scientist can observe data objectively. Historians are objective too, but they are also frequently subjective. Historians become involved in the past as they endeavor to understand the mood of a time or the nature of someone's personality or many other intangibles of the past. The material of history, concerned about things such as cultural forces, social contexts, and human beings of the past, is simply different from that of the scientist. It yields a different type of understanding than that which the scientist seeks. So historians differ from scientists -- and also from social scientists to the degree that the latter tend to think of themselves as scientists.

In fact, differences between social scientists and historians are numerous. Consider the following statement made in explanation of the study of political behavior by the political scientist David Easton. "There are," he contended, "discoverable uniformities in political behavior. These can be expressed in generalizations or theories with explanatory and predictive value."[7] Such a study of political behavior, indeed, would be scientific, but it would have little to do with an historical inquiry. Easton, of course, did not speak for all political scientists, just as the present writers do not express the opinion of all historians. But the thrust of Easton's comment does underscore a definite difference that exists. There are others. As contrasted to historians, social scientists tend to be more interested in constructing models, in factor analysis, in establishing regularities they perceive present in their data, in linking together theory and research, and in using the past to substantiate theories offered in explanation of social concepts. Historians, on the other hand, study particular things in the past, and, more than social scientists, place greater stress on original sources and on narrative in their studies; and unlike social scientists, they accept intuitive insight as a viable element in their inquiry.

Any consideration of how history relates to the humanities and social sciences and where it should be positioned is useful. It helps to

---

[7]David Easton, *A Framework for Political Analysis* (Englewood Cliffs, N.J.: Prentice Hall, Inc., 1965), 7.

sharpen one's understanding of the nature of history and helps to define what history can and cannot do. The novice tackling a serious historical investigation for the first time would be well advised to read a few of the better known statements on the subject by historians.[8] History is sometimes perceived as in part one of the humanities and in part one of the social sciences since it contains elements of both art and science.

But is such a hybrid definition correct? Both science and art were known when Herodotus and Thucydides wrote, yet they thought of their investigations as unique studies. As we have previously seen, history has a number of distinguishing characteristics. They are all clues to its separate identity. The renowned English historian R.G. Collingwood once explained that the "prime duty of the historian" is found in "a willingness to bestow infinite pains on discovering what actually happened."[9] The object of that discovery is some particular thing of the past. History, it should be remembered, is the study of human deeds. It is about real human beings who lived in the past, their lives and sayings, successes and accomplishments, and their sufferings and failures. It is also about particular events and movements and the change that occurs within them. Since no other study of human experience has these hallmarks, one is led to conclude that historical study can be distinguished from other investigations of the past. It can be understood as an autonomous approach to the past.

However the scholar views the various disciplines, one must be careful not to adopt a perspective that is artificially limited. The view adopted recently among some communication scholars and in graduate communication training, that the research methods of social and behavioral sciences are the only truly legitimate ones for the study of communication questions, is shortsighted and holds much potential danger. All research methods have some value, and only the scholar of narrow perspective would argue that only his or

---

[8]Among the better books on the subject are the following: G. Kitson Clark, *The Critical Historian* (New York: Basic Books, Inc., 1967); Paul K. Conkin and Roland N. Stromberg, *The Heritage and Challenge of History* (New York: Dodd, Mead and Company, 1971); G. R. Elton, *The Practice of History* (New York: Thomas Y. Crowell Company, 1967); H. Stuart Hughes, *History As Art and As Science* (New York: Harper and Row, Publishers, 1964); Arthur Marwick, *The Nature of History* (London: Macmillan and Co., LTD., 1970); and Pardon E. Tillinghast, *The Specious Past: Historians and Others* (Reading, Mass.: Addison-Wesley Publishing Company, 1972).

[9]R.G. Collingwood, *The Idea of History* (London: Clarendon Press, 1946; reprinted, London: Oxford University Press, 1956), 55.

her method is correct. Communication researchers, including historians, must be familiar with all methods that can help shed light on problems and answer questions. The historical method has a number of advantages. First, it can be used, unlike particular social and behavioral science methods, to study a wide range of problems covering many aspects of the human condition. Second, while soft-science methods generally are limited to an examination of situations that presently exist, the historical method provides the only adequate way to study topics from the past. Third, while social and behavioral sciences tend to view the human mind as being mechanistic, the historical method assumes a freedom of thinking apart from the biological mechanics of the brain to account for the diversity of human thought and action. Fourth, the historical method can and should make use of all other methods when they will help study the problem at hand, including the techniques used in behavioral and social sciences.

But the fact that the historical method is so versatile should not mislead the historian into thinking it is easier to master than are other methods. If anything, the opposite is true. Historical method requires more rigorous thinking than any other. While the communication researcher working, for example, with opinion surveys may use established methods to draw a random sample or to determine margins of error, the historian frequently must make sound judgments without such formalized mathematical equations. Historical research, therefore, requires the development of a highly critical mind that must be able to evaluate a wide range of material, subject it to intense scrutiny without the aid of formulae, and arrive at thoughtful conclusions.

The Purpose of History

Without exaggeration, one can say that people have found purpose in history since the Greeks invented it. For the Romans it was an inspiration for their imperial confidence and vision. Medieval monks and scholars produced various works that kept alive the tradition. And, even if they bent it to their own purposes, who can doubt that it offered the society of their day an historical vision. Following the Middle Ages, history grew in prominence as a form of knowledge until the nineteenth century when it entered its golden age. Whether written as a national epic, biography, science, or a revelation of historical destiny, its purpose was not questioned. It was central to the age. Never before or since has it enjoyed such position. The literature of that century is crowded with the great works written by historians across the Western world.

In the twentieth century people continue to pursue history as a subject worthy of serious investigation. They do so for different reasons. In the United States, for instance, early twentieth-century Progressive historians used history to underscore the progress of enlightened democracy that was so important to their hopes of reforming contemporary society. More recently, "new left" historians have attempted to radicalize history and make it an instrument of social transformation. The Marxist historian Herbert Aptheker claims that history must serve the needs either of the oppressed or the oppressors. To that comment, the well-known Lincoln scholar Richard Current recently responded: "Though that may be good Marxism, it may also represent the fallacy of the excluded middle. Surely there are historians who try, not wholly in vain, to write and teach for the sake of neither oppressors nor oppressed but for the sake of historical truth."[10] He provides an important clue with that comment, for most American historians are neither new leftist nor Marxist nor devotees of any special school of history. Most simply pursue their studies hoping to produce a significant, convincing, honest, authentic, and engaging product.

If in the twentieth century, with many new competitors in the field, history has failed to retain its nineteenth-century position, it surely has held its vitality. It remains today a major form of knowledge pursued both as a popular and professional study. It continues, moreover, to enjoy a flourishing existence in schools and colleges and constitutes a significant genre of writing. Yet, it is still possible and profitable to inquire into its purpose. Like all subjects and forms of investigation, history has its detractors as well as its supporters. Moreover, in a culture such as ours in which present-mindedness, practicality, vocationalism, and materialism are so pronounced, the questions sometimes raised about the value of historical study fail to surprise one. Such questions find their logical answers in an understanding of the purpose of the study.

What is it, then, that historians hope to do when they make their inquiries into the past? The first part of the answer to that question is simple. They hope to explain particular things of the past with fullness and truth. In studying those distinctive things, which might be called historical problems, they seek to produce a rational reconstruction of the particular object of investigation from the inside out. They hope to capture and relate the thought and feeling of a time past as they are associated with the problem under consideration. The meaning sought cannot be imposed from without. Such study,

---

[10]Richard N. Current, "Fiction as History: A Review Essay," *The Journal of Southern History* 52 (February 1986): 87.

therefore, can subordinate itself neither to religious or anti-religious passion, nor to political or social ideology, nor to deterministic theories, nor to the social scientist's "models," and still be history. History investigates things that have happened and seeks to comprehend them in their fullness of meaning. In that manner it hopes to be informative about human behavior, about how people have related to one another, and about how they have interacted with the conditions of their time.

Indeed, it is possible to perceive a number of purposes in a study of particular things of the past pursued from the inside out. Within the context of the problem under investigation, it affords the opportunity to produce wholeness and to be informed about the nature of man and historical truth. The purpose of history is neither to justify an action of the past nor to offer facile judgments about the past nor to suggest careless analogies between past and present. It is rather to provide reasonable explanation for the complexity of evidence for some part of the past. As such, its purpose involves the painstaking willingness to search for the truth of a past situation and, by doing so, to set a standard of excellence in comprehending the subject of the inquiry.

By their separate inquiries, historians contribute to the authentic record of human experience. But is that record worth the effort? What use does it have for society? Consider the proposition that history has purpose from a slightly different angle than that found in the previous discussion. Most historians believe that their discipline provides information important for identity and background. It helps us to know ourselves both individually and collectively, and it provides knowledge valuable in helping us to understand the world as we find it.

By way of example, consider a few events much studied by historians. The revolution that began on the field of battle in 1775 gave birth to our American republic. No one expects our country to experience another revolution of that sort. Since it probably will not recur, should it be studied? Can Americans living more than 200 years after the event be informed about themselves as a nation by studying this event? Or, consider the Soviet Union today. Given birth by the Bolshevik revolution of 1917, it is in fact the product of a revolutionary movement whose roots reached far back in Russian history. By studying that movement and the upheaval of 1917, are there significant things to learn about the Soviets today? In the 1930s the Nazi movement surfaced to disrupt Western society and to occasion one of history's bloodiest wars. No one expects a Nazi revolution to happen again in Germany or elsewhere, though it is always possible that it might. Should that terrible historical event be studied? Everyone hopes for international peace. Is there any profit to derive from studying the causes of previous wars or the success and failure of peace settlements? They will never occur again in exactly the same way they did in the past. Or, take the case of Britain, the first country to industrialize in the modern world. Can we benefit from a knowledge of what the results of that industrialization were and what policy measures were made in an effort to cope with the problems inherent in the new industrialized order? One could ask hundreds of questions of this type, and their answers surely suggest that history has a purpose for anyone who hopes to be a responsible and informed person, particularly in a democratic society.

The purpose of history involves the significance and particularity of the object studied. Its significance lies in the historian's conviction that something selected from the past for study has an ongoing importance. Its particularity stems from the idea that it investigates things in context, things about particular problems, people, places, and times.

History and Communication History

Scholars involve themselves in historical investigation for many reasons. Some seek to close gaps in some important segment of the existing historical record. Others aspire to advance a new idea. Whether the aim is to supplement or to supplant previous historical knowledge, they know that they will produce no final answers, for none exist in historical study. The object of the historian's quest is to provide an honest understanding of something in the past based on the best evidence available. The past, of course, is a vast domain; no one can know it all. Serious-minded specialists, each moved by his or her own particular interest, select what amounts to slices of the past to study.

The great variety of history now becomes apparent. Some specialists choose to work within the framework of an established period limited by time and place. One might, for instance, be drawn to a study of nineteenth-century America or to twentieth-century Europe. Others are drawn to national history or to area studies; and yet others to special topics such as reform or industrialization. Biography attracts some; social groups, others. Some incline toward economic studies; others, toward political, diplomatic, religious, or military ones. There are viable historical dimensions to practically every major contemporary entity or institution, and they too attract the historian's attention. All historians pursue special interests of some sort in the past.

Communication history, with its particular focus on mass

communication, is one such specialized study. Nevertheless, the more one inquires into its nature, the more it can be understood as a part of the mainstream of history. In a sense, it is more general than communication studies, which mostly deal with current problems and tend to employ the methodology of the social and behavioral sciences. Communication history can be broadly defined as part of history because its subject matter is integrated into the general currents of history and, as we explained earlier, cannot, with integrity to its subject, be separated from it. Communication history has a natural position in general history and can be considered a part of it.

It is a vast area of study that can accommodate numerous interests. For instance, within its scope fall a great variety of subjects related to the news media in the past. Communication historians are concerned with these media in terms of their content and audience and the various forms they have taken. They are interested also in the development, control, and effects of those media as well as with the people who have influenced their existence. The formation of opinion interests communication historians as well as the circulation and influence that opinion has had in society.

It is, in fact, difficult to place boundaries on communication history. Its study is an invitation to investigate not only the media in the past but also subjects such as publicity, propaganda, public opinion, censorship, and civil liberties. Communication historians are interested also in opinion-policy relationships. Their studies, consequently, deal with many aspects of how people communicated and how communications interacted with society in the past. Therefore, their inquiries have little validity if they concentrate solely on communication media.

Communication history is the pursuit of a certain dimension of the past. It examines something that happened in the past and cannot be understood if separated from the context in which it occurred. Historians interested in this variety of history must inform themselves about "historical time"; they have to acquire a sense of the particular time in the past associated with their inquiry. They must acquire knowledge of the personalities, events, and forces that influenced not only the object of their investigation but also those that influenced the particular time in which it existed. Can one understand figures such as William Cobbett, William Lloyd Garrison, James Gordon Bennett, Edward R. Murrow, or Frank Capra without knowledge of the times in which they lived? The more one appreciates the many dimensions of communication history and the way they connected to so many aspects of the past, the more it becomes clear that communication history has a place in the mainstream of social, economic, cultural, and political history.

Some scholars have recognized this claim for many years. The American historian James Ford Rhodes once wrote: "The story of the secession movement of November and December, 1860, cannot be told with correctness and life without frequent references to the Charleston *Mercury* and the Charleston *Courier*. The *Mercury* especially was an index of opinion and so vivid in its daily chronicle of events that the historian is able to put himself in the place of those ardent South Carolinians and understand their point of view."[11] How many other occurrences of the past can be vivified and given meaning by use of the media as record?

Let us consider just one additional example. It is perhaps the most famous case of its kind, and it demonstrates that to construct the historical record without including a place for the media would grossly distort the record. The case deals with the Spanish-American War. In explaining that war, historians place a special emphasis on the role newspaper sensationalism played in causing the conflict. The newspaper war between Joseph Pulitzer and William Randolph Hearst, they reason, helped to cause war between Spain and the United States. Other interpretations of causation notwithstanding, this contention has some merit. To understand it, however, one needs to know a good deal about the nature of the press and the society at that time. Who and what forces were involved in the sensational press? Was "yellow journalism" a thing of the moment or had it been long in coming? Our questions cannot be limited to the press alone, for the press exists in society. Accordingly, we must know something about the public of that time. Why was it so receptive to sensational journalism? Then, there is the factor of government to consider. Did the influence of the sensational press reach into the chambers of political power? If so, can that influence be documented? Once one has answered such questions, then alternate explanations for the cause of the war can be sought and studied in order to place the factor of the press in its proper perspective. To remove that factor from consideration, however, would damage the history of the event under investigation.

Historians are interested in communication history for many reasons. Just as the media today help the public to gain understanding of current issues, so the media of the past enlighten historians about past public problems. Today's media influence the public's perception of the present world. So it was with the media in the past. Media are a part of the past that cannot be removed from it. To some degree, they have always reflected public whim, taste, and opinion,

---

[11]Lucy Maynard Salmon, *The Newspaper and the Historian* (New York: Oxford University Press, 1923), 471.

and to some degree they have shaped public and individual perceptions and opinions about aspects of society too numerous to mention. Have they been a mirror of society, a source of entertainment, a branch of commerce, or a forum for news, opinion, and business? Obviously they have been all of these things, though the mix varies according to time, place, and circumstances. Mass media are essential elements in modern political life. What modern revolutionary movement has neglected them? Or, consider modern democracy. Its history is bound up with the history of the media. In a democratic society journalists have the responsibility to report and interpret news and to watch authority from the perspective of the governed. They exist as an irreplaceable unit in the public debate. Consider how important the media were to the revolutionary mentality that emerged at some point before the start of the American War for Independence. Think of the role the media played in every great issue (expansion, slavery, reform, isolation, entrance into wars, etc.) that has permeated this country's history.

The record of the mass media, consequently, is one of the richest of historical sources, and it deserves the serious attention of historians. In order to study these media as parts of the past, historians must acquire a workable knowledge of their characteristics at a particular time in the past. How were they organized? What type of influence did they have and why? Take the case of one medium, the newspaper. Historians need to know much about a newspaper to understand it as an historical source. Who produced it and how and why? What type of influence did it have and why? Was it known equally for all of its contents? Were there restraints placed upon its opinion, or did that opinion conform to some outside interest? There are, of course, many other questions that can be asked about a newspaper as an historical source or as an object of historical inquiry. Such a medium -- and it is but one among those that attract the attention of communication historians -- must receive the same scrutiny that historians devote to other historical sources and subjects. Historians, however, are not the only group to have a special interest in communication history.

Journalists and other participants in the mass media have a special interest in their professional predecessors. As the distinguished British journalist and writer Sir Linton Andrews contended, there is much for one to learn from the career and lives of key figures in journalism history, even those whose work falls within recent generations. It is important, he said, to know "what made them journalists? What qualities made them excel? What did or do they see as the proper function of the press? Have they expanded its influence? Have they made it more powerful for ensuring the public good?" Once these questions can be answered, he explained, "the better equipped we shall be to face present challenges in the world of communication."[12] He might have added that one does not have to read far into the history of the twentieth-century media to discover that many of its successful practitioners have themselves had a lively curiosity about their own predecessors.

It stands to reason that communication professionals themselves should have a natural curiosity about the development of that which they are a part. As in any other craft or profession, it is valuable to have a knowledge of how things were done previously in the field, or to have an awareness of problems that once existed (and perhaps still exist) and how they were handled, or some grasp of past successes and failures, or some understanding of how the forces and features of modernization such as technology have influenced its development. Principles and problems, potential and pitfall can all be underscored by such knowledge. At the very least, knowledge of what others have done before helps one to understand what it is possible to do.

The appeal of communication history is obviously many sided and well deserved. Like any other division of historical study, its record goes back into time. In order to comprehend that record, in part or in full, one must also understand the historical setting with which it is associated. If the media have influenced society, they surely have been influenced by society in return. The fact of interaction between media and society has to be one of the fundamentals of communication history. There is, however, another fundamental to grasp. If communication history is to reach its potential and acquire the stature it deserves, it must reach the standards of excellence of any serious historical investigation. In ensuing chapters those standards will be discussed along with many practical matters. They all contribute to the construction of sound history. But first, let us consider how previous historians approached the subject of communication history.

---

[12]Andrews and Taylor, XX.

2

Interpretation in History

History is more than the story of what happened in the past. It is not simply an account of certain events occurring on certain dates and of certain individuals doing certain things. Dates, names, and places provide little more than the raw data for history. Anytime we advance beyond such basic details, we soon realize that history well researched and effectively told does more than provide chronologies and lists. If we attempt to determine, for example, whether a particular journalist or an event had an impact on American journalism or if we attempt to explain what that impact might have been or the extent of the impact or its value, we immediately find that history is no longer a simple statement of what happened. It has become an attempt to explain what happened.

In that process of explaining, historians have not always shared the same views. One historian might approach a subject from a starting viewpoint that varies either in small or large degree from that of another. Thus, in the nearly two centuries that American historians have been writing about their media's history, they have given accounts that differ widely. One historian might condemn the party press for its partisanship, while another might praise it for its contributions to the American political system. One historian might rebuke the media for propaganda during World War II, while another might salute them for contributing to Allied victory. Such differences can frustrate students who wish to have the "true" history of communication, but they actually provide one of the most valuable features of historical study. Differing perspectives among historians result in pictures and explanations that are multi-dimensional rather than flat, multi-colored rather than monotone.

The most valuable historical writing is always interpretive. Every time a historian selects material or advances a generalization based on that material, interpretation occurs. Every time one attempts to explain causation or to probe into the nature of change, one interprets. Without interpretation, historical study remains superficial, with no probing beneath the surface of facts to determine why events occurred and why people acted as they did. With no attempt to determine why, historical study provides mere chronology. Too frequently, the study of history is approached with the attitude that the past is a static story of facts, names, dates, and other details - a study of "how things were" -- rather than a dynamic, changing story. The truth is that the story of communication history is an ever-changing one. One purpose of good history is to provide understanding of change. That it does through interpretation. It is the need for interpretation that accounts for the periodic rewriting of various episodes in history. As the present views and perspectives on communication change, so also do our understanding and explanations of communication history. The notion that history needs no rewriting is held only by those people who believe that the world does not change or that historical study can determine the precise truth. It cannot.

Yet, interpretation should not be predetermined. The good historian does not set out with a theory and marshal facts to fit the theory. The best history is always a search for truth. As facts are gathered to find the truth, they may lead to a theory, but theory should never be used to determine facts. Interpretation arises implicitly from the gathered facts. Spurious historians ask how they might select and interpret facts to fit their theory. The result is, at best, didactic history. It offers little benefit except to those historians who have a particular view to propound. The historian should gather all the relevant facts and then ask what conclusions may be drawn from them.

Differing interpretations of communication history have arisen for three primary reasons. The most important is that historians' attitudes have been influenced by the conditions and beliefs of the times in which they wrote. Successive generations of historians have tended to view the past in terms of the ideas of their own time. Every generation believes that it knows more than the previous generation, that it has a more penetrating and accurate view than the generation that preceded it. Every generation is influenced by events and conditions of its own time. The existing conditions of mass communication -- not to mention politics, social situations, economics, and a multitude of other aspects of the surrounding culture -- have helped determine the ways historians have looked at the past. In effect, the way in which historians explain history reflects, to some degree the culture of their own times. No historian is immune to those conditions that shape his or her own day. At the same time, historians within the same generation have brought to their study different beliefs and assumptions. Therefore, historians writing at the same time have taken the same body of material and have come to differing conclusions about the past.

The second reason is that new material, new facts, from the past is being discovered constantly. One would think that generations of study of the press in the American Revolution would have exhausted the resources, but then an historian turns up letters in a depository heretofore overlooked. Or a student of the penny press of the 1830s discovers copies of a newspaper long forgotten. Or another scholar examines radio program transcripts in a university archives never before seen by historians. Or, as so often happens, a historian thoroughly reads the files of a newspaper taken for granted by others and provides a whole new insight into the paper and its era. The new information makes possible a fuller insight than has been possible before and sometimes provides a startling new explanation that turns on head long-held assumptions.

The third reason for new interpretations is the availability of new research tools for examining the past. A new generation of scholars may be trained in new techniques of inquiry. In the 1970s, for instance, many historians began to use quantitative methods in their studies as well as computer technology as it became available. They borrowed both methods and theories from social scientists and, to some extent, from historians in other countries and applied them where feasible in their investigations. As a result, historians today have heightened awareness of methodological options of inquiry, and their studies reflect that diversity.

Thus, the idea that history is a static account of dead details from the past is made meaningless. Historians disprove that idea in all they do. They not only use the skills of interpretation in constructing all the elements in their inquiries, but they are also aware of the broader interpretations into which communication historians can be grouped. Awareness of these schools of history is essential. It helps historians to delineate the changing nature of their subject, to grasp the reasons that explain that change, and to respond to the broad achievement of previous scholars according to the dictates of their own judgment.

Based on their perspectives or interpretations, communication historians may be grouped into several schools. By understanding these schools, the student not only may recognize why historians present such diverse explanations of the past; he or she may draw from the various schools those perspectives that seem best to explain history, apply them to one's own study, and thereby provide a fuller, deeper explanation in one's work.

Generally speaking, interpretation of mass communication history in the United States has gone through six broad stages: Nationalist, Romantic, Developmental, Progressive, Consensus, and Cultural. Although a handful of historians have written within Marxist and other schools, historians in the first six have provided by far the most extensive work.

The Nationalist School

The historians of the early nineteenth century, writing during an era in which pride in American progress and achievements was popular, took a nationalistic approach and explained the mass media, primarily newspapers, and journalists as influential and important patriotic figures who contributed to the progress of America and her institutions. These Nationalist historians looked on the history of America as the advancing revelation of the nation's leadership role in mankind's improvement. To them, America was the nation chosen to lead the world to the fulfillment of mankind's destiny: greater and greater freedom and liberty.

Influenced by the ideas of the Enlightenment, with its emphasis on natural rights and progress and the people's role in determining their government, these historians displayed a particular interest in the subject of freedom of the press. Working within a framework of the unfolding advance of mankind and its social and governmental institutions, they attempted to reveal the progress of freedom of the press within an overall story of the developing liberty of mankind and, in particular, of the American people. Most Nationalist historians wrote about freedom of the press in terms of the political splits of early America, between colonists and British authorities and between Patriots and Tories. Their attention centered on the colonial and revolutionary periods, when Americans had struggled to free themselves from oppressive British rule, and they virtually ignored the early years of American independence. Fulfillment of human freedom, they believed (unlike many historians in the twentieth century), had been accomplished with the separation from England. The sides in the conflict over freedom were pictured as those who advocated the natural rights of liberty and those who supported authoritarian government.

Isaiah Thomas, America's first journalism historian, expressed the Nationalist interpretation of the struggle in classic Enlightenment terms. Thomas had been a leading Patriot printer during the Revolution. In *History of Printing in America* published in 1810, he explained that "the rulers in the colonies of Virginia in the seventeenth century judged it best not to permit public schools, nor to allow the use of the press and thus, by keeping the people in ignorance, they thought to render them more obedient to the laws, and to prevent them from libelling the government, and to impede the growth of heresy, &c."[1] Like Thomas, most other Nationalist historians viewed the history of the press in terms of America's struggle for freedom and the advance of mankind against repressive British authority. They identified the great forces in that history as liberty, progress, and the American nation.

The Romantic School

While the Nationalist interpretation continued strong throughout the nineteenth century, it was altered beginning in the 1830s by the influence of Romanticism. Romantic historians shared their predecessors' belief in the progress of mankind, in liberty as the ultimate goal of history, and in America's special role in leading the world to that goal. The press, they believed, was one of the institutions of primary importance in mankind's advance, and they considered America as the high point in the development of civilization. But they added a new flavor to history. Most Romantic historians were men of leisure who had spare time to pursue historical study as an avocation, men of the professional classes, or journalists who had an inclination toward historical study. Frequently, they had known their subjects or had participated in the episodes about which they wrote. Personal reminiscences therefore often served as the basis for their histories.

While the Romantic historians usually were amateurs, many attained a high degree of chronological accuracy and literary quality. The Romantic movement in the arts -- with its emphasis on pictorial descriptions and narrative, its fascination with the past, and its accentuation of the role of great men in history -- greatly influenced these historians. They thought of history as one of the literary arts, and they mainly wrote narrative biographies in a romantic style designed to appeal to larger audiences.

Romantic historians frequently told the history of the press against the panorama of politics. Primarily from New England and New York, they took as their predominant subject printers and editors from those same regions and described them as men larger than life who imprinted their newspapers with their own characters.

---

[1]Isaiah Thomas, *History of Printing in America* (Worcester, Mass., 1810), 7.

Since Romantic historians typically were gentlemen from socially and politically elite families, they especially favored printers and editors who respected established values and traditions. Tending to be conservative in politics, they reacted negatively to the shift away from the aristocrats' participation in government which had occurred with Thomas Jefferson's and Andrew Jackson's elections to the presidency. As a result, they tended to treat conservative printers and editors (Federalists and Whigs) favorably, while blaming Jeffersonian Republicans and Jacksonian Democrats for the exclusion of men of higher principles from public office and for their replacement by men who pandered to the desires of the mass public.

The Romantic interpretation was readily apparent in the work of Joseph T. Buckingham. A journalist who, among other achievements, founded the Boston *Courier*, a pro-Whig newspaper, in 1824, he had worked with many of the journalists about whom he wrote and was intimately acquainted with many of the episodes. One of the earliest histories of the American press, Buckingham's *Specimens of Newspaper Literature: With Personal Memoirs, Anecdotes, and Reminiscences,* published in 1850, combined narrative history with autobiography. Composed primarily of pleasant and anecdotal descriptive biographies, it emphasized journalists whom Buckingham had known and extracts from their papers, most of which were in New England.

Romantic historians' predilection for respectability was typified by another major work of the mid-nineteenth century, James Parton's *Life and Times of Benjamin Franklin.* Published in 1864, it provided one of the earliest biographies of an American journalist. Sometimes called the father of American biography, Parton drew a revealing contrast between Benjamin Franklin and his older brother, James. He especially praised Ben's competence as a businessman, editor, and owner of the *Pennsylvania Gazette* and his success in making it the best newspaper in colonial America. His achievement was based on his talent and respectability. But for his brother James, Parton had few kind words, in contrast with most twentieth-century historians, who have praised James for his defense of freedom of the press against encroachments by the political and religious establishments. Parton was a critic of radical democratic movements in American history and thus was not inclined to agree with James' attitudes and practices. He criticized James' *New-England Courant* for being the first American newspaper based on sensationalism and roundly condemned it for its sarcasm and ridicule of civil and religious authorities. By the time Parton's biography appeared, however, a change was taking place in American journalism, and with it a change in historical interpretation.

The Developmental School

In 1833 Benjamin Day had founded the New York *Sun*, America's first successful general-interest penny newspaper. It created a revolution in journalism, in attitudes about what the nature of newspapers should be, and in historians' views about communication history. From this changed perspective emerged what came to be the predominant, most pervasive, and longest-lived approach to communication history, the Developmental interpretation. Beginning with the publication in 1873 of Frederic Hudson's *Journalism in the United States, from 1690 to 1872,* the Developmental interpretation has provided the underlying assumptions of most histories of American mass media and continues today as the most commonly held perspective.

It is based on the concept of the professional development of the press, viewing the history of journalism as the continuing evolution of journalistic practices and standards. While other interpretations have been strong at various times, the concept of the developmental progress of the media has been persistent since the last decades of the nineteenth century. In addition to working as an independent interpretation, it also has operated in combination with the other interpretations and frequently served as an underlying assumption of historians in the other schools. Thus, Nationalist historians, for example, thought of the development of the press as an aspect of the progress of mankind, while Progressive historians in the twentieth century evaluated the press as it developed as an instrument of reform. In its purest form, however, the Developmental interpretation has been based on the concept of the professional, journalistic progress of the press. How the press became a journalistic instrument was the primary concern of Developmental historians. Like other historians, they tended to view the past in terms of the present, but they attempted to explain and evaluate history by its contributions to present journalistic standards.

Hudson's *Journalism in the United States* was the first survey history of American journalism written after the appearance of the penny press in the 1830s, and in its interpretive basis it provided the approach used by most later historians. Hudson had been managing editor of the New York *Herald*, the newspaper which more than any other emphasized news over opinion as the proper function of newspapers and which had been the most successful mass newspaper in American history. Assuming that such characteristics were the appropriate ones for newspapers, he tended to explain earlier journalism in terms of how it performed in accordance with the successful practices of the *Herald* and how those practices had developed in the past. His Developmental perspective can be made clear by an examination of his evaluation of the party press, which immediately preceded the penny press in American history.

With his news-oriented background, Hudson evaluated earlier newspapers in terms of how they conformed to the concept of a newspaper as a news medium and a journal popular with the masses of readers and independent of influence by political parties. He concluded that the party press, although important and influential in politics, was primarily political in nature, that it was vituperative, and that the partisan period was a negative one for journalistic development. The primary problem, he said, was that politicians controlled the press and prevented it from developing professional standards. Newspapers had been necessary to build a solid political foundation for the nation, but journalism "had not yet become a profession." The press "was a power with the people," but it ultimately failed because "it was managed by ambitious political chiefs, as armies are maneuvered by their generals." During the party period, Hudson admitted, the press had progressed in some areas, but "its views and opinions on public affairs were the inspiration of politicians and statesmen....Editors...were bound to party. Independence of opinion and expression, outside of party, was political and financial ruin." Despite such problems in journalism, Hudson could see with the historian's hindsight that the penny press would emerge soon, and thus he observed that "the world was moving, and its soul was marching on."[2]

As mass communication began to professionalize in the late 1800s, interest in its history began to grow. As a result, historical studies increased in number. Although differing on a few particulars, they largely echoed Hudson's themes. Most later historians came out of the mass communication professions, and many in the twentieth century taught in professionally oriented college programs in journalism, broadcasting, and advertising. Because of their professional perspective, they considered the penny press, with its emphasis on news, mass appeal, and political autonomy, to have been the origin of the "modern journalism" of their own times. They believed the professional standards that had developed over time to be the appropriate and proper ones for the media, and they began to apply even more universally the concept of professional progress in the history of communication.

The Developmental interpretation had a pervasive impact on historical assumptions because most textbooks for college courses in communication history were cast in terms of the professional

---

[2]Frederic Hudson, *Journalism in the United States...* (New York: Harper and Row, 1873), 142.

framework. With textbooks such as James Melvin Lee's *History of American Journalism*, published in 1917, and Willard G. Bleyer's *Main Currents in the History of American Journalism*, published a decade later (1927), the Developmental interpretation became entrenched in historical thinking. Studied by generations of students and future historians, they tended to reinforce the explanation that the history of American mass communication was the story of how the media evolved in their professional characteristics. Developmental historians focused often on determining the origins of media practices and on the individuals who had made contributions to media progress. Textbooks and other studies, being generally positive about the professions in mass communication, also exercised a major importance by providing a favorable view of the American media and reinforcing a pro-media outlook among communication students and professionals.

Although Bleyer's was the most widely used of the early textbooks, it was superseded by Frank Luther Mott's *American Journalism; A History of Newspapers in the United States Through 150 Years: 1690 to 1940*. Through its three editions (1941, 1950, and 1962) Mott's book provided the basis for the historical study by most students for four decades. The foremost practitioner of the Developmental interpretation, Mott primarily concerned his study with documenting the progress of journalism and its practices. The concept of progress provided the thematic structure for Mott's entire narrative, and he established it with his treatment of America's earliest newspapers. Viewing the past as the story of how journalism had reached its modern state, he entitled his narrative of the colonial press "The Beginners, 1690-1765." The chapter illustrates the essence of the Developmental interpretation.

Mott detailed such topics as the earlier European patterns upon which American publications were based, pamphlets and other forerunners of the newspaper, and early episodes involving freedom of the press. Among the journalistic "firsts" he chronicled were the first American newspaper, Benjamin Harris' *Publick Occurrences; Both Foreign and Domestick;* "the first continuous American newspaper," John Campbell's Boston *News-Letter*; and the appearance of entertainment and the first American newspaper crusade, both in James Franklin's *New-England Courant*. To these were added narratives of such items as the "first American newspaper consolidation," the "first serial story in an American newspaper," the "first titled series in an American paper," the first illustration, and so on.

While Mott appreciated the fact that colonial newspapers operated under journalistically unsophisticated conditions, he tended to explain the early press in terms of later standards. Thus, he observed that the Boston *News-Letter*, because of its content and writing style, "seems very unexciting to a modern reader" and that Campbell's "theory of the presentation of foreign news [emphasizing an organized historical record over recency] gave little consideration to timeliness." Methods of newsgathering, page appearance, the job of the editor, the absence of editorial pages, and other such aspects of the colonial press -- Mott explained all with an implicit comparison to later practices.

In general, Mott evaluated the colonial press as relatively crude by twentieth-century standards, but found satisfaction in the fact that it had provided a solid foundation for journalistic practices and achievements that were to come later. While he found much lacking in the toddler attitudes and performance of many early printer-editors, he believed some -- such as James Franklin with his attempt to free the press from control by authorities, Benjamin Franklin with his several innovations, and the Bradford family of Pennsylvania with their high standards for printing and their sense of the role of the press -- had recognized what journalism was supposed to be and do and had made contributions to the quality and development of the American press.[3]

Mott's work provided the apex of the Developmental school, and most later historians labored in his long shadow. To a large extent, they provided elaboration or extension of his ideas. After World War II, several events contributed to the expansion of the professional concept of the news media as entities which ideally should be autonomous from outside authority and independent of other parts of society. Influenced much by the media's role in such episodes as the civil rights movement of the 1950s and 1960s, the Vietnam War, and the Watergate political scandal, Developmental historians -- while retaining the concept of professional progress -- sometimes viewed history as a clash between the media and established institutions such as government, religion, the military, big business, and the white racial majority. Thus, whereas Progressive historians, for example, had emphasized the media as a means of working within society to achieve social and political change, Developmental historians tended to emphasize such historical trends as press freedom and media-government relations in which the media confronted other units of society. In the view toward nationalism the newer Developmental historians differed markedly from their predecessors. Earlier historians had viewed nationalism positively and the media as contributors to it; recent historians sometimes seemed

---

[3]The quoted material is taken from Frank Luther Mott, *American Journalism*... (New York: Macmillan, 1941), 3-70.

anti-nationalist. The devotion of the media, they suggested, should be to journalistic ideals rather than to a nation. Thus, they showed considerable concern with such issues as the media's autonomy in the area of national security, press freedom during wartime, and the media as propaganda agents for governmental activities.

The Progressive School

Contrasting with the Developmental interpretations, a fourth school -- that of Progressive history -- emerged around 1910. In place of the Developmental school's professional progress explanation of history, Progressive historians substituted a concept of ideological conflict. The Progressive school grew, in part, out of a change that had taken place in the study of American history in the late 1800s. Professional historians began to replace the gentlemen historians and amateurs; and, under the impact of discoveries in the natural sciences, they began to think of the study of history as a science rather than as an art. While professional journalists continued to write many of the historical works, many communication historians in the early 1900s were educators from the emerging departments of journalism at various universities. Because American universities opened their doors to everyone, the new professional historians came from various levels of society. Representing various geographic regions, they began to shift some of the emphasis away from journalism in New York and New England to that in other sections of the country.

Influenced by the ideas of such Progressive American historians as Frederick Jackson Turner, Charles A. Beard, Claude Bowers, and Vernon L. Parrington, many reform-oriented communication historians began to view the past as a struggle in which editors, publishers, and reporters were pitted on the side of freedom, liberty, civil reform, democracy, and equality against the powerful forces of wealth and class. They believed the primary purpose of the media was to crusade for liberal social and economic causes, to fight on the side of the masses of common, working people against the entrenched interests in American business and government. The fulfillment of the American ideal required a struggle against those individuals and groups which had blocked the achievement of a fully democratic system. Progressive historians often placed the conflict in economic terms, with the wealthy class attempting to control the media for its own use. Progressive historians, as earlier historians had done, viewed history as an evolutionary progression to better conditions. They thought in ideological terms, perceiving the media as an influential force in helping assure a better future.

Sympathetic with the goals of the Progressive reformers of the early twentieth century, these historians wrote in such a way as to show the media as tools for social change, progress, and democracy. They explained the past in cycles of democratic and journalistic advance, which occurred when the media improved in serving the masses in America. They praised journalists and episodes that had contributed to greater democracy, while criticizing those favoring an elitist society and political system.

While Progressive historians reevaluated every major period in American communication history, works by three historians in the 1920s and 1930s epitomized their ideological approach and their use of history to change conditions of their own time. The first was Oswald Garrison Villard. Deploring what he considered to be crass materialism on the part of most of the American press, he argued that the best newspapers were those that led the fight for improved social conditions. In *Some Newspapers and Newspapermen*, published in 1923, he claimed that newspapers too often had deserted their leadership role in molding public opinion and instead appealed to public tastes in scandal, racial hatred, and social animosities -- all because owners thought the best way to make money was to appeal to public passions. He described, for example, Adolph Ochs' New York *Times* as racist and a promoter of discriminatory separation between blacks and whites. In *The Disappearing Daily*, published in 1944 as a revision of his earlier book, Villard argued that fighting crusades was more important than providing news, and he scorned the trend toward pictures, features, and a generally soft approach to news. Believing that the role of the media was to keep a wary eye on the government in order to protect the public, he claimed that too few newspapers championed enough causes. The problem with American journalism, he concluded, was that newspapers treasured profit more than principle.

The second historian, George Seldes, in two major works in the 1930s, attacked wealthy owners' self-serving use of their newspapers. In *Freedom of the Press*, published in 1935, he argued that big business' control of the media was destroying press freedom. A big-business, big-money oligarchy owned and manipulated the American press, he claimed, and its intent was to destroy the democratic foundation of the American political system. No section of journalism went untouched. Advertisers, public utilities, big business in general, and propagandists colored and suppressed the news and corrupted both the media and the public. The Associated Press, Seldes declared, always sided with authority, no matter how corrupt, while the New York *Times* spoke without exception for the conservative status quo, and William Randolph Hearst advocated privilege and possessed no social conscience. Seldes denounced the media for their opposition -- despite the great need for social reforms -- to the rights of organized labor, support of child labor for purely financial reasons, emphasis on scandal, invasion of privacy, interference with trial by jury, and critical treatment of the American Newspaper Guild (the reporters' labor union). When a majority of American newspapers published propaganda, he concluded, simply because to do so was profitable, it was impossible to have freedom of the press and unconcealed truth. Seldes followed his first work with *Lords of the Press* in 1938. Employing the same theme of the pernicious effect of wealthy moneymakers' ownership, he argued that the media typically were ultra-conservative and failed to ensure fair news treatment of labor or social and economic reforms.

One of the most trenchant Progressive attacks on the conservative media came from Harold L. Ickes, Secretary of the Interior under Franklin Roosevelt and director of the Public Works Administration. In the 1939 book *America's House of Lords*, a caustic criticism of publishers who opposed Roosevelt's New Deal, Ickes argued that the shortcomings of the press resulted from modern publishers being businessmen more interested in running their newspapers as business enterprises than journals of news. Publishers, he said, imparted to their papers an upperclass outlook and sought to make them profit-seeking businesses rather than public-spirited agencies concerned with social good. As a result, the emphasis on business endangered the free press required by a democracy and led to a lack of fairness in newspaper pages, unreliability, suppression of information, and fabrication of news.

The Consensus School

While the Progressive interpretation greatly influenced the study of American history in the first half of the twentieth century, the fact that America faced major crises during that same period encouraged a diametrically opposing interpretation. With the nation confronting external threats from world war and domestic problems caused by the Great Depression, a number of historians sought to present a picture of America and its mass media that was characterized by basic agreement and unity. These Consensus historians reasoned that America's past was marked more by general agreement than by conflict and that Americans, rather than sundered by class differences, tended to be more united than divided. While Americans from time to time might disagree on certain issues, their disagreements took place within a larger framework of agreement on underlying principles -- such as a belief in democracy, human freedom, and constitutional government -- that overshadowed their differences. Generally, Consensus historians claimed that American history was not marked by extreme differences among groups; and in their hands the Progressives' villains such as industrialists, businessmen, and media owners were molded into less evil people who made constructive contributions to America, while Progressives' heroes such as reformers and the labor press were painted as less idealistic and more egocentered.

Forsaking the critical attitude that had characterized much Progressive writing, Consensus historians tended to emphasize the achievements of the United States and its mass media, with the intent of showing a national unity among Americans. The Consensus outlook had a major impact on the interpretation of numerous aspects of communication history. It explained the American Revolution and the press' role in it, for example, as democratic rather than economic or social, as Progressive historians had argued. It viewed the media's role in America's entry into World Wars I and II in terms of the general agreement among Americans that involvement was necessary. Consensus historians viewed the media's performance during the World Wars positively, crediting the media and government for providing adequate information in a way that helped make possible the defeat of democracy's enemies. They praised media owners, whom Progressives had castigated for their conservatism, as entrepreneurs who had made the American media system into the freest and most effective in the world. In these explanations as in others, Consensus historians generally approached communication history from the viewpoint that the media should work with the public and government to solve problems rather than create divisions by emphasizing problems and conflicts.

The foremost advocate of this interpretation was Bernard Bailyn. He expounded the argument first in his 1965 work *Pamphlets of the American Revolution, 1750-1776* and then elaborated it in *The Ideological Origins of the American Revolution*, the 1967 winner of both the Pulitzer Prize and the Bancroft Prize for history. Pamphlets provided the most important forum for the expression of opinion during the revolutionary period, according to Bailyn. They revealed that the American Revolution, rather than being a class struggle, was above all else an ideological, constitutional, and political struggle. Colonial leaders feared that a sinister conspiracy had developed in England to deprive citizens of the British empire of their long-established liberties. This fear lay at the base of the views expressed in the pamphlets. The ideas in the pamphlets then became the determinants in the history of the revolutionary period by causing colonists to change their beliefs and attitudes. These ideas challenged British authority and argued that "a better world than had ever been known could be built where authority was distrusted and held in constant scrutiny; where the status of men flowed from their achievements and from their personal qualities, not from distinction ascribed to them at birth; and where the use of power over the lives of men was jealously guarded and severely restricted."[4]

The Consensus viewpoint tended to be especially strong at those times when the United States faced grave dangers. Thus, a number of studies of the media during World War I, for example, appeared in the years surrounding World War II. Consensus historians believed that the media should aid in defeating the threats and solving the problems faced by the nation. To them, history revealed that the media had performed best when they contributed to national unity. They believed that the media's endorsement of America's entry into both World War I and II had been responsible and reflected the consensus of the American people and that the proper role of the media during the wars was to support the aims of the nation. Against the Progressive argument that propagandists, profiteers, and reactionary publishers misled the public and led America into the wars, Consensus historians declared that the position of the media mirrored the opinions of the majority of the American public and that the enormity of the threat from America's and democracy's enemies fully justified media support of the war effort.

Consensus historians also broke sharply with the views of Progressive and recent Developmental historians on the issues of freedom of the press and government control over information. While other historians sometimes argued that freedom of the press should be absolute or that cooperation of the conservative media with government posed the danger of compromising liberal, honest journalism, Consensus historians believed absolute freedom and independence of the media could result in an irresponsible journalism that ultimately could endanger the nation and the democratic system that made press freedom possible. To merit freedom, Consensus historians argued, the media must perform responsibly in relation to the rest of the society, with the welfare of the nation as a whole rather than of the media alone of primary importance. This view led Consensus historians to the natural conclusion that restrictions on media freedom during wartime may be acceptable and that such restrictions -- because of the circumstances under which they are implemented -- do not abandon the concept of freedom in a democratic philosophy.

---

[4]The quoted material is taken from Bernard Bailyn, ed., *Pamphlets of the American Revolution, 1750-1776* (Cambridge, Mass.: Harvard University Press, 1965), "Introduction."

Similar to the Consensus interpretation -- indeed, sometimes classified as part of it -- has been the Neo-conservative approach to history. Beginning in the 1920s, it provided an abrupt departure from the interpretation of Progressive and some Developmental historians. Its reinterpretation has been most evident in a number of biographies of media owners. Progressive historians had portrayed owners as selfish, conservative profiteers. Neo-conservative historians argued that owners often had made lasting constructive contributions to the media, and that they symbolized some of the fundamental positive aspects of the American character. Whereas Progressive historians had viewed most owners with suspicion, Neo-conservative historians described them as individuals of high principle.

Although the appellation "Neo-conservative" may be applied appropriately to this approach, it also may be thought of in many respects as a "business history" school. Following the leadership of scholars in the prestigious Harvard Graduate School of Business Administration in the 1920s, business historians developed their own approaches to explain American industrial history. Those historians who studied the mass media argued that owners were not predatory profit seekers but farsighted, thoughtful entrepreneurs whose contributions to the American media system were considerable. Owners' goals were not simply to accumulate money but to bring new efficient methods of management to the media industries and in the process to serve better the information needs of the American public. Business historians also rejected the Progressive critique of media owners as enemies of democracy and freedom. They argued instead that owners, by providing efficiency and larger operations, gave America the best media system in the world and thereby actually contributed to greater democracy and freedom.

The most highly acclaimed work from these historians was Gerald Johnson's *An Honorable Titan*, published in 1946, a biography of Adolph Ochs, publisher of the New York *Times*. Ochs, Johnson said, was one of the financial giants of the late 1800s who had so much to do with making industrial America what it is. Unlike many of the industrialists who were materialists and rogues, however, Ochs was an honorable businessman committed to the ideal of the newspaper as a public institution: impersonal, reliable, responsible, and devoted primarily to serving the public with news. Daring and honest, he made the *Times* successful through faith in traditional values, hard work, common sense, and self-reliance. Believing journalism's first obligation was to inform the public, he refused to be influenced by advertisers and maintained a low editorial profile. His journalistic career exemplified principle, and the history of the *Times* under his direction provided a story of advancing journalism. Ochs, Johnson wrote, broke with the personal journalism of the past, while shunning the sensational techniques of Joseph Pulitzer and William Randolph Hearst. In emphasizing serious news, rather than sensationalism or opinion, he adapted the *Times* to conditions of his era and of the future and thus laid the foundation of modern quality journalism. As the *Times* quickly acquired a reputation for excellence, its owner gained a reputation for honor, character, and integrity.

The Cultural School

The sixth major school of interpretation -- that of Cultural history -- gave little attention to any such ideology, neither conservative nor liberal, its fundamental premise being that the media operated in a close interrelationship with their environment. The major works in the Cultural school were written by university professors trained in communication history and often in communication and behavioral sciences. The impetus for the Cultural interpretation may be traced to a work on urban sociology by Robert E. Park, one of the members of the prestigious school of sociology at the University of Chicago. In "The Natural History of the Newspaper," published in 1925, Park argued that the evolution of American journalism resulted from its interaction with the surrounding culture. The press, he said, was "the outcome of a historic process in which many individuals participated without foreseeing what the ultimate product of their labors was to be. The newspaper, like the modern city, is not wholly a rational product. No one sought to make it just what it is. In spite of all the efforts of individual men and generations of men to control it and make it something after their own heart, it has continued to grow and change in its own incalculable ways."[5] The primary factors in determining the nature of the newspaper, Park stated, were the conditions of the society and the system in which the press operated.

While some historians in other schools had attempted to explain the media as institutions somewhat separate from society, Cultural historians considered the media as a part of society and therefore influenced by various factors outside the media themselves. Thus, such questions as what factors accounted for the founding of newspapers and radio stations and under what

---

[5]Robert Park, "The Natural History of the Newspaper," in Park, Ernest W. Burgess, and Robert D. McKenzie, *The City* (Chicago: University of Chicago Press, 1925), 88.

financial conditions the media operated began to involve the historians' interest. Whereas most historians had assumed the media had a major influence on society, Cultural historians were interested in the reverse effect: the impact of society on the media. This perspective accounted for a major change in historical outlook. Until the 1950s media influence was so widely accepted that historians often had based their studies on the concept of influence. With behavioral research studies in the 1950s beginning to suggest that the persuasive power of the mass media was limited, historians largely downplayed the idea of direct persuasive media influence on society and substituted for it the concept that the media themselves were a product of social influences.

The changed perspective on influence had other effects. One result was a virtual disappearance of the "great man" explanation of communication history. Rarely did Cultural historians frame their studies around the role that an individual had played in affecting the media. More and more studies also shifted their focus from the media giants in the Northeast to journalists on the frontier and in other sections of the nation. While some of the shift in interest was caused by the emergence in the Midwest of the major doctoral programs in journalism education, followed by other programs in the South and West, the frontier studies placed an emphasis on the environmental conditions in which the media operated and their effect on the media.

The most productive historian from the Cultural school was Sidney Kobre, who in a number of works attempted to explain the mass media as a product of environment. Labeling his perspective as "sociological," he argued that the development of American journalism could be explained best in terms of how the media had been influenced by economic, political, technological, sociological, geographic, and cultural forces working on them from the outside. In his 1945 article "The Sociological Approach in Research in Newspaper History,"[6] the fullest treatise on Cultural interpretation, he declared that without consideration of such factors, media history could not be understood. Kobre applied his sociological approach to explain media history in five major books, *The Development of the Colonial Newspaper*, published in 1944, *Foundations of American Journalism* (1958), *Modern American Journalism* (1959), *The Yellow Press and Gilded Age Journalism* (1964), and *Development of American Journalism* (1969). In the first, a study of the years 1690-1783, he attempted to show how "the changing character of the American people and their dynamic social situation produced and

---

[6]*Journalism Quarterly* 22 (1945): 12-22.

conditioned the colonial newspaper." The first American newspapers were products of economic, social, and cultural conditions, including city growth, the public's desire for political and commercial news, and the need of business for an advertising medium. The character of the colonial newspapers was affected greatly by the public's and printers' ideas about political self-determination, a new American philosophy then taking shape. Colonial publishers, Kobre argued, "altered the character of their products to conform to...transformations in society....Expensive machinery, large personnel and extensive office buildings and plants were not necessary. Given these economic and technological conditions, a free press was easily secured for the people."[7]

In *Modern American Journalism*, Kobre studied the twentieth-century media from the same perspective. Emphasizing the development of the modern news media in terms of their interaction with their environment, he argued that gigantic forces including population changes and growth, industrialization, labor organization, and a spirit of social reform transformed America in the first half of this century and thus drastically altered the nation's news media. As the media mirrored the changes in economics and society, they changed to conform to new conditions. Thus, there developed a greater emphasis on interpretive journalism and newspaper column writing to explain a complex society to readers. Journalism schools and associations of journalists grew in importance as their profession grew more sophisticated. Technological developments in radio and television altered traditional media practices. Because of rising costs of labor and newsprint, publishers consolidated newspapers and formed chains to save money and to buy production material on a larger scale, mirroring similar developments in such other businesses as grocery store chains. Unlike Progressive historians, Kobre thus explained -- as did several other Cultural historians -- the business growth of the media as harmonizing with the tremendous changes in industrial, social, and economic conditions of the twentieth century. While the harmonizing frequently occurred in very dynamic ways, Kobre concluded that changes in the media were natural results of the social and economic environment.

A notable impetus in encouraging studies from a particular kind of "cultural" perspective was provided in 1974 by publication of James Carey's article "The Problem of Journalism History" in the inaugural issue of the journal *Journalism History*. By claiming

---

[7]Sidney Kobre, *The Development of the Colonial Newspaper* (Pittsburgh: Colonial Press, 1944).

that a "cultural history of journalism" would be a "new" interpretation, Carey overlooked the fact that many works already had
been written by Cultural historians; and the approach he called for
was closer to what general semanticists term *perception of reality*
than to cultural history. Similarly, historians who have tried to
apply the approach have normally used the term "symbolic
meaning," which more accurately describes their assumptions than
does the word "cultural." Carey limited his definition of "cultural"
history to the relationship between the media and human "consciousness" and stated that historians studying journalism should
be concerned principally with the "way in which men in the past
have grasped reality." The role the press played historically in that
process of grasping reality, he said, is the key to journalism
history.[8] Although little historical evidence exists to document such
a media-reality theory, Carey's article probably has been the most
influential in the last few years in encouraging theory-oriented
historians to look at the media from a particular perspective. Their
attempts to employ their "symbolic meaning" assumptions remain,
however, primarily on the philosophical level.

The Necessity of Interpretation

Understanding schools of historical interpretation is essential to the
communication historian. Historians have two primary jobs. One
is to describe the essential nature of the past. The other is to explain
why that essential nature was as it was. Interpretation helps provide
explanation. Without explanation, history is dry if not dead. The
presentation of data without explanation of why or to what effect
offers little insight or understanding. Explanations grow out of
historical perspectives; without a perspective in which it is based,
historical writing tends to wander. It is a traveler with no road map
or destination -- who takes one road or another and never arrives
anywhere because he had no place to go. While the historian or student may find none of the six interpretations discussed in this
chapter fully satisfying and while none is without faults or offers
the full answer in the search for historical understanding, without
them or other interpretations historical study would offer little more
than accumulations of data. An understanding of interpretation is
invaluable not only in understanding the histories that have been
written. It is essential to the historian who wishes to add to our

---

[8]"The Problem of Journalism History," *Journalism History* 1 (1974): 3-5
and 27.

understanding of communication history and make significant contributions to historical study.

3

The Fundamentals of 'Good' History

The quest for excellence in communication history is by no means new. More than a quarter of a century ago, Allan Nevins, a journalist turned historian, called attention to many of the problems that account for the thin and uneven quality of writing in "this branch of history." Nevins, then president of the American Historical Association, urged that journalism history be held to the same standards as other branches of history, but observed, "of such history we have as yet the barest beginning."[1] Since that time, the level of communication history has improved, yet it is still uneven.

The craft of history includes people from many different backgrounds. Statesmen, diplomats, generals, businessmen, journalists, and others join the academicians to compose its ranks. So it is also with communication history. Some communication historians were previously practicing journalists; some are academicians. Moreover, academicians who are interested in communication history come from various scholarly orientations. Such diversity, of course, attests to the widespread interest in the subject, but it also can cause problems. Criteria for excellence in scholarship can differ from field to field.

What then are the standards of excellence that communication history should embrace? In the 1850s when that gifted churchman John Henry Newman undertook to found a Catholic University in Ireland, he realized that an explanation of the principles of a

---

[1]Allan Nevins, "American Journalism and Its Historical Treatment," *Journalism Quarterly* 35 (1959): 412.

university would help mitigate doubts and opposition regarding the creation of such an institution in Dublin. He developed that explanation in a series of lectures that became the basis for his much heralded *The Idea of a University*. Those lectures rested on the fundamental proposition that a Catholic university must first be a good university. Newman's premise applies to communication history since the first prerequisite of any serious history is that it be "good" history. Assuming that serious students consider it absurd to have the creation of poor history as their goal, the foregoing proposition seems simple and correct enough. In fact, it delivers us to the edge of a serious and long debated problem.

To define "good history" is a dubious task. That is the problem. History has no single methodology; its practitioners hold many different persuasions about the discipline. To define that which is characterized by such diversity, indeed, would be presumptuous. Nevertheless, people who wish to engage in a serious pursuit of history, particularly those whose scholarly background lies in another field, should know about the standards of excellence that have general recognition in the field. In the case of those interested in communication history, we shall assume that they have or will acquire knowledge of the mass media as an institution. They also should deepen their understanding of the schools of communication historians mentioned in the previous chapter. A knowledge of the history of historical writing might also illuminate the principles and controversies associated with history as a major dimension of human inquiry. They should at least become familiar with the life and works of a few of the master historians, if they have not already done so. They should be familiar with the historical literature already written about their field. As they pursue their scholarly interest in communication history, however, an introduction to the basic standards of history will also be of value to them. The first part of this chapter focuses on those standards as they are generally perceived today. In the final two sections, we shall consider some matters related to the ongoing effort to produce better history.

The Criteria of "Good" History

Purists, of course, might quarrel with anyone's delineation of the hallmarks of "good" history. Yet historians do recognize and attempt to comply with a number of basic standards. We have listed here seven of these standards, which we believe describe fundamental elements of good history. In each case, we have provided a brief elaboration by way of introduction. More will be said later on most of the elements themselves.

1. *Topic Definition.* Although this task may appear uncomplicated, it is one of the most difficult of all those involved in historical research. A topic should be chosen according to the established rules of selection; it should be clearly defined and significant. It must make sense in terms of time and space, and it must have continuity of content. To satisfy these requirements, one has to shape, limit, and sometimes reshape the boundaries and purpose of an investigation.

2. *Bibliographic Soundness.* A well-developed bibliography is essential to any serious historical work. Given the abundance of historical literature, establishing a proper bibliography can be a problem. All varieties of primary sources and secondary literature that are germane to the topic should be compiled. Standard authorities on a subject must be included as well as all monographic and periodical literature that bears direct relation to the topic. The monographic and periodical search might well carry one across disciplinary borders.

3. *Research.* Evidence is the grist of history, and research involves finding it, evaluating it, and reconstructing a segment of the past based upon it. When historians speak of producing a well-researched study, they mean one that rests upon primary sources with secondary sources employed only with discretion as the circumstances of narration merit. The evidence of history, its sources, may be found in either published or unpublished form, but sound history stands upon sound research. There are four basic activities involved in research: (1) compiling a complete record, (2) evaluating the sources that compose that record, (3) understanding the explicit and implicit meaning of those sources, and (4) explicating the essence of those sources in the history one produces. Researchers must master all four of these activities to achieve effectiveness in their work. To do so requires time, patience, imagination, knowledge, and discipline. It depends on one's ability to find and to analyze.

4. *Accuracy.* There can be no substitute for accuracy in both the research and writing of history. In regard to research, one must attempt to reach the truth of the matter. Did Dr. Samuel Johnson witness or manufacture those parliamentary speeches he reported in the British press? He once admitted that he had only visited the gallery in the House of Commons one time. If he did not hear them, then who heard them and related them to him? Were they faithful reports or invented ones? In communication history sources one frequently encounters exaggerated reports, examples of views shaping news, and even invented interviews. What is truth in such cases? In research one must try to reach the truth of the matter, to understand circumstances related to it, and to analyze the elements

of a given problem as exactly as possible. In short, one must establish not only the authenticity of data but also its meaning. Accuracy is also the cornerstone of good historical writing. It must govern one's presentation of evidence and handling of generalization as well the details of writing such as sharpness of particular references, the correct use of names, titles, and offices; the selection of the precise word or phrase of description; and the proper employment of quotations, figures, and footnotes.

5. *Explanation.* Previously, we spoke of the explication of sources. That is, indeed, an important element of explanation that runs through the construction of good history. In this case, we are attaching a broader meaning to explanation and are using it to mean the elucidation of the various processes involved in producing history. Explication of sources is part of the larger process, but the latter also includes other tasks historians perform in handling their material. There will be facts to explain, generalizations to form, and interpretations to offer. The quality of one's work depends on how well one explains the component parts of the subject under investigation as well as the full subject itself.

6. *Historical Understanding.* Occasionally in our discussion to this point, we have made reference to *historical understanding.* That term merits special attention, for it is central to good history. It may well be the most illusive of all the elements in history, but its presence enhances all good historical writing. By historical understanding one can mean having understanding of the circumstances and personalities pertaining to a study. It also can be taken to mean an understanding of historical movement, cause, and change. It can mean an understanding of life as it was in the past. So in their effort to understand some figure or episode, historians probe beyond the documents as such into contextual information. Sometimes this exercise involves closing gaps in the documented record or making connections. Sometimes it involves creating settings. To achieve understanding, one must develop an awareness of "time" regarding circumstances now vanished. "What distinguishes history from other humanistic disciplines," wrote Trygve Tholfsen, "is overriding interest in the role of time in human life."[2] Historians often speak of the need to avoid "present-mindedness" -- that is, viewing the past in terms of the present -- and stress the need to recapture the sense of the spirit of the times surrounding a study, to comprehend the feelings, persuasions, and emotions that once were real, to grasp how things happened in some

---

[2]Trygve R. Tholfsen, *Historical Thinking: An Introduction* (New York: Harper and Row, Publishers, 1967), 247.

past age, or to comprehend the nature of the forces that conditioned life in the past. Surely, communication historians must be able to comprehend past consciousness. An understanding of time, therefore, lies at the core of historical understanding. Without it there will be little comprehension of the reality that surrounded past figures and events.

7. *Writing*. The narrative element is essential to history and is another one of its distinguishing characteristics. It cannot be equated with excellence in popular writing nor even in journalistic writing, genres that adhere to their own standards. Historical narrative must be carefully crafted in terms of the elements of good writing and in terms of the elements of history. The latter involves the ability to integrate into the narrative the previous six attributes of history introduced in this section. To be sure, it relies on factual record, and must be faithful to it, but the historical narrative also tells a story. "Good history," Lester Stephens reminds us, possesses literary qualities; and "history which is drab, prosaic, and devoid of aesthetic value often merits the little attention it is likely to receive."[3]

The Historian Between Past and Present

Can there be truth in history? The same question can be asked of journalism. In the case of the latter, there are always a wide array of variable factors to consider such as the disposition of the journalist involved, the nature of news, the demands of the audience, the imperfect quality of sources, and the pressure to make journalism a paying business enterprise. Is the result propaganda or truth, and if it is somewhere between the two, is it presented as such? Even in the case of today's investigative reporting, there are limits to the time, expense, and effort that can be spent in researching a story. Journalistic writing, by its very nature, can only imperfectly reproduce the full reality of a current episode. Suppose the journalist had the time of the historian to publish. The results of the investigation might, indeed, be improved in degree of accuracy reflecting a more extensive use of sources and perhaps the benefits of detachment. But sources are never perfect, and the detachment of time has to measure against the loss of the sense of the moment. Consequently, if journalists find truth elusive in their explanation of all but the most obvious reportable data, it can be argued that historians might also.

---

[3]Lester D. Stephens, *Probing the Past: A Guide to the Study and Teaching of History* (Boston: Allyn and Bacon, Inc., 1974), 13.

The problem revolves around a double axis. In part it relates to evidence; in part, to the investigator.

Historians, like journalists, often despair at the yield of evidence. They frequently need more evidence, or more explicit evidence, to resolve a particular problem of interpreting data. Even in this day of the growth of archives and the abundant accumulation of printed and other evidence, one must wonder if the historian is forever at the mercy of the evidence that happens to survive. Today more documents are being produced than in previous times. The typewriter, the word processor, the tape recorder plus those now indispensable photocopying machines have provided quantity of record. Have they increased the accuracy of sources? The same technological culture that produced them also produced the greater means for people to communicate with one another without making that communication a matter of record. The same revolution that gave us speed of communication also increased personal contact, privacy, and potential secrecy. Beyond this present circumstance, historians have to deal with evidence that is far from satisfactory, much in the manner familiar to journalists in their engagement of sources. Are there gaps in the record? Can substantive contradictions found in them be reconciled. And, even if the record is complete, is it a biased account of truth? How many individual experiences become embellished with dramatic flourishes when recollected? The rules of evidence can help one, whether historian or journalist, to handle such problems in a fair way. They cannot guarantee, however, that the outcome will be at one with truth, nor can they ascertain that all people of all ages perceive fairness in the same way. Based on this imperfect record, the historian proceeds to advance explanations. By necessity, what part of them is incomplete? How much is hypothetical? What part is artistry or, in extreme cases, even artifice? In our own time, if we have witnessed a remarkable broadening of the definition of historical sources, which we have, we have failed to experience an end to the inherent problems of sources. Their limitations are simply part of the discipline; there is no prospect of their vanishing in the future.

Consequently, the fact of partiality of record permeates the nature of history. Complete truth cannot be known about anything other than the merest superficial elements associated with past episodes. When historians pursue the "how" and "why" of past episodes and when they discuss facts (as opposed to data) and ideas of times gone, they have to acknowledge an appropriate sense of restraint regarding conclusions. It is a characteristic that becomes a part of their professional judgment and a part of the tone of their narratives. It would be unrealistic for any audience to expect the full truth about a segment of the past from historians and arrogant of them to think they had discovered it. What can be expected is that they be truthful to the greatest extent possible, that they work to understand the past on its own terms, and that they demonstrate judgment that is honest, perceptive, and balanced. There is, then, a definite personal element in history related to the historian's stance between past and present and to his or her limited knowledge of both spheres.

This personal element deserves further attention for a number of reasons. Like journalists, historians are products of their own social environments; they can never completely escape the conditions that shaped and continue to shape them. They all have emotions, persuasions, and ethical standards, some of which are shared in part with others of similar background and some of which are uniquely their own. Religion, nationality, geography, class awareness, ideology, education, occupation, knowledge, and experience give definition to human perceptions. To what extent do these perceptions become habits of thought, perhaps even biases, either recognized or not, that enter into the writing of history, thus imperiling the reconstruction of the true past? One cannot easily forget the comment of the then elder British statesman A.J. Balfour about Churchill's multi-volume account of the First World War: "Winston has written an enormous book about himself and called it The World Crises."[4]

History is, after all, a reconstruction by an individual of things past. How much of ourselves do and should we put into it? Modern historians, particularly those cast in the Rankean mold of scientific history, may have extolled the goals of impartiality and objectivity for history, but others have pondered either the possibility or plausibility of such well-intended aims. In fact, in recent years New Left and radical historians, like those journalists who prefer advocacy to objectivity, have rejected such neutrality in favor of a more active search for and development of history as a tool to employ in solving present problems and improving society. In the process, if they are able to reconstruct an accurate version of the past, they have enhanced history. If not, as David Hackett Fischer observed, they become "methodological reactionaries." In fairness, it must be admitted that radical historians do not hide their opinions. Among historians of the mainstream, that has not always been true. Moreover, many communication historians have tended to believe they could tell history as objective truth. Other writers in previous generations have produced histories based on their conviction that they were on the side of truth and thus have subordinated history to cause. Present-mindedness has distorted much historical writing,

---

[4]Quoted in Marwick, *The Nature of History,* 135.

as has historians' tendency to view history from the perspective of the mass communication professions rather than as detached observers. Most journalism historians have judged the past by their own generation's journalism standards. Nevertheless, let us return to the fundamental question, what part of oneself do and should historians put into their history?

The presence of the personal factor is manifest in all of history from its inception to the final act of composition. It is, in fact, one of the strongest links between history and journalism. The well-known foreign correspondent Herbert Matthews once explained: "That a journalist has, at all times, his bias and sympathies is certain, since he is only a human being. That those feelings color his choice and presentation of news, without his being conscious of it, is also obvious....It all boils down to the impossibility of achieving perfection or complete precision, and we journalists could write as many books on that subject as the philosophers have written."[5] Much the same comment could be made of historians. They reveal preference in choice of topic, selection of evidence, and the words they employ to describe and explain their subject. The demands of narrative and explanation force historians to become a part of their scholarship.

Historians interpret past figures and events to the present, and in doing that they not only evaluate sources but also exercise judgment. At some points in their reconstruction of past happenings those judgments may be value judgments. Then it is only fair to ask, whose values? Who was right in the partisan press wars of the early 1800s or in the ideological conflicts of the muckraking era? What was the good life for one group in society may have been exploitation or oppression to another group. The freedom of the press rights that were given to newspapers may have been denied to radio in the 1930s. Was that proper? Or, what serves the purposes of journalism may hinder the conduct of government. In the epic of man's past experiences one can find many contradictory, even irreconcilable, convictions, honestly held in their day. They may have appeared as manifestations of national, religious, class, economic, political, professional, environmental, or generational differences and peculiarities. Moreover, who can doubt that standards change, culture evolves, opinions shift, styles come and go, and commitments rise and wane. Such uncertainty is part of the complexity of the past, and historians must explain such things. They are also

---

[5]Herbert L. Matthews, *The Education of a Correspondent* (New York: Harcourt, Brace and World, Inc., 1946; reprint ed., Westport, Conn.: Greenwood Press, 1970), 59.

expected to reflect upon it, to put the best of their thought into it.

Should that reflection involve them in moral judgment? No one expects contemporary history to be a moral narrative, but one might expect it to reflect judgment that goes beyond explanation as such. History's audience is a present one, and it is interested in knowing the meaning of past episodes. Meaning, of course, can be found in explanations of human achievement and failure and in many aspects of individual and collective past human action. In reflecting upon meaning, upon that which is of significant quality, might a comment expressing an ethical value be in order? There are, indeed, ethical and moral dimensions of past human behavior. Every age has its obscene, criminal, and evil elements. Should historians avoid comment on such things? There was an Adolf Hitler, and genocide did occur, as have many other terrible acts in history. Simply to explain man-made disasters and dramatic failings in human conduct stops short of saying whether it was right or wrong. As C.V. Wedgwood, who has probed this matter with restraint matched by wisdom, observed: "...from explaining an action we move insensibly towards justifying it, and from thence towards a general blurring of moral issues and a comfortable belief that circumstances are always to blame, and men and women are not....This outlook steadily and stealthily fosters the conviction that nothing is good or bad in itself but only in relation to its surroundings."[6] That observation touches the nerve of the issue. Historians, like all writers who describe the human experience, make moral judgments all the time in their use of language (e.g., one person's order is another's oppression). Would it not be better to recognize the habit and discipline oneself to handle it with discernment and precision? Moreover, when it comes to unethical acts in the past of a dramatic sort, the historian's audience expects reflection about such matters. Historians have a responsibility to provide that, not to overdo it, but to do it with a broadness and sense of honesty that will enhance meaning about significant questions. Finally, let us remember history can be a source of inspiration to some people. That being the case, the historian's responsibility includes being ethically responsible. There is a great deal of common sense in Barbara Tuchman's statement "to take no sides in history would be as false as to take no sides in life."[7]

Without the historian acting as a responsible interpreter of past

---

[6]C.V. Wedgwood, *The Sense of the Past: Thirteen Studies in the Theory and Practice of History* (New York: Collier Books, 1967), 48.

[7]Barbara Tuchman, "The Historian's Opportunity," *Saturday Review* 25, February 1967, p. 31. Also cited in Stephens, *Probing the Past, 55.*

happenings, it would be difficult to have a deep awareness of self, to be intellectually honest, to seek understanding of the past on its own grounds, and to recognize that there is a time and place for ethical judgment. Historians stand between past and present and must engage both with imagination, integrity, and a sense of responsibility. The creation of that delicate balance represents one of the greatest challenges in historical scholarship. As one contemporary authority on the relevancy of history to the present writes: "A mastery of the techniques of scholarship does not necessarily...guarantee good history, which is also the matter of the human equation, the sum total of the man or woman using the techniques."[8]

The Open Borders of Knowledge

All historians wish to have the fullest grasp of their subject that they can acquire. To that end, they traditionally have been informed by many specialties of knowledge such as paleography, epigraphy, diplomatics, numismatics, heraldry, genealogy, linguistics, and statistics. Quite naturally too, they have had a long reciprocal relationship with the social sciences.

The relationship between geography and history, for instance, is pronounced; these two collateral studies logically intersect at many junctures. Geography explains the physical setting in which history resides and enlightens one about nature's violent and quieter influences on mankind. Knowledge of geography is as important to historians writing today as it was to their counterparts hundreds of years ago. At the very least, as W. Gordon East observed in his thoughtful volume *The Geography Behind History*, history raises "the familiar questions Why? and Why then? but also questions Where? and Why there?"[9] Historians, of course, understand that communication is interwoven with the history of mankind from the earliest times. Trade, transportation, and communication are bound together over time in many ways. When the great historical studies are written on that theme, who can doubt that geography will be present in them? Surely the development and practice of communication, and of media themselves, have been influenced by climate, habitat, town settlement and growth, and urban development as well as by the earth's physiographical features --

---

[8]Carl G. Gustavson, *The Mansion of History* (New York: McGraw-Hill Book Company, 1976), 334.

[9]W. Gordon East, *The Geography Behind History* (New York: W.W. Norton & Company, 1965), 4.

subjects on which the geographer can inform the historian. The same thing can be said of communication history and technology, economics, politics, and numerous other specialized areas.

Important differences, of course, both in style and substance exist between history and the social sciences. An extensive literature exists on that point, and this is not the place to review it in depth. Suffice to say, the differences are real enough, but they do not apply totally. Indeed, there are many points of convergence between the studies. Historians and sociologists, for instance, may use a common body of information for different purposes, perhaps less so today than a generation ago; yet an overlapping between the two occurs at point of contact with many topics. Communication historians today profess a new interest in many things about the past such as public opinion, newspaper readership, advertising influence, sensationalism, the media and violence, newsroom organization and social change, to mention only a few current topics, that also interest sociologists. They are interested also in how people behave in groups and in the mass. To proceed in investigating such topics in communication history without knowledge of what sociologists have said about them would be unwise. The same, of course, can be said of sociologists who explore the same questions, for there is a definite historical element in any sociological explanation. By making that statement, one is not suggesting that history become sociology or that sociology become history. The point is simply that two disciplines can overlap in terms of subject, and at those points it is logical to expect intellectual interaction to occur.

Communication historians explore subjects that frequently fall between the disciplines. If one were to take the case of the press in the Soviet Union during Stalin's time, to comprehend the subject one would need to know about political theory as well as history. Or, consider again history's convergences with sociology, a borderland familiar enough to communication historians. Today, for instance, one topic that attracts historians' attention is the subject of riots that occurred in the past. It attracts the interest of sociologists too. More is known about riots in America between the 1740s and the 1770s and between the 1830s and 1850s than those that occurred during the intervening decades. Only recently have historians focused on American riots between 1780 and 1830. Newspapers of that era, so important as a source to both the historian and the sociologist, we are told, "seldom covered riots: politics and trade were much more important than local news...[and] local news which detracted from the commercial reputation of a community was especially taboo."[10]

---

[10]Paul A. Gilje, "'The mob begin to think and reason': Recent Trends in

Communication historians already have helped to explain that particular circumstance, and they will no doubt have much more to say on this topic and similar ones that social historians are bringing to the surface. In doing so they will want to know about the questions sociologists have asked of such phenomena and the varieties of explanations they offer about them. The findings of social psychologists on the subject should interest them too. In order to understand the individual and collective experience of past periods, the communication historian needs, as always has been true of historians, an understanding of time and place. As all historians, they also need to be broadly informed about their subject -- not only about the media themselves but about the many sides of knowledge regarding them at any given time in the past.

In fact, communication historians operate in an extremely fluid area of history. Since the media have influenced, and have been influenced by, so many facets of modern life, their history is multi-sided. So too is most history that is worthy of consideration. To understand the media in modern history, historians must be able to comprehend a good deal about business technology, ideology, politics, public opinion, national power, international relations, etc. So, again we see them pursuing topics across disciplinary borders from an historical base.

Moreover, there is the individual in communication history to consider. Was Joseph Pulitzer, for instance, an average man? Quite to the contrary, he was an extraordinary man of tattered nerves, many maladies and eccentricities, a remarkable man to be sure, and a genius as a publisher. How can a communication historian grasp, let us say, Pulitzer's driving and inexhaustible energy? Or, in writing about the behavior of correspondents in battle or the shaping of public opinion in a nation at war and many other subjects, communication historians can sharpen their comprehension of the subject by knowledge of what psychologists and sociologists have said about such questions.

If the goal of writing communication history is to write good history, then one must be broadly informed about the various dimensions of the subject being studied. As we have indicated, communication historians may have to stray into divisions of knowledge related to history but in many respects different from history. How far and in what manner should they travel along these lines? Before proceeding farther, we must consider the use of psychoanalysis and quantification in history. Both have excited a good deal of discussion and controversy among historians.

Psychohistory

First, let us consider the use that some historians wish to make of psychoanalysis. The desire to probe deep into the mind and behavior of individuals and groups in the past, in fact, has been alive in history since the days of its inception in ancient Greece. So it might be reasoned that some form of psychological thinking has long been alive in historical inquiry.

What historians have come to call *psychohistory*, however, goes beyond the limits of the more informal previous use of psychological generalization because it is a response to the development of psychology as a modern field of behavioral research. It also reflects the intention, which can be traced back to the nineteenth century, of some historians to make historical inquiry more scientific in nature. Since contemporary society so esteems science and considers whatever is "scientific" to have a high degree of objectivity and intellectual sophistication, one can understand the desire to use science to increase the accuracy and truth of history. In his much heralded presidential address to the American Historical Association in 1957, William L. Langer encouraged historians to deepen their understanding by exploiting "the concepts of modern psychology," by which he meant psychoanalytical thought and development.[11] More than a quarter of a century has elapsed since Langer's address, and during that time historians have revealed a heightened interest in psychoanalysis as a useful tool in their inquiries. The most notable use of psychoanalysis in communication history is Richard Hofstadter's *The Age of Reform* (1955), which attempted to describe muckrakers of the early 1900s as motivated by "status anxiety."

During this same time, apprehensions about applying psychoanalysis to history surfaced and could not be dismissed. Part of the reason is that a number of important psychological biographical studies, such as Erik H. Erikson's *Young Man Luther* (1958) and Sigmund Freud and William C. Bullitt's *Thomas Woodrow Wilson: Twenty-Eighth President of the United States: A Psychological Study* (1967), contained, in the judgment of many historians,

---

[11]William L. Langer, "The Next Assignment," *American Historical Review* 63 (January 1958): 284.

serious flaws.[12] Even Hofstadter, surely one of the most prestigious American historians of his generation and an advocate of applying psychological analysis to history, was criticized for his handling of psychological theory in *The Age of Reform.*

The reasons for the historian's apprehension of psychohistory, however, go beyond criticism of particular works. They deal with perceived differences between psychology and history and the difficulties of applying the former to the latter. Communication historians should consider these apprehensions about psychohistory as well as the reasons for using it, for they frequently operate in an area of history that calls for an illumination of personality, persuasion, and motivation. Their work often necessitates the ability to recapture the emotional edge of an historical moment; and, one must admit, in dealing with the journalists of the past, they have more than their fair share of eccentric personalities to decipher.

Basic to historians' uneasiness regarding the practice of psychohistory are concerns about the approach and evidence. To begin with, they tend to suspect that a psychological approach to history imposes prefixed theories on human actions in the past. Thomas A. Kohut, a scholar trained both in history and psychology, in a recent examination of this question observed: "...the psychohistorical method relies on theory, particularly psychoanalytic theory, to provide understanding and explanation. Figures and events from the past are not comprehended or made comprehensible on their own terms but are understood and explained primarily by psychological theory. Too often, when employing the psychohistorical method, the historian comes to the past with an understanding and explanation already in hand; the understanding and explanation do not emerge from the past itself but are the products of a theoretical model."[13] Traditional historians are no strangers to theoretic thought about the past; most students of the past have thoughts about and possible answers to questions they intend to pursue in mind when they approach

---

[12]For an example of the many reviews on the Freud and Bullitt study of Wilson, see A.J.P. Taylor, "Silliness in Excelsis," *New Statesman* 12, May 1967, pp. 653-54. Erikson's study of Luther received considerable criticism from historians, though the more thoughtful of their critiques also recognized Erikson's achievement. See, for instance, Roland H. Bainton, "Psychiatry and History: An Examination of Erikson's *Young Man Luther*," and Lewis W. Spitz, "Psychohistory and History: The Case of Young Man Luther," in Roger A. Johnson, ed., *Psychohistory and Religion: The Case of YOUNG MAN LUTHER* (Philadelphia: Fortress Press, 1977), 19-88.

[13]Thomas A. Kohut, "Psychohistory as History," *American Historical Review* 91 (April 1986): 337-38.

their investigations. Furthermore, historians approach their study with an awareness of the modes of thought of their own society. They should not, however, seek to impose a theoretical model on the past. To the greatest degree possible, they believe that the past should be allowed to speak for itself. Accordingly, historians are committed to understanding particular events and figures of the past as much as possible on their own terms. The application of psychological theory to past experiences can mar historical explanation since to be historical the latter must emerge from the evidence of the past itself.

Beyond these considerations on approach there is the matter of causation to consider. Historians tend to see particular experiences of the past in their full complexity and usually depend on a mixture of motives to explain human action. Psychological interpretations might suggest an unhistorical reductionism in causative explanations.

The question of evidence in psychohistory involves several considerations. Again there is the problem of psychoanalytic theory to confront. Historians use evidence of the past, but, as Kohut once again cautioned, "psychohistorians, when they rely on theory, also accept evidence from the present to validate their interpretations."[14] Their theories, he noted, are normally derived from contemporary evidence rather than from past evidence. His observations -- and they are not those of a detractor of psychohistory -- deserve close attention, since evidence lies at the core of historical inquiry.

Some historians feel that every age is unique. Conditions of one time are never repeated. Therefore, ideas and theories fashioned under the conditions of one time may be quite erroneous when applied to those of another. Surely it would be careless thinking to suppose that people in the past were the same psychologically as people are today, or will be in future generations. Their psychological responses to fear, anxiety, and suffering were influenced by a variety of social and cultural realities that were particular to their day. Moreover, it would be reckless to assume that the record of the past with which the historian normally works is similar to that which psychoanalysts handle in the routine of their work. The clinical relationship is missing. The historical "patients" cannot be questioned, and the records they leave behind are far from complete. In many cases those records are spotty. Perhaps they were randomly kept in the first place. Or, perhaps they were carefully chosen for posterity. Consequently, although the psychohistorical method may be a valuable tool, it does have limitations.

Nevertheless, historians are more and more coming to

---

[14]Ibid.

appreciate psychoanalysis as useful in probing human conduct in the past. They agree that it is not the one and only tool, that it must be substantiated by sufficient historical evidence, that what it produces must be placed in realistic perspective, that the psychoanalytic interpretation is simply an interpretation that might help to explain a particular past human action, and that the lack of psychoanalytic training is a problem for most historians. Indeed, the reasons for accepting properly applied psychoanalytical thought as a tool of historical inquiry are compelling. Historians, after all, are interested in human behavior, in human motivation and reaction. They should prepare themselves to understand these things as sharply as they can. Suppose, for instance, in the course of a study they become convinced that a person in that study was mentally ill. Knowledge of psychoanalytic explanations of mental illness would be useful in such cases.

But beyond that type of extreme instance, psychological generalization can help the historian to elucidate past human behavior. Historians are not interested, as a practicing clinician would be, in the proper treatment for the patient. Rather they are interested in understanding human action and reaction in the past and describing it with sophisticated accuracy in their explanations. Feelings and emotions were realities in a given past human episode and must be understood in their fullness.

A number of recent studies have shown that human behavior does and has changed over time. Those studies underscore the credence of the traditionalist historian's concern about the autonomy of a past period. But is that autonomy complete? It is difficult to quarrel with the recent conclusion of Peter N. Stearns and Carol Z. Stearns that psychohistorians need to pay greater attention to the fact of "change in emotional behavior over time...while admitting that certain psychological findings probably do describe human realities that may be immune to change." To that they add: "After all, we are animals with biological constraints; it is curious that many historians and social scientists have ignored biological factors in their studies of emotion."[15] Current treatment of mental disorders, which is based on medicine as well as on therapy, tends to confirm their point.

Regarding the traditionalist's concern about the use of psychological theory in history, current literature on historical methodology suggests two conclusions. First, it is not a tool for all historians

---

[15]Peter N. Stearns with Carol Z. Stearns, "Emotionology: Clarifying the History and Emotions of Emotional Standards," *American Historical Review* 90 (October 1985): 824.

to use; and, second, those who decide to use it should consider it only one of the methods they employ in their scholarship and as one of the factors to consider for purposes of explaining thoroughly examined historical material.

Quantification in History

Now let us consider the use of quantitative methods in history (also known as quanto-history or simply as quantification). Communication historians should study the debate surrounding their use since many people active in the field, but by no means all, approach the study with a background in communication studies, a field that is much involved in quantitative methodology and other skills associated with the social and behavioral sciences. Many were introduced to quantitative methods in their communication research courses.

Should those methods be applied to communication history? Richard L. Merritt in his study of the growth of American nationalism in the eighteenth century and others have demonstrated that quantification can be applied with success.[16] There are, in fact, a number of places in communication history where one can use quantitative techniques to advance and sharpen understanding of subject. They can be of use, for instance, in probing into the social, economic, and demographic aspects of the field. In grappling with the statistics of publishing, circulation, and readership these techniques are of obvious value. The same can be said about efforts to comprehend the currents of historical public opinion. Quantitative methods can sharpen the process of content analysis and aid in the development of collective biography. But, useful tool though it may be, like any other new historical source or technique, quantification has not shown that it can or should replace traditional methods.

It is natural enough that a number of contemporary historians find this methodology attractive. Interest in quantification in history increased as a new interest in social and economic factors grew among historians. Naturally the growth of statistical sources in recent generations and the advent of the computer with its capacity to store, index, and manipulate vast quantities of data were bound to foster interest in this method.

Quantification, of course, can have several meanings. To

---

[16]Richard L. Merritt, "The Emergence of American Nationalism: A Quantitative Approach," *American Quarterly* 17 (Summer 1965, supplement): 319-34.

some, it means the simple counting of figures of enumerative data, an old tradition in the practice of history. Others perceive it as a procedure by which such data can be tested in ways more common to social scientists than to historians. This second group of historians finds quantification a systematic method for historical scholarship, an invitation for historians to use hard data to test the validity of their generalizations and to develop explicit designs in the manner of the social scientist. These advocates are themselves divided. William Aydelotte, for instance, deems quantification an appropriate method for studies that lend themselves to it. Others, like Lee Benson, are attracted to it as a means by which history might acquire a genuinely scientific methodology and thereby become itself a social science. It is easy to understand why quantification, therefore, has been the source of controversy among historians.

The historians' reaction to this assault has been several sided. In part, it must be admitted, the responses of those among them who were suspicious of quantification were reactions to that which they intuitively disliked simply by means of their own professional temperaments. As C. Vann Woodward noted, they saw "their authority challenged, their humanistic values threatened, their canons of criticism ridiculed...." Besides, they found little comfort having "their cherished classics derided as 'soft,' impressionistic and unscientific."[17]   Then, too, did not quantifiers practice the techniques of the social sciences and perhaps even hope to use them to carry history away from its traditional moorings? Nevertheless, as more traditionally-minded historians have adjusted themselves to the presence of quantification in current historical research and perhaps even admit its usefulness in analyzing certain evidence, some fundamental questions regarding it remain.

Essentially these questions reflect three concerns: sources, object, and narration. Regarding sources, most historians maintain that a great deal of historical data is such that it cannot be quantified and that too great a reliance on statistical data will lead to distortion. Personal feelings and social and cultural forces and pressures are as important to the historian as so-called "hard" data. Can such things be measured? At the very least they suspect that an emphasis on quantification could lead to greater concentration of the already disturbing stress on recent history, since statistical data is less abundant and reliable for the more distant past. There is also reason to question if quantifiers too readily choose their data because of its recurrent or serial relationship to other data. Too much

[17]Quoted in Richard E. Beringer, *Historical Analysis: Contemporary Approaches to Clio's Craft* (New York: John Wiley & Sons, 1978), 193-94.

historical data defies placement into well-delineated categories and series. Moreover, the warning that "historical facts are unique in character, space, and time" does indeed restrain historians "from trying to fit them into a rigid theory or fixed pattern...."[18] Quantifiers rely on material that has the capacity to be measured. That thought led Arthur Schlesinger, Jr., to suggest the often repeated argument "that almost all the important questions [in history] are important precisely because they are *not* susceptible to quantitative answers."[19]

A particular approach which has become popular among communication historians in the last few years has been content analysis. Because some have relied almost solely on it for their research, it has created several misconceptions and problems. The popularity of content analysis stems from the fact that doctoral programs in mass communication have emphasized quantitative methods for social and behavioral research, and content analysis seems to historians to be the method most adaptable to historical research. In essence, content analysis is a method for the objective, systematic, and quantitative description of various characteristics of communication. Some historians use it simply to count the number of various items that appear in a publication and then group them according to similarities.

Often, historians have used content analysis alone as the means of research for particular studies. From it they not only have described the nature of the content but sometimes have attempted to imply various reasons underlying history, including writers' and publishers' motivations. Content analysis, however, can do only one thing: describe content. It cannot show, for example, a cause-effect relationship, and it cannot establish motives. It does not prove, for instance, that because a newspaper had a conservative economic policy its publisher's motive was to gain advertising from conservative businessmen.

To be generous to content analysis, however, we might add that it can suggest or hint what motives or relationships might be. But once it has offered its hint, the historian cannot jump to a conclusion. One must examine other historical sources, such as diaries or private correspondence or business records, that might establish evidence. By itself, content analysis is inadequate to provide the research material necessary in historical study. It provides only a

---

[18]Carl Bridenbaugh, "The Great Mutation," *American Historical Review* 68 (January 1963): 325.

[19]Arthur Schlesinger, Jr., "The Humanist Looks at Empirical Social Research," *The American Sociological Review* 27 (December 1962): 770.

part of the raw material the historian must use. Historical study requires thorough examination of not only the content of newspapers, for example, but of private papers, relevant political or religious or economic material, demographic data -- and on and on. The point for the historian is this: Content analysis can do nothing more than describe content, which is, after all, only one very small aspect of historical material. It cannot go beyond the material itself; and -- this point is particularly important for the communication historian -- it can *never* answer the question of "Why?"

The remaining two concerns about quantification relate closely to the first. Regarding the object of history, traditionalists are quick to point out that history must recreate real life. That deals not only with elements of historical setting but also with motives of the individual and of the many in the past. Suppose it is possible to explain that people acted in one way or another economically. One still wants to know if they were motivated by economic rationality. There are, moreover, cultural and social motives to consider. Did the newspapers that supported slavery in the nineteenth century or those friendly to Nazism or opposed to Communism in the twentieth assume their positions for solely economic reasons? Most important of all, do the mathematical models of the quantifiers, which grow more involved as the data grow in complexity, convey a sense of what it was like to have lived and to have been moved to action in some previous time? Even when history deals with the many, historians must strive, as Carl Bridenbaugh observed, to "show them as individuals whenever it can." That was what he had in mind in his 1962 presidential address to the American Historical Association when he warned historians not to "worship at the shrine of the Bitch-goddess, QUANTIFICATION."[20] Though vigorously put, his point merits pondering.

The final concern about quanto-history is the simplest to explain but equal in importance to the previous two. Will reliance on quantification impair the narrative element in history and its ability to communicate to a wide audience? Peter Laslett's outstanding study of pre-industrial England, *The World We Have Lost* (1965), stands as proof that this need not be the case. Most communication historians who rely on quantification have, unfortunately, made their texts read more like clinical reports than historical narratives. Good historical writing does more than provide a formulized description of the method by which the research was performed and of the findings it revealed. Mechanical structure and style is one of the injuries content analysis and other soft-science research

---

[20]Bridenbaugh, "The Great Mutation," 326.

methods have inflicted on historical writing in communication. Some historians rely so exclusively on content analysis that their article manuscripts and papers consist almost solely of a detailed description of the method employed. However, while research methods, whether quantitative or traditional, are critical in historical study, probably no more than one paragraph of a narrative should be devoted to the description of the methods. The quality of the research should be evident from the narrative. All that is needed -- even if a technique such as content analysis took a year to complete -- is a brief summary stating the most essential details.

The problem for writing created by quantitative methods in communication history appears to be a result of the uncertainty that communication scholars have about the academic and "scientific" validity of their field. Communication historians generally have not attained the maturity in research to have confidence in their performance. They feel compelled to defend the adequacy of their methods. The solution is study of historical methods -- and a mastery of them. Through such study, communication historians may one day be so rightly confident of the soundness of their methods that they will know it is evident from the results they present. Research methods should be so good that the reader will *know* from the findings that are narrated, rather than from the historian's minute detailing of how the methods were performed.

Nevertheless, the quantifiers have a strong argument, if quantification is understood as part of the aggregate whole of history. There are quantitative as well as non-quantitative elements and characteristics of the past. Quantification has the potential to expand and sharpen historical knowledge. The work of Lawrence Stone, Charles Tilly, Peter Laslett, and a number of other non-communication historians has proven that proposition. On a smaller research scale, some communication historians have used quantitative methods effectively in examining such topics as journalists' professional attitudes, the origins of sensationalism, the nature of media content, and the shift in American newspapers from foreign to domestic news. As a method, quantification has much to offer in understanding that part of historical evidence that can be handled by mathematical means. It can help historians to examine vast amounts of historical data and to search that information for characteristics, uniformities, and variations.

Based on their own explanation of their methodological principles and on the contribution their studies already have made to history, it is only fair to conclude that quantifiers can and do provide enlightenment on a wide range of historical problems including some of general historical interpretation. Several leading exponents of the method recently offered this perspective:

"What is attempted in quantitative research, as in other research, is not full knowledge of reality but an increasingly closer approximation to it....These techniques, even if they cannot produce the ultimate, can at least bring us increasingly closer to a position that we can urge with a certain amount of assurance."[21] Historians can and should acknowledge the value of quantification as well as its limitations. "History is still basically a humanistic study," as Lester Stephen reminded us, "and quantification is useful to historical research only insofar as it helps us to understand human beings in the past."[22] With that thought in mind, its present usefulness can be confirmed as well as its promise for the future.

Good history, we can conclude, should manifest many qualities. In contemplating them, we are reminded of its diversity. The variety of people who find the study significant enough to involve themselves in the labors of doing history continue to enhance and expand the study. The fascination that attracts them to historical scholarship should not be lost. It is one of history's richest resources. In the words of C. V. Wedgwood, "the mansion of history" has many rooms. Enough, Wedgood said, "to accommodate all of us."[23] To continue that metaphor, one can add that the mansion has many entrances and a sturdy foundation. History remains history, a form of inquiry with acknowledged standards but one that features elasticity in scope and method. It continues to bear kinship to the humanities and to experience a "love-hate" relationship with the social sciences. Seeking to recapture the human element in the past, its practitioners still recognize the importance of audience and stress the communicative element, the art, that has so long been one of its distinguishing characteristics. It still tries to comprehend the past on its own terms as far as is possible and to probe into the truth of a past episode, restrained always by the uncertainty inherent in all the larger aspects of the subject. History continues to depend on the historian, on that person's integrity, imagination, historical grasp, and professional inclination. Communication historians should consider the reasons that make Richard W. Steele's "The Great Debate: Roosevelt, the Media, and the Coming of the War, 1940-1941"

---

[21]William O. Aydelotte, Allan G. Bogue, and Robert William Fogel, eds., *The Dimensions of Quantitative Research in History* (Princeton, N.J.: Princeton University Press, 1972), 11.

[22]Stephens, *Probing the Past*, 109.

[23]Quoted in Gustavson, *The Mansion of History*, I.

such a fine article.[24] Its excellence as a piece of history is due less to the fact that it reflects or fails to reflect new techniques available to historians than to the fact that it successfully engages the accepted standards of good history.

---

[24]Richard W. Steele, "The Great Debate: Roosevelt, the Media, and the Coming of the War, 1940-41," *Journal of American History* 71 (June 1984): 69-92.

Basic Procedures and Techniques

How should one begin a project in history? Let us assume the project is one of considerable length -- a seminar or convention paper, a journal article, or a longer work: a thesis, a dissertation, or even a book. There are basic procedures to follow. At the start of a project, however, one must ask: What is it that I want to do with this study? How can it be done? What are the practical considerations to take into account? What will make it a worthwhile study? With such questions in mind, one can appreciate the fact that beginnings are never easy. So much is at stake. Barriers, known and unknown, lie ahead. There is vastness to confront and manage. Mistakes made at this point can haunt one throughout the entire study. They can even ruin it. In this chapter we shall consider some basic procedures that one should follow at the outset of a project.

Preliminary Reading

When students and scholars contemplate research in history, in any part of history, they already have started to think about a subject to investigate. From either general interest or previous courses, they have acquired at least a semblance of knowledge about a particular subject. The task they face now is that of sharpening the degree of knowledge they have, and general reading about the subject in its larger historical setting is a logical place to begin. How much of this general or preliminary reading is necessary? The answer depends on the person involved in the task. We all approach research with varying degrees of knowledge about a field that attracts our interest.

Even the seasoned scholar can drift from one historical area to another. Consequently, preliminary reading can be just as necessary for someone who has spent years in serious historical scholarship as for the student beginning a major research project for the first time. Let us, however, focus our attention on a student trying to start work on a research project in communication history. Several recent textbooks which include the subject to be investigated provide a sensible first source to consult. A student's advisor can offer guidance about which ones to use, but in the case of an area such as communication history, one in that area and one in general history can be recommended. Since the media do not exist alone in time, the duality suggested in this recommendation will become a major feature of the ensuing research.

The idea of beginning by using textbooks will cause some eyebrows to raise. Indeed, if one already has a firm grasp on the larger aspects of a research subject, this step might be skipped. But even in cases where there is an absence of such knowledge, purists can argue that a textbook might shape one's perception of a subject. Why not go to the sources and form your own perceptions? The point is logical and laudable, but unrealistic. By this time in a student's education, general perceptions of the subject already have been formed. That is one reason for the choice of a particular subject in the first place. Moreover, throughout the course of a research project, one will interact with what other scholars have said on the subject. It can, therefore, be helpful at the start to know how previous historians have shaped the subject and how they have presented it to the general audience.

For the next step in preliminary reading, logic suggests that one proceed to consideration of an appropriate volume in an extensive cooperative survey of a large field of history into which the subject falls. These multi-volume studies offer a synthesis of traditional and new information and interpretation (new to the date of publication). Many also contain excellent bibliographical essays. Two of the best known of these cooperative surveys are *The New American Nation Series* and *The Rise of Modern Europe* (Harper and Row Publishers). Let us say the subject of investigation is "The American Press and Europe During the First Years of World War I" (a topic that would need additional refinement). In that case, the following two volumes, one from each of the cooperative surveys mentioned above, should be considered: Arthur S. Link's *Woodrow Wilson and the Progressive Era, 1910-1917* and Bernadotte Schmidt's *The World in the Crucible 1914-1917*. Both Link and Schmidt are major historians, both provide a sophisticated introduction to the general times into which the subject falls, and both include numerous references to the press and journalists in their bibliographies.

Unfortunately cooperative histories, indispensable though they are, frequently can be dated since they represent a scholar's mature comment resulting from prolonged study of a subject. It is also unfortunate for communication historians that no cooperative survey exists for their particular field. Consequently, they should continue their general reading on communication aspects of their topic by pursing bibliographic leads cited in the textbooks consulted. In this case that would connect them with studies on censorship, propaganda, war correspondence, etc. They also should consult their advisors about authoritative communication studies that cover the subject in part. No doubt, in this instance, they would be directed to Robert Desmond's *Windows on the World: World News Reporting 1900-1920*, the second volume in his four-volume survey of world press history.

How long should one spend on preliminary reading? In a sense it lasts for the duration of a study as part of the ongoing general reading the study will entail. But when should one move on to the next stage? Bear in mind that any manual (including this one now in the reader's hands) oversimplifies divisions between stages for purposes of illustration. Still, it can be recommended that once you gain familiarity with the general dimensions of your subject (e.g., recognition of its basic political, economic, social, institutional, and biographical aspects), you are ready to proceed with further study. The next step involves defining a precise topic within the chosen area.

Topic Selection

A perfect topic is a rarity, particularly among those that students choose toward the beginning of their investigations. There are no guaranteed criteria for all occasions regarding selecting a topic, but the following suggestions are worth considering:

1. *Significance.* Is the topic important, and can its importance be demonstrated? Does it relate in an explainable way to things considered consequential in the past? Does it relate to matters that are important for society to know? If not, it is only of antiquarian value and fails to qualify as a viable topic. Moreover, in establishing the significance of the topic to one's satisfaction, attention should be paid to whether it is historically justifiable. Where does it fit into older work on the topic if previous studies have been conducted? Is this one needed? The answer to these questions takes us back to the purpose of history and assumes a bibliographic awareness that must mature as the investigation proceeds.

2. *Ability*. Researchers must ask themselves if they have the necessary skills needed for this investigation. If not, are they willing to acquire them? One would have to have knowledge of the Russian language, for instance, to investigate the Soviet press during Lenin's time. Communication history can involve so many aspects of life and society that the range of expertise regarding language, economics, politics, religion, and many other things related to it is also great. Without the expertise that will allow you to understand the topic in its historical setting and to understand sources, the topic will suffer. In such cases, one is well advised to select another.

3. *Workability*. Is the topic workable in terms of availability of sources? Remember, history depends on evidence, and that evidence must exist in sufficient quantity to provide answers for significant questions that will be asked of it. Moreover, some topics, however fascinating they might be, are unknowable. For instance, what was the source of the sense of humor that President Lincoln displayed so often in his dealings with reporters? Can it be known beyond description? In short, selection involves establishing the feasibility of investigating a topic. Curiosity and interest are important, but they can be taken for granted. Feasibility counts.

Once chosen, a topic must be delineated or restricted in terms of time, space, and content. A researcher can accomplish this task by considering the who, what, where, and when of the topic.

1. *Who*. Decide who or what groups or people will be included in the investigation.

2. *What*. Determine what aspect of communication (the issue, one might say) the study will examine. What are the important questions about the subject that have confronted previous historians? Does the topic have unity of its own? Every topic is related to others in close proximity to it, yet the successful topic should lend itself to individual treatment. The extent of that individual treatment, of course, depends on the researcher's preference and on the logical connectedness of the topic itself. It might be quite extensive and inclusive. In the end, however, it must lend itself to intelligible explanation on its own.

3. *Where*. Define the precise geographical area of the topic.

4. *When*. Determine a particular span of time to cover. Be sure it has a logical beginning and end.

By such procedures as described here, the researcher should be able to make the necessary and careful initial topic selection. Once made, it is possible though doubtful that the selection will hold until the end of the project. Either common sense or acquired knowledge may dictate topic redefinition as the research progresses. That adjustment, though sometimes painful to execute, might be needed for the eventual success of one's investigation. Research should proceed with an ongoing concern for the viability of the initial selection of the topic as well as for whatever redefinition of the topic one has made.

We would recommend that historians (but not necessarily students) look for topics of large scope. Small topics are chosen frequently because they are the only ones that a scholar can find which have not been "done before." They therefore frequently are insignificant and make little contribution to our understanding of communication history. All topics, even small ones, require a large investment of time and work; and one convention paper or one article seems little reward for so much. Thorough familiarity with literature already produced in communication history should suggest important topics that need to be reconsidered or new topics to be studied.

When searching for a topic, the historian might ask whether it is worthy of book-length treatment. Many topics in communication history need such study. When an appropriate topic is found, it offers several benefits over the smaller one. First, the topic will have to be significant. Second, it will make the historian realize that extensive research must be done. That is an advantage because it forces the historian to do thorough research. Third, once the research has been conducted, the historian has the raw material for several papers and articles in addition to a book. Hour for hour, then, time is spent more economically on a large rather than on a small topic.

Organization

Researchers use a number of basic techniques to organize their investigations. As their topics grow, for instance, they create timelines of events and actions. These timelines may be designed to cover the entire chronological scope of the topic or, in more integral detail, any of its component parts. They make a practice of creating a number of files to keep for instant references. Files on basic data and on biographical data, for example, can be indispensable tools in a researcher's work. Many also keep a file of ideas, thoughts they have about various aspects on their investigation. By actually putting ideas about their subject in writing, they sharpen them and, in the process, discipline themselves to think with precision as well as with imagination about their topic. Every researcher, of course, will develop his or her own version of devices such as these, and it is important to anticipate as early as possible in a project the type of information needed to have on instant recall.

An outline is one of the most useful of all organizational

devices. It should be designed early in the investigation as evidence is gathered, but it should not be allowed to dominate that evidence. The purpose of an outline is structural and functional. It helps one to perceive a possible order and framework for the study. It helps one to detect gaps in research and to strengthen its continuity. In short, it is a device for integrating old and new subject matter and for providing structure and direction for the project. Remember, however, that the past should be allowed, as far as possible, to stand on its own. Therefore an outline should not be considered a straitjacket for selecting evidence. To the contrary, it should be used as a tentative organizational device, which itself will probably have to be redesigned as the research mounts. Researchers will find it a useful instrument to use in pulling together the diverse but related data collected. As the project evolves, the original outline will undergo numerous changes, gradually becoming a tool for producing a usable structure for the narrative itself.

Let us suppose now that a student has begun a serious inquiry into an historical subject. We shall assume preliminary reading and organizational preparation have been done as far as possible at this point. What next? Questions must be asked: What does one want to discover about the topic? Everything? Do certain conclusions seem to fit before one finds the evidence to substantiate them? Everyone with any knowledge about a general historical subject has a hunch about answers to many questions within it. Sometimes it is even a well-known hunch. Nevertheless, in regard to a specific project, a researcher will do well to keep in mind this advice that Sherlock Holmes once gave to the faithful Dr. Watson: "I have no data yet. It is a capital mistake to theorize before one has data. Insensibly one begins to twist facts to suit theories, instead of theories to suit facts."[1] That sound if idealistic advice should serve as a restraint for students and scholars involved in historical research at least in forming the overarching structural framework of the study and in advancing conclusions.

Nevertheless, every researcher has thoughts about material at first contact with it and has certain questions in mind needing to be answered. In a sense, the process of selection of evidence has already started. Does that mean that distortion also has begun? Topic selection involved selectivity, and now questions to be asked of the material begin to emerge. Will not the simple presence of those questions guide the choice of evidence? Does the use of an outline structure research too much and force an artificial selection of

---

[1]Sir Arthur Conan Doyle, *The Complete Works of Sherlock Holmes* (Garden City, N.Y.: Doubleday & Company, Inc., n.d.), 163.

evidence? Moreover, what happens to evidence once one begins to formulate a hypothesis? Might that encourage reductionism or perhaps reflect bias in the selection and use of evidence?

Understanding the place of hypothesis in historical investigation can be of use in responding to these questions. A hypothesis is a tentative assumption, a proposition to be proven, modified, or rejected. For example, a hypothesis might be: the American press became a tool of propaganda during World War I. Once stated, that proposition would then have to be proven by evidence or changed. "The hypothesis," as Lester Stephens said, "usually plays a more crucial role in scientific investigation than it does in history."[2] Historians today tend to refer to the "working hypothesis," by which they mean a concept to use in approaching evidence. It involves the advancing of a possible explanation for evidence as research progresses. By its nature, it is a tentative device subject to accommodation forced by the sway of evidence. A hypothesis may be vague at first, but it is unrealistic to think that hypothesis formation can be delayed. Thought about a topic begins as soon as the mind starts to contemplate it. It can be recommended, therefore, that attention be given to crystallizing a working hypothesis (or working hypotheses) as part of the ongoing involvement with evidence.

The student might also find it useful to pose the topic in the form of question. The proposition that "the American press became a tool of propaganda during World War I" might be rephrased as the interrogative, "Did the American press serve as a propaganda tool during World War I; and if so, how and to what extent? If it did not, what role did it serve?" Stating the topic as a question forces the student to formulate it in a concrete and precise form. Concreteness and precision assist the researcher in determining what data he or she finds is relevant and what is not. As research progresses, other smaller questions may be raised in precise manner, and each should be answered.

Similarly, when the student first states the question to be studied, he or she should determine whether it really is the essential, most important, most interesting question. Both students and scholars are prone to ask questions that actually only scratch the surface rather than getting to the heart of history and their interest in it. A good way to find the heart is to ask the question "Why?" repeatedly, every time the student or historian thinks he or she has answered it. Suppose the question of study first proposed is "What were the attitudes about journalism held by penny press editors in the 1830s and 1840s?" The historian should then ask, "Why do I want to know?"

---

[2]Stephens, *Probing the Past,* 31.

The answer might be, "I want to know whether they thought of themselves as journalists and originated modern journalism, as many historians have claimed, or whether they thought of themselves in some other way and, if so, how?" Each "Why?" and its answer moves the historian closer to the essential question and to a topic of real importance in the study of history. At the foundation of every question may be one of true significance if only it can be uncovered.

The danger of forcing an artificial selectivity on evidence, however, remains. Researchers can take several precautions to minimize such dangers when dealing with working hypotheses. First, keep in mind that a hypothesis must be in accord with evidence. All available evidence must be considered. Indeed, it is contradictory evidence that usually forces modification or even rejection of a hypothesis. Second, do not avoid a basic step in research, that of gaining familiarity with the evidence. If you are dealing, let us say, with the personal papers of a nineteenth-century journalist, study those papers to the greatest degree possible. Use your imagination; let your natural curiosity lead you to examine evidence in the collection that bears little relation to your topic. Try to acquire a sense of such figures on their own terms. Be generous in your notetaking. Include items that inform one about general circumstances of the time as well as those that have direct relation to the topic being investigated. Pursue and clarify questions about the material at hand until you are satisfied that you have a basic understanding of it. It is unrealistic to suppose that in this process of familiarization you will have no hypotheses and questions in mind. They should be, however, more tentative than those that emerge as research progresses, and remember that even the latter are only working hypotheses, ideas to be tested against evidence. Finally, and this takes us back to the purpose of history, recall that the goal of history is "to reconstruct the past as accurately as possible."[3]   That goal involves modification of hypotheses and questions until one becomes convinced that the reconstruction is valid. Any methodological device such as constructing a hypothesis is simply a tool to use. It should not be allowed to master those who employ it.

Notetaking

Taking research notes is a more involved process than one might expect. It necessitates the mastery of some mechanics as well as thought. Consequently, even in this day of photo-duplicating machines and computers, a few comments about this most basic of

---

[3]Ibid., 32.

research techniques are in order. The fundamental rules to follow are these:

1. Always start by citing the source for the note.

2. Along with that citation, include a topical reference on the note.

3. Be consistent in where you place the citation and other references on the note.

4. Develop a method of consistent usage for copying direct quotations, particularly those long ones that will cover several pages of notes.

5. Make sure that a note is self-explanatory and that it will make sense when viewed a week, a month, or even years later.

6. Try to enter only one item on each note. Remember that the notes have to be filed in some coherent order.

7. Make accuracy of information a fetish. Double check your notes as you make them.

8. Never write on the reverse side of a notecard or a page of notes.

The arrangement and storage of notes can be a problem for communication historians because of the sheer bulk and variety of size of materials that can be gathered. Therefore, one has to develop some scheme of arrangement. Suppose the topic is "American Filmmakers and the Great Depression." Should notes be arranged according to topic, area, chronology, or person? Should notes reflect the organizational pattern of your project? Or should they be arranged into a collection of material to be employed as needed in the project, and perhaps in later ones too? If the last method is chosen, an effective indexing system will have to be developed.

We mentioned previously that notetaking involves thought as well as the mastery of mechanics. The thought referred to concerns what you attempt to tell yourself in a note. Notes are not only reminders of what you have seen but also a record of your observations of what you perceive in the sources. Some notes may be a paraphrase of lengthy materials. If that is the case, you must become skilled in the art of reducing long items to comments of manageable length. Some notes are your own reflections about either external or internal aspects of the source. Regarding the former, you might wish to know who initiated a series of letters and what their frequency was, or what type of document is under consideration, or how a newspaper that is being used for opinion or news can be described. Regarding reflections about internal aspects, you might wish to write a note interpreting a source or offering some explanation of how the information fits into broader patterns of thought and action. Explanatory notes can be as valuable as ones containing quotations or basic data. They must, however, be an accurate reflection of the source.

Everyone will develop his or her own habit of notetaking and storage. Nevertheless, it can be concluded that notes should be uniform, accurate, and complete. A system of arrangement and storage, whether in files of your own design or in a computer, should be logical, clear, manageable, retrievable, and expandable. Normally, sources have to be revisited and notes reexamined as one's own comprehension of the subject grows. The task of notetaking involves a person in the central function of historical research, the continuing interaction between historians and their sources.

The Library as a Reference Tool

Earlier in this chapter, we mentioned that researchers create their own informational files. These devices are useful in both research and writing. They provide the exact background information needed for identifying historical figures and defining data in your work. The information for these files, along with other items of reference you may need in your study, can be found in your own university library. Answers to all the questions of a general informational sort (e.g., identification of people and references to particular items, etc.) that emerge as one encounters historical records can never be found. Yet, a great deal of such information can be located by an imaginative use of reference tools available in a university library.

The Reference Room of a library will become the familiar habitat for a historian. It is a storehouse of information that enables one to find facts and to locate other information. In fact, the number and type of reference books can appear overwhelming. The Reference Room of any university library will be well stocked with general encyclopedias as well as a number of general historical surveys such as the *New Cambridge Modern History*. They represent, however, only a few of the reference works available for historical research. You also will discover lining the shelves of a Reference Room an array of almanacs, guidebooks, yearbooks, historical and current atlases, historical dictionaries, special subject encyclopedias, registers of events, and companion volumes to particular studies. Communication historians, for instance, would find *The Encyclopedia of American Journalism* (1983), *Mass Media: A Chronological Encyclopedia of Television, Radio, Motion Pictures, Magazines, Newspapers, and Books in the United States* (1987), and *Newspapers: A Reference Guide* (1987) useful sources.

To help you establish the "who," "when," and "what" about people, there are a number of sources to consult. Some are standard works and national in design, such as *Current Biography*, the *Dictionary of American Biography*, *The National Cyclopedia of American Biography*, *Who Was Who in America*, and *Who's Who in America*. Others are more focused, such as the *Dictionary of American Negro Biography* (1982), *Great North American Indians: Profiles in Life and Leadership* (1972), and *Notable American Women 1607-1950: A Biographical Dictionary* (1971). Yet others have an ethnic or religious focus or are specialized according to region, topic, or occupation. All are valuable sources for communication historians. So too are dictionaries of portraits and volumes on genealogy. Of special value to communication historians are references devoted exclusively to journalists, particularly William H. Taft's *Encyclopedia of Twentieth-Century Journalists* (1986) and Perry J. Ashley's three volumes: *American Newspaper Journalists 1690-1872* (1985), *American Newspaper Journalists 1873-1900* (1984), and *American Newspaper Journalists 1901-1925* (1983). Ashley's works appear in the Dictionary of Literary Biography series published by the Gale Research Company that contains other volumes of related interest for communication historians. For a comprehensive and classified listing of biographical sources and other reference works useful in historical inquiry, one might wish to consult Helen J. Poulton's *The Historian's Handbook: A Descriptive Guide to Reference Works* (1977), Francis Paul Prucha's *Handbook for Research in American History: A Guide to Bibliographies and Other Reference Works* (1987), and John R. M. Wilson's *Research Guide in History* (1974). Eugene Sheehy's *Guide to Reference Books* (10th ed., 1986) is the classic general guide to reference sources.

It is important for researchers to gain familiarity with key reference sources in the libraries they use most. What sources are available? How should they be used? The first question is easy to answer. Browse around a Reference Room and observe the sources held by the library. Take the time to make some notes on the sources that attract your particular attention. Make your own guide for these sources taking care to include their location and potential use. The books mentioned earlier and the Card Catalog, which we shall describe in the next chapter, can help you designate specialized reference works (e.g., special subjects source books and encyclopedias) that you may want to include in your guide. Regarding how these reference works should be used, it is important to study the Preface or Introduction for each work you select. Examine those sections for information on the work's arrangement, scope, and possible bias. Also, note the publication date of the work to see if it is up to date. A few words of caution are in order about the use of reference works. These are, as the name implies, for "reference." They are aids to research that provide basic information, an introduction to a subject, or particular information regarding definition and description. Consequently, they should not be cited as bibliographic entries in a research paper. (Major historical surveys that might be classified as reference works such as the Oxford and Cambridge histories are exceptions to this rule.) Reference works such as historical dictionaries, handbooks, and encyclopedias are tools to be used for research. They are not to be employed as substitutes for historical sources.

A Working Bibliography

What books and sources to consult? That question is central to any research endeavor from start to finish. A bibliographic foundation, for instance, must be established before work can be proceed on a topic. After that the bibliography will grow and will be defined to accommodate the topic as it develops. In the next chapter, we shall see that there are many tools to use in compiling a bibliography. There is, however, no perfect previously prepared bibliography to serve one at the outset of an investigation. Bibliographies compiled during research have an organic quality about them. It would be more accurate, therefore, to refer to a bibliography during the time of research as a "working bibliography." At the start of a project one compiles such a working bibliography as a guide to books and sources to consult. As work proceeds, some items are disregarded; others, added. It becomes a record of material to be consulted. The working bibliography, which is usually compiled on cards for purposes of convenience, becomes the basis for the proper "Bibliography" that will appear at the end of the completed study.

A working bibliography, then, is a tool, an evolving record of sources consulted and to be consulted. It should be complete in terms of time and type of sources. Both old and new books should be included. Older ones are worth at least a cursory consideration. They sometimes contain information not found elsewhere and may have different perspectives on material that can be found in newer studies. Older perspectives at least enhance a person's grasp of the historiographical setting of the subject.[4] Regarding type, it is necessary to have a working bibliography reflect the full range of works and sources available. In terms of published works, that usually means major works and documentary collections as well as

---

[4]The term "historiography" has several meanings. It is used here in reference to the history of historical writing.

biographical, monographic, and periodical literature. Beyond that, whatever oral, visual, and written records you intend to consult should be included. Leave nothing to memory. Finally, a working bibliography should be imaginative in its construction. It should include published works in related areas that may be relevant.

As early as possible in their bibliographic work, students will find it useful to identify "standard authorities" who have produced studies on or related to their project. Students may recognize them from a previous course in the field, or they might begin to gain awareness of them from study of bibliographical, historiographical, and review literature, or perhaps they will learn of them from conversation with their advisors. Regardless, they must consult these standard authorities. Sometimes a major historian will have written directly on a topic now selected for investigation from a different perspective. That work must be studied. For example, who would wish to conduct an investigation into the history of the American newsreel in the 1920s without studying Raymond Fielding's work on that subject? Or, who would wish to investigate the topic of foreign correspondence in twentieth-century wars without consulting works by Robert Desmond, John Hohenberg, and Phillip Knightley? Sometimes a topic fits into a particular larger area of historical investigation. For instance, should one decide to investigate the topic "American Immigrants and the Press in the 1890s," the works of Oscar Handlin and others on the more general topic of American immigration become key sources to consult. These standard authorities should be known, studied, and, if merited, confronted in a new probe into the subject. They represent the most significant scholarly statement on a general subject and sometimes on a particular topic. Most topics, of course, also involve an extensive monographic and periodical literature that one must search for information and interpretations. This literature, too, contains much that is authoritative.

The Computer and the Historian

In our technological age computer usage has expanded as one expected it would. Today its application extends far beyond fields such as applied mathematics, engineering, the natural and physical sciences, and business, where it was first adapted. The social sciences have been applying the computer to their studies for several decades. Can the computer be of value in historical inquiry? There is good reason to believe that it can be. In 1966 the journal *Computers and the Humanities* began publication, and there is a growing literature on the subject. At professional conferences, increased attention is now devoted to possible ways to apply the computer to historical study. Moreover, contemporary historians in general now view the computer like any other machine, as a tool to be used when appropriate.

The computer's speed and capacity in handling information, in fact, make it a fascinating tool. Its potential usage stretches from what you can do with an individual word processor, to what a large computerized bibliographic system can do for you in your pursuit of source materials, to how it can manipulate and organize data. A computer can facilitate work in compiling not only bibliographies but also indexes and concordances. It can store and assist one in handling numerical data. Computers can also be useful as tools for conducting literary and content analysis. Regarding written records, they can be programmed to find particular words or groupings of words, to search for key subjects, and to locate similarities and differences in the use of languages between texts. Indeed, the current status of computer technology suggests that in the future it will have an even greater role to play in textual analysis. Optical character readers are available today that can read a typed page. Some can read a printed page. In fact, there are optical character readers now in use that are able to read medieval text.

Nevertheless, computers have their limitations in historical research. They cannot do what historians must do to be historians. They cannot imagine the past, nor can they establish contact with the mind of the past, nor can they perceive the "climate of opinion" of a past age, nor comprehend what it was like to have lived at some other time and place in history. Moreover, they cannot establish truth beyond the quality of evidence that one feeds them, and that evidence, including numerical data, is far from perfect, as we shall see in a later chapter. One authority on the subject reminds us that "a computer does not do any thinking and cannot make unplanned decisions....Computers do not solve problems -- people solve problems. The computer carries out the solution as specified by people."[5] Consequently, the computer is a tool for historians to use. It will allow them to do certain things, surely in processing massive amounts of data, that otherwise would be beyond their capacity. Like all tools, the computer has its limitations for historical inquiry, and one should remain mindful of them. Nevertheless, because of its

---

[5]Donald D. Spencer, *Basic Programming* (New York: Charles Scribner's Sons, 1983), 17 and 19. Quoted in Jacques Barzun and Henry F. Graff, *The Modern Researcher,* 4th ed. (New York: Harcourt Brace Jovanovich, 1985), 101.

potential, beginning researchers should familiarize themselves with computerized technology and its possible application to history.

5

Searching for Historical Materials

Research depends on evidence and on access to it. Though that statement is the most apparent of truisms, it is an imperative one to grasp at this point in our discussion. A researcher might have to spend time at a major research library such as the Library of Congress in Washington, D.C., or the Center for Research Libraries in Chicago, or, perhaps, some other similar institution in another country. Or one might have to spend time working in some archives such as the National Archives in Washington D.C., or the Public Record Office in London. Visits to state and local historical societies may be in order. Some material is in private possession, and researchers may have need to locate and use it, too. Even in the case of books and other published or produced historical materials, historians have to learn which ones their own library holds and which ones have to be ordered. The search for historical materials can be an involved problem, but numerous bibliographic tools are available in a university library to help resolve it.

The Card Catalog as a Bibliographic Tool

Let us consider that venerable assemblage of file drawers known as the Card Catalog. Recently, a number of libraries have introduced a microfiche catalog system. Others use a microfilm system. The former allows hundreds of printed cards from a traditional catalog to be reduced and placed on one fiche. A computerized catalog system appears even more promising in solving problems of storing catalog information, and some academic and research libraries have begun to use an on-line computer system. Nevertheless, because of the time and expense of conversion, most libraries that use a computerized system will not place the contents of their existing catalog on-line. Therefore, researchers can expect to encounter a variety of catalog formats. The average college library still uses the traditional Card Catalog, and even those that have introduced a computerized catalog will probably use it in conjunction with a traditional catalog or cards reproduced in some type of microform in the foreseeable future. In any case, the historian needs to understand the principles of organization of the Card Catalog itself.

The Card Catalog is an index to all the books contained in a particular library. It is organized according to a selected classification system. The vast majority of university libraries in this country use the Library of Congress classification system rather than the older and more limited Dewey Decimal system. Each card in the Card Catalog or each on-line citation provides basic bibliographic information about a book, and each includes a "call number" indicating where this book can be found in the library. These catalog cards are arranged alphabetically in the drawers according to the author, title, and subject. Citations in on-line catalogs can be accessed similarly at terminals. Researchers may encounter two types of Card Catalogs. In one, called a "dictionary catalog," the author, title, and subject cards are filed together; in the other, called a "divided catalog," they are separated into two parts -- the "author-title" catalog and the "subject" catalog.

When using print or on-line catalogs, it is necessary to understand several important filing rules. Regarding author and title cards or citations, remember:

1. Articles *a, an,* and *the,* and their foreign equivalents, if they appear first in the title, are not considered part of that title for filing purposes. They are, however, considered part of it when they appear internally in the title.

2. Abbreviations are treated as if they were spelled out in full. (Dr. is found as Doctor, St. as Saint, etc.)

3. *M', Mc,* and *Mac* are all filed as if they were *Mac.*

4. Numbers in a title are filed as if they were spelled out in full (50 is found as Fifty).

5. Prefixes such as *de* or *von* usually are not considered part of a person's surname according to the standard rules of filing.

One also should be aware that organizations and agencies are considered as authors when issuing publications. They may be public ones such as the United States Office of Censorship and the United States National Archives, or they may be private ones such as the Institute of Early American History and Culture or the Association for Education in Journalism and Mass Communication.

Since researchers may know neither the name nor the title of books pertaining to their topic, particularly in the early stages of a biblio-graphic search, they tend to find subject cards more useful. For pur-poses of dicsussion these subject cards will be referred to as the "subject catalog" with the understanding that in a library that has a "dictionary catalog" they would be interfiled alphabetically with the author and title cards.

The subject catalog has much to offer researchers, yet at first its arrangement might appear illogical. Subject cards or citations are filed alphabetically for the sake of convenience. Consequently, a sequence of subjects may be unrelated. To correct this incongruity, catalogers add "see also" cards and citations. The researcher should not confuse them with the "see" references that direct one to a proper subject heading in cases where the subject heading one has in mind is non-existent in the classification system. A "see also" ref-erence serves a different function. It directs one to other existing subject headings related to the one under examination. This cross-reference system can be used to round out the extent of one's subject according to the possibilities that the system provides. For example, the "see also" reference for the subject "Journalism" would lead one to additional and related subject headings such as "College and School Journalism," "Press," and "Reporters and Reporting," which would not be filed in the subject catalog in proximity to the subject heading "Journalism." According to standard rules of cataloging, "see also" references are placed at the end of the first general division of a subject run. Subject headings are filed with the general subject category coming first, followed by the various sub-divisions of that subject. For example, consider "the Press" as a subject heading. Entries in the subject catalog for that subject begin with a general category labeled "the Press." Directly after that there are various subdivisions into which catalogers separate the subject, "the Press," such as "Press -- History," "Press -- Argentine," etc. "See also" references appear at the end of the section "the Press." When justified, they also may be found at the end of any subdivision of the subject where there is an appropriate cross-reference to make. The subject catalog, however, only lists subjects for which a particu-lar library has holdings. Most libraries that use the Library of Congress classification system have the two-volume set, the *Library of Congress Subject Headings* (1986), near the catalog. This set is the authority for subjects in that library's catalog and can lead the user to other useful headings.

Subject headings can appear confusing at first. Using them calls for a little knowledge, imagination, and some patience too, but the results can be rewarding. It helps to understand a few basic rules that govern the arrangement of the subject catalog. There are four basic types of subject headings:

1. A single noun without adjective modifiers and undivided (e.g., "History" or "Journalism").

2. A noun followed by subject divisions (e.g., "History -- Bibliography" or "Journalism -- U.S.").

3. A noun and an adjective modifier in either uninverted (e.g., "Political Cartoons") or inverted (e.g., "Journalism, Commercial") form.

4. A phrase composed of two nouns (with or without modifiers) linked by a conjunction or a preposition (e.g., "Press and Politics").

These basic divisions are often subdivided according to form, topic, geography, and chronology. Form and topical subdivisions are listed first, followed by geographical and chronological ones. Consider the following examples. (These headings and those that follow were chosen as examples of general order and are not consecutive runs. In a Card Catalog, one will find intervening entries.)

Propaganda
Propaganda -- Addresses, Essays, Lectures
Propaganda -- Bibliography
Propaganda -- Collections
Propaganda -- History
Propaganda, American
Propaganda, British
Propaganda, Chinese

and,
United States -- History
United States -- History -- Addresses, Essays, Lectures
United States -- History -- Bibliography
United States -- History -- King Philip's War 1675-1676
United States -- History -- King George's War 1744-1748
United States -- History -- Revolution 1775-1783
United States -- History -- Constitutional Period 1789-1809

Beginning researchers should note that it is worthwhile to follow a subject heading division through all the levels of its divisions. In the following case of a run of subdivisions, someone interested in journalism and the Spanish-American War of 1898 would miss much of consequence to that topic by failing to consider the full listing of subdivided subject headings:

United States -- History -- War of 1898
United States -- History -- War of 1898 -- Cartoons
United States -- History -- War of 1898 -- Journalists
United States -- History -- War of 1898 -- Personal Narrative

A little detective work combining knowledge of subject and thoroughness of approach will produce the greatest yield from the subject catalog. Because its value increases as one's knowledge of the subject grows, researchers will find themselves re-consulting it many times during their work on a given topic.

The library catalog, however, has its limits as a bibliographic tool. A cataloger may assign a number of subject headings to a book, but these cannot always accommodate the complete contents of the book. Moreover, the subject headings used are frequently broad. At the beginning of a project, therefore, a researcher might encounter difficulties due to these circumstances. Furthermore, the catalog is limited to the holdings of a particular library, and normally it does not list parts of books, essays in anthologies, newspapers, or preiodicals. Most important of all, it provides little direct help in locating those manuscript sources that are so valuable to historians. To remedy these limitations, a researcher must turn to other bibliographic resources found in the Reference Room.

Locating Historical Materials

It is possible to find historical materials almost anywhere. Nevertheless, when one speaks of historical materials -- the records upon which research in the field rests -- it is usually collected, organized, or classified materials that one has in mind. Although some may be held privately, the researcher will find materials of this sort most often in a library or some other institution that involves itself in storing, organizing, and preserving sources of history. Your own university library contains many such materials; not only books but also documents, newspapers, periodicals, etc., are to be found there. In some cases your library may have an archives or a rare-book collection. Accordingly, researchers can find some materials for their inquiries in their own institutions. Sometimes, however, they may have to travel to a library that has needed manuscript materials or to an institution that holds significant archival materials. For a comprehensive discussion of how to locate materials in their own library and in other libraries and archives, researchers should consult Thomas Mann's *A Guide to Library Research Methods* (1987).

Archival and manuscript material is of prime interest to

historians. Their research rests on the foundations of these types of resources more than on anything else. Before proceeding further, therefore, a brief explanation of terms is in order, for the distinction made between these two types of records is not always understood. There is, in fact, reason for the confusion, since some similar items may be found in either a library or an archives. But, although a library might contain or be "the custodian for" an archives, a library is not an archives. A library collects items, some published and some in manuscript form. Manuscript materials may be found in an archives too, but when encountered in a library they are more individualized; and, since they are frequently the private papers of an individual, it can be said that they are also more personalized than records found in an archives. Accordingly, in the William Allen White Papers at the Library of Congress one will find the correspondence, documents, original drafts of published works, and all other such times that White, or his family, kept and made part of the collection, or items that the library has added to that collection. Frequently, in such manuscript collections, the materials are uneven; items may not have been kept with preservation for public use in mind. At the very least, they are the papers of an individual person or thing.

For an archives, to the contrary, it is not the records of an individual that dictate inclusion, but rather how those records might fit into the kept materials of an organization or agency, or perhaps a special type of preserved historical record. This is a major difference. One will, for example, find the records of the Committee on Public Information that President Wilson created during the First World War in the National Archives,[1] while the papers of its chairman, George Creel, will be found in the Library of Congress. The placement of materials in an archives depends on public or private "functional activity" that occurred and falls into the scope of interest of a particular archives.

In terms of the traditional distinction made between the two

---

[1] A brief explanation of the "National Archives" is in order. In 1935 the United States established a National Archives, the last major nation to do so. Some years later, in 1949, it was transferred to the newly created General Services Administration, and its name was changed to the National Archives and Records Service. In 1985 the National Archives became an independent agency, the National Archives and Records Administration. Today the National Archives occupies a large, imposing building in Washington, D.C., located halfway between the White House and the Capitol. There are now three additional Washington and suburban D.C. locations for United States government records; and, beyond that, the National Archives operates twenty-three other archives and records centers around the country.

terms, a library is a "collecting agency," whereas an archives is a "receiving agency." The latter receives the records of groups, organizations, agencies, etc., and it arranges that material according to place of origin (i.e., by organization or agency, etc.). Such materials are cataloged by groups and series under the organization or agency, or some subdivision thereof, that created them. In terms of classification, therefore, it is well to bear in mind the explanation of one authority on the subject: "The librarian catalogs his material while the archivist describes his in guides, inventories, and lists. The librarian selects his materials, while the archivist appraises his; the librarian classifies his material in accordance with established classification schemes, while the archivist arranges his in relation to organic structure and function; the librarian catalogs his materials, while the archivist describes his in guides, inventories, and lists."[2]

Manuscript collections and archival materials are found in many places. The Manuscript Division of the Library of Congress is the most important manuscript repository in North America. In Britain the British Library of the British Museum holds a similar distinction. Yet in both countries many manuscript collections are found elsewhere.

In this country, they may be in one of the presidential libraries, in state libraries and historical societies, in academic libraries, and in a variety of other repositories. The National Archives is, of course, the major federal archival repository in this country as the Public Record Office in London is Britain's central repository for national records. But a great deal of diversity characterizes archives in both countries. In this country, for instance, there are state and local archives, and even federal records are dispersed among the National Archives in Washington and various regional federal archives and record centers. There are, in fact, a variety of archives other than state, local, and national ones available to researchers. For instance, there are the National Film Archive in London, Vanderbilt University's Television News Archives, and the data Archive of the Inter-University Consortium for Political and Social Research in Ann Arbor, to name only a few of the types of archives that have appeared in recent decades. Before using archival and manuscript materials, a beginning researcher might wish to consult Philip C. Brooks' *Research in Archives: The Use of Unpublished Primary Sources* (1969), which continues to provide a

---

[2]T.R. Schellenberg, *Modern Archives: Principles and Techniques* (Chicago: University of Chicago Press, 1957), 23-24.

most useful introduction.

There are, in fact, many types of repositories for historical materials. They might be found in special libraries such as the library of the American Newspaper Publishers' Association Foundation in Washington, D.C., or the Wisconsin State Historical Society Library. Special collections can be found in these and many other libraries. Perhaps your own university library holds some. Regardless, whether you are dealing with manuscript materials, archival records, or published or produced items, the problem of identifying the materials you need from the multitude of those existing is formidable. To assist one in handling this problem, a number of bibliographic tools are available.

Bibliographic Sources: A Selected Listing

Where and how can a researcher find all the items to examine in his or her inquiry? A library provides numerous tools to assist in this task. They include published guides, catalogs, bibliographies, indexes, abstracts, and many other such items. For the remainder of this chapter we shall refer to them, for purposes of description, as "sources," meaning bibliographic sources, and we shall refer to the records of history themselves as "materials."

It is important to understand that it would take a separate volume of considerable length to describe all the bibliographic sources that one might use. The following listing is not exhaustive. It contains a selection of two types of sources. First, we chose many of the standard bibliographic sources to include. Most of these can be found in university libraries, though every library will exercise discrimination in purchasing sources that it considers unnecessary or repetitious. Leads to additional standard sources can be found in *Handbook for Research in American History* (previously cited). Second, we selected sources of particular interest to communication historians. Space does not permit inclusion of all sources for the many topical subdivisions of communication history. Researchers, therefore, also might wish to consult M. Gilbert Dunn and Douglas W. Cooper's "A Guide to Mass Communication Sources" (*Journalism Monographs,* No. 74, November 1981), which contains numerous listings of bibliographies and sources of historical material. Although now dated, it is an invaluable guide for communication historians. They should not, however, expect to find leads to material of interest to them only in sources designated as "Communication Sources." Many general historical bibliographic sources are rich in references to materials that are useful, indeed indispensible, in communication history.

In terms of geographical scope, we emphasize sources pertaining to the United States. Some British sources are also included for several reasons. Before 1783, American history was also British history and can be studied with profit either from the perspective of British history or British imperial history. Moreover, many trans-Atlantic connections and influences characterize the historical nature of the media in both countries.

1. Bibliographies of Bibliographies

(All of the sources contained in this list are cited with titles placed first for the convenience of the researcher. Most bibliographic tools are known by title. In the interest of brevity, annotations have been kept to a minimum or have been omitted. For serial and continuing publication, only the inclusive dates are given. For example, *Humanities Index* is cited simply as *Humanities Index* [1974-], indicating that it has appeared in regular intervals since 1974 and continues to date.)

American History: A Bibliographic Review (1985-). Its articles, features, and reviews are devoted to "American historical bibliography" broadly interpreted.

Bibliographic Index (1937-). A valuable current index that now appears twice a year and examines about 2,600 bibliographic sources annually. It includes bibliographies published either separately or as parts of books and articles. To be listed a bibliography must have fifty or more citations.

Bibliographies in American History: 1942-1978: Guide to Materials for Research, Henry Putney Beers (Woodbridge, Conn., 1982).

A World Bibliography of Bibliographies, Theodore Besterman, comp., 4th ed., 5 vols. (Totowa, N.J., 1963). Updated by Alice Toomey, 1977. A massive compilation of separately published bibliographies covering over 16,000 subjects. International in scope, it is the best known work of this type of bibliographic literature.

Comment. Researchers should make a practice of consulting on a regular basis the book review and appropriate special feature sections in scholarly journals relating to their studies. The *American Historical Review,* for instance, includes a "Documents and Bibliographic" section, and *Journalism Quarterly* has an extensive coverage of books and articles in the field including bibliographic sources. Also, researchers should be aware that in 1978 a group of bibliographers, historians, and librarians organized the Association for the Bibliography of History. This group later established the

National Registry for the Bibliography of History located at Georgetown University. Since its beginning in 1981, the Registry has recorded work now underway in all fields of historical bibliography.

2. Basic Bibliographies in United States History

General United States History Sources:

Bibliographical Guide to the Study of the Literature of the U.S.A., Clarence Gohdes and Sanford E. Marovitz, 5th ed. (Durham, N.C., 1984). Directed mainly to American literary history, but it covers many other subjects of interest to communication historians.

Bibliographies of the Presidents of the United States. Carol Bondhus Fitzgerald, ed. (Westport, Conn., 1987-). This a projected fifty-volume collection of annotated bibliographies covering all the American presidents to be published by Meckler Publishing Corporation between 1987 and 1991.

A Guide to the Study of the United States of America: Representing Books Reflecting the Development of American Life and Thought, Donald H. Mugridge and Blanche P. McCrum (Washington, 1960); *Supplement 1956-1965,* Oliver H. Orr, Jr. (Washington, 1976).

Harvard Guide to American History, Frank Freidel, ed., rev. ed., 2 vols. (Cambridge, Mass., 1974). The best comprehensive bibliography for United States history.

History of the United States of America: A Guide to Information Sources, Ernest Cassara, ed., 3 vols. (Detroit, 1977).

Writings of American History, 1962-73: A Subject Bibliography of Articles, James J. Dougherty, comp. and ed., 4 vols. (White Plains, N.Y., 1976). Should be used in conjunction with *Writings on American History: A Subject Bibliography of Books and Monographs 1962-73* (cited below). Together they represent a continuation of a series begun in 1904. The subsequent volumes in that series have appeared at varying intervals, and there are some gaps in the years covered. Recent volumes in the series including those cited here are standard bibliographic sources in United States history.

Writings on American History: A Subject Bibliography of Books and Monographs 1962-73, James R. Masterson, comp., 10 vols. (White Plains, N.Y., 1985). See the above citation.

Comment. There are two extensive bibliographical series for United States history that provide a comprehensive up-to-date coverage of the field: the "Gale Information Guide Library" published by the Gale Research Company and the "Goldentree Bibliographies in American History" published by Harlan Davidson.

Autobiographical and Biographical Sources:

American Autobiography, 1945-1980: A Bibliography, Mary Louise Briscoe, et. al., eds. (Madison, Wis., 1983).
American Diaries: An Annotated Bibliography of American Diaries Prior to the Year 1861, William Matthews, comp. (Berkeley, 1945). An older source than the following one but still deserving of mention. *American Diaries: An Annotated Bibliography of Published Diaries and Journals.* Vol. I, *Diaries Written from 1492-1844,* Laura Arksey, et. al. (Detroit, 1983). The first of a two-volume work designed to supersede Matthew's guide, which was the original satisfactory guide in the field.
A Bibliography of American Autobiographies, Louis Kaplan, comp. (Madison, Wis., 1961). Should be used together with the newer work by Briscoe mentioned above.

Comment. There are a number of bibliographic computer and telecommunication systems available for researchers today such as the Online Computer Library Center (OCLC) in Dublin, Ohio. Another similar and important system is the Research Libraries Information Network (RLIN), which is used by about twenty-five major research libraries. The RLIN contains the *Eighteenth-Century Short Title Catalogue* database that cites British and Colonial publications in English printed throughout the world. Over 330 American libraries are now contributing to this British Library created database that aims to list 500,000 items when completed.

3. Bibliographies in Communication History

Standard Sources:

"The American Jewish Press, 1823-1983; A Bibliographic Survey of Research and Study." Singerman, Robert (*American Jewish History,* 1986: 422-44).
American Journalism History: An Annotated Bibliography. Wm. David Sloan (Westport, Conn., 1989).
An Annotated Journalism Bibliography 1958-1968. Warren C. Price and Calder M. Pickett (Minneapolis, 1970).
Basic Books in the Mass Media: An Annotated Selected Booklist Covering General Communication, Book Publishing, Broadcasting, Film, Editorial Journalism and Advertising. Eleanor

Blum, 2nd ed. (Urbana, Ill., 1980).

Bibliographies and Lists of New York State Newspapers: Annotated Guide. Paul Mercer, comp. (Albany, 1981).

A Bibliography in the History and Backgrounds of Journalism. Robert X. Graham, comp. (Pittsburgh, 1940).

A Bibliography of the History of Printing in the Library of Congress. Published by Horace Hart (Springwater, N.Y., 1987).

A Bibliography of Literary Journalism in America. Edwin H. Ford (Minneapolis, 1937).

"The Black Press to 1968: A Bibliography." Armistead S. Pride, comp. (*Journalism History,* 1977: 148-153).

Blacks and Media: A Selected, Annotated Bibliography, 1962-1982. J. William Snorgrass and Gloria T. Woody, comps. (Tallahassee, 1985).

"Chicanos and the Media: A Bibliography of Select Materials." Felix Gutierrez and Jorge Reina Schement, comps. (*Journalism History,* 1977: 52-55).

Contributions to Bibliography in Journalism. Various authors (Lincoln, Neb., various years).

The Dutch Language Press in America: Two Centuries of Printing, Publishing and Bookselling. Hendrik Edelman, (Nieuwkoop, The Netherlands, 1986).

"English-Speaking Caribbean Media History: Bibliographic References and Research Sources." John A. Lent (*Journalism History,* 1975: 58-60).

Freedom of the Press: An Annotated Bibliography and *Freedom of the Press: A Bibliocyclopedia, Ten Year Supplement (1967-1977).* Ralph E. McCoy (Carbondale, Ill., 1968 and 1979).

"A Guide to Mass Communication Sources." M. Gilbert Dunn and Douglas W. Cooper (*Journalism Monographs,* No. 74, 1981).

Historical Bibliography of the Press. International Committee of Historical Sciences (1930-1935).

History of Journalism in the United States, a Bibliography of Books and Annotated Articles. Edwin H. Ford (Minneapolis, 1938).

Information Sources in Advertising History. Richard W. Pallay (Westport, Conn., 1979).

Journalism: A Bibliography. Carl L. Cannon (New York, 1924).

"Journalism as Art: A Selective Annotated Bibliography." Fleda Brown Jackson, W. David Sloan, and James R. Bennett (*Style,* 1982: 466-487).

The Journalist's Bookshelf, 8th ed., Roland E. Wolseley and Isabel Wolseley (Indianapolis, 1986).

The Literature of Journalism: An Annotated Bibliography. Warren C. Price (Minneapolis, 1959).

"The Literature of Women in Journalism History." Marion Marzolf, Ramona R. Rush and Darlene Stern, comps. (*Journalism History*, 1974-1975: 117-128), and "The Literature of Women in Journalism History: A Supplement." Marion Marzolf (*Journalism History*, 1976-1977: 116-123).

"Media Ethics: A Bibliographical Essay." Joseph P. McKerns (*Journalism History*, 1978: 50-53, 68).

News Media and Public Policy: An Annotated Bibliography. Joseph McKerns (New York, 1985).

Newspapers: A Reference Guide . Richard Schwarzlose (Westport, Conn., 1987).

"A Preliminary Bibliography: Images of Women in the Media, 1971-1976." Virginia Elwood (*Journalism History*, 1976: 121-123).

The Religious Press in the South Atlantic States, 1802-1865. An Annotated Bibliography with Historical Introduction and Notes. Henry Smith Stroupe, (Durham, N.C., 1956).

Sources for Film, Radio, and Television:

British Broadcasting 1922-1972: A Selective Bibliography. John Houle, ed. (London, 1972).

Broadcasting and Mass Media: A Survey Bibliography. Christopher Sterling, ed. (Philadelphia, 1974).

The Critical Index: A Bibliography of Articles on Film in English, 1946-1973, Arranged by Names and Topics. John C. Gerlach and Lana Gerlach (New York, 1974).

Effects and Functions of Television: A Bibliography of Selected Research Literature, 1970-1978. Manfred Meyer and Ursula Nissen, eds. (Hamden, Conn., 1979).

The Film Audience: An International Bibliography of Research, With Annotations and an Essay. Bruce A. Austin (Metuchen, N.J., 1983).

Film Research: A Critical Bibliography with Annotation and Essay. Peter J. Bukalski, comp. (Boston, 1972).

Film Study: A Resource Guide. Frank Manchel (Rutherford, N.J., 1973).

The Macmillan Film Bibliography: A Critical Guide to the Literature of the Motion Picture. George Rehrauer, 2 vols. (New York, 1982).

Moving Pictures: An Annotated Guide to Selected Film Literature with Suggestions for the Study of Film. Eileen Sheahan (Cranbury, N.J., 1979).

Radio Broadcasting and Television: An Annotated Bibliography. Oscar Rose (New York, 1947).

Television: A Guide to the Literature. Mary B. Cassata and Thomas D. Skill (Phoenix, Ariz., 1985).

The Whole Film Sourcebook. Leonard Maltin, ed. (New York, 1983).

Related Sources:

American Popular Culture: A Guide to Information Sources. Larry N. Landrum (Detroit, 1982).

Communication and Society: A Bibliography on Communication Technologies and Their Social Impact. Benjamin F. Shearer and Marilyn Huxford, comps. (Westport, Conn., 1983).

Communication and the United States Congress: A Selectively Annotated Bibliography of Committee Hearings, 1870-1976. George D. Brightbill, comp. (Washington, 1978).

Handbook of American Popular Culture. M. Thomas Inge, 3 vols. (Westport, Conn., 1978-1981). A source rich in bibliographic references to many subjects of interest to communication historians.

MLA *International Bibliography of Books and Articles on the Modern Languages and Literature,* Eileen M. Mackesy (New York, 1922-). The most comprehensive of the literary bibliographies.

Propaganda and Promotional Activities: An Annotated Bibliography. Harold D. Lasswell, Ralph Casey, and Bruce Smith, eds. (Ann Arbor, Mich., 1939, reissued 1969). A standard source.

Photographic Literature: An International Bibliographic Guide to General and Specialized Literature on Photographic and Processing Techniques, Theories.... Albert Boni, ed., 2 vols. (New York, 1962, 1972). Includes citations back to the nineteenth century but mostly technical ones.

Comment. Communication historians may have reason to consult sources relating to the creative arts or to critical commentary about them. If this is the case, one should consult the Card Catalog (subject card section) for sources to a particular branch of the creative arts (e.g., "Drama-Bibliography").

4. *Sources for Periodical and Less-Than-Book-Length Publications*

Access: index to little magazines (1976-).

Alternative Press Index (1969-).

America: History and Life (1964-). Originally an abstracting publication. In 1974 it expanded into four parts: Part A, *Article Abstracts and Citations;* Part B, *Index to Book Reviews;* Part C, *American History Bibliography (Books, Articles and Dissertations);* Part

D, *Annual Index*. Its coverage is limited to the history of the United States and Canada.

American Humanities Index (1975).

Arts and Humanities Citation Index (1977-). A permutern subject index derived from identifying key words in a title. It covers over 6,000 journals.

Books Review Index (1965-). An index to current reviews from over 455 publications.

British Humanities Index (1962-). Formerly entitled *Subject Index to Periodicals*. It mainly indexes popular periodicals but includes a number of scholarly ones too.

Canadian Periodical Index (1948-). Indexes 137 major magazines in French and English.

Combined Retrospective Indexes to Journals in History 1838-1874. Carrollton Press, Annadel N. Wile, exec. ed., 11 vols. (Washington, 1977-1978).

Current Contents: Arts and Humanities (1977-). A weekly publication that reproduces in each issue tables of contents in about 200 journals as they appear. It covers many historical journals.

Essays and General Literature Index (1900/1933-). A subject index to essays and articles found in hundreds of anthologies, collections, and other miscellaneous publications.

Humanities Index (1974-). A basic source for scholarly articles that, along with the *Social Science Index*, supesedes the *Social Science and Humanities Index* (1965/1966-1973/1974). The latter was formerly the *International Index* (1920/1923-1964/1965) which, in turn, originally appeared as the *Reader's Guide Supplement* (1907/1915-1916/1919).

An Index to Book Reviews in the Humanities (1960-). Indexes about 375 periodicals.

Index to Free Periodicals (1976-).

Index to Periodicals by and about Blacks (1950-). A retrospective index is also available for this subject, *Blacks in Selected Newspapers, Censuses and Other Sources: an Index to Names and Subjects*. 3 vols. (1977).

Index to Southern Periodicals. Sam G. Riley, comp. (Westport, Conn., 1986). This is a companion volume to the author's *Magazines of the American South* (Westport, Conn., 1986). It contains references to nearly 7,000 non-newspaper publications and is part of the series Historical Guides to the World's Periodicals and Newspapers, published by Greenwood Press.

Index to U.S. Government Periodicals (1970-). See citation below under "Sources for Government Publications and Documents."

Poole's Index to Periodical Literature, 1802-1906. 7 vols., rev. ed. (New York, 1938). Usually considered the most important index of its kind for nineteenth century periodical literature. It covers the years 1802-1906. *The Nineteenth Century Reader's Guide to Periodical Literature 1890-1899* serves as a supplement for the years designated in the title.

Public Affairs Information Service Bulletin (1915-). Commonly known as PAIS. It is an instrumental interdisciplinary index in the social sciences. PAIS covers subjects related to public policy and issues.

Popular Periodical Index (1973-). Indexes about forty periodicals not included in *Reader's Guide to Periodical Literature*.

Reader's Guide to Periodical Literature (1900/1904-). The standard index for twentieth-century popular periodical literature mainly published in the United States.

Recently Published Articles (1976-). Published three times annually by the American Historical Association. This is the best source for journal articles in all fields of history.

Social Science Citation Index (1973-). A permutern subject index covering about 2,000 journals.

Social Sciences Index (1974/1975-). See the above citation for the *Humanities Index*.

Comment. Researchers can stay current through computerized searches of on-line counterparts of a number of the above cited indexes. Also, since there are indexes covering an array of subjects that are too numerous to mention, one might wish to consult "Abstracts and Indexes," a listing in *Magazines for Libraries*, Bill Katz and Linda Sternberg Katz, eds., 4th ed. (1982).

5. *Sources for Audiovisual Materials*

America on Film and Tape: A Topical Catalog of Audiovisual Resources for the Study of United States History, Society and Culture. Howard B. Hitchens, ed. (Westport, Conn., 1985).

The British Film Catalogue 1895-1970: A Guide to Entertainment Films. Dennis Gifford (New York, 1987).

The British National Film Catalogue (1963-).

Early Motion Pictures: The Paper Print Collection in the Library of Congress. Kemp Niver and Bebe Bergsten (Washington, 1985). An invaluable collection covering films from 1894-1915. It includes newsreels and "documentaries" (i.e., films of actual people and events) as well as drama and other film genres.

Index to Motion Pictures Reviewed by "Variety." Max Joseph Alvarez (Metuchen, N.J., 1982). Covers foreign and American films and short subjects reviewed by *Variety*, which neither *Reader's Guide to Periodical Literature* nor any other continuing periodical index includes.

International Index to Film Periodicals (1972-).

Magill's Survey of Cinema: English Language Films. Frank N. Magill, ed., 1st Series, 4 vols. (Englewood Cliffs, N.J., 1980); 2nd Series (Englewood Cliffs, N.J., 1981). This is the core set of Magill's survey of films past and present. Since its appearance, he has added several more sets: *Magill's Survey of Cinema: Silent Films* , 3 vols. (Englewood Cliffs, N.J., 1982) *Magill's American Film Guide,* 5 vols. (Englewood Cliffs, N.J., 1983); and *Magill's Survey of Cinema: Foreign Lanuage Films,* 8 vols. (Englewood Cliffs, N.J., 1985). In 1982 he also began an annual review, *Magill's Cinema Annual* (1982-). The various Magill series are compilations that provide critical essays as well as basic data about outstanding films.

The Motion Picture Guide. Jay Robert Nash and Stanley Ralph Ross, 12 vols. (Chicago, 1985-1987). This work is more than a guide. It provides a synopsis of content and criticism for each of its 35,000 entries covering English-language and notable foreign films.

Motion Pictures: Catalogue of Copyright Entries. Library of Congress, 5 vols. (Washington, 1951-1971). Covers films copyrighted 1894-1969.

Picture Sources Three: Collections of Prints and Photographs in the United States and Canada. Ann Novotny, ed. (New York, 1975).

Radio Broadcasts in the Library of Congress, 1924-1941: A Catalog of Recordings. James T. Smart, comp. (Washington, 1982).

Retrospective Index to Film Periodicals 1930-1971. Linda Batty (New York, 1975).

Scholar's Guide to Washington, D. C., for Audio Resources: Sound Recordings in the Arts, Humanities, and Social, Physical, and Life Sciences. James R. Heintz (Washington, 1985).

Total Television: A Comprehensive Guide to Programming from 1948 Through 1979. Alex McNeil, rev. ed., (New York, 1985).

6. *Abstracts and Digests*

Abstracts in Anthropology (1970-).

Abstracts in English Studies (1958-).

Abstracts in Military Bibliography (1967-).

Abstracts of Popular Culture (1976-).

America: History and Life, Part A (1964-). This is the standard source of abstracts in United States and Canada history.

Book Review Digest (1905-). Provides excerpts from and citations to nearly 100 American, Canadian, and British periodicals.

Communication Abstracts (1978-).

"Communication History Abstracts." Susan J. Henry, comp. (*Journalism History,* 1977: 101-103; 1979: 26-27, 64; 1980: 34-37, 79-80; 1981: 34-36; 1981-1982: 112-114; 1982: 73-75; 1982-1983: 108-110; 1983: 35-6, 64-66).

Dissertation Abstracts (1952-). Compiles abstracts of doctoral dissertations microfilmed. It does not cover all dissertations written in the United States, only those from institutions listed in each issue.

Historical Abstracts (1955-). A standard source of historical abstracts that is international in scope. Since 1975 it has directed researchers interested in historical abstracts for United States and Canadian history to consult *America: History and Life.*

International Political Science Abstracts (1951-).

Journalism Abstracts (1963-). Abstracts master's theses and doctoral dissertations written in departments and schools of journalism and communication in the United States.

Media Review Digest (1970-). Covers material in 150 periodicals about films, videotapes, slides, maps, etc. Formerly (1970-1972) called the *Multi Media Reviews Index.*

Sociology Abstracts (1953-).

Comment. Researchers might wish to consult a current news digest. *Facts on File: A Weekly World News Digest with Cumulative Index* (1940-) is the basic one published in this country. *Keesling's Contemporary Archives: Weekly Diary of World with Index Continually Kept Up-to-Date* (1931-) is its British counterpart. They might also wish to consult specialized digests such as the *African Recorder: A Fortnightly Record of African Events with Index* (1962-), the *Asian Events with Index* (1955-), or the *Current Digest of the Soviet Press* (1949-).

7. Statistical Sources

Guides

American Statistics Index (1973-). Indexes unclassified statistical information of the federal government. It covers over 800 federal perodicals and reports, and its second part abstracts most of the material indexed. This source should be used in conjunction with *Statistical Reference Index* (cited below).

Foreign Statistical Documents: A Bibliography of General International Trade and Agriculture Statistics, Including Holdings of the Stanford University Libraries. Robert Gardella, comp., Joyce Ball, ed., Hoover Institute on War, Revolution and Peace, Bibliographical Series 28 (Stanford, Calif., 1967). A guide to statistics covering foreign countries.

Guide to Resources and Services 1985-1986. Inter-university Consortium for Political and Social Research (Ann Arbor, Mich., 1986). A catalog that indexes the holdings of the Consortium, the largest data archives of its kind. Its coverage is international and goes back to the nineteenth century. For the United States, it includes data available from 1789.

Guide to U.S. Government Statistics. John Androit, ed., 3rd ed. (Arlington, Va., 1961).

Population Information in Nineteenth Century Census Volumes. Suzanne Schulze (Phoenix, 1983). The author has continued this index in a second volume, *Population Information in Twentieth Century Census Volumes: 1900-1940* (Phoenix, 1985).

Statistical Bulletins: An Annotated Bibliography of the General Statistical Bulletins of Major Political Subdivisions of the World. Library of Congress (Washington, 1954, repr. 1978).

Statistical Reference Index (1980-). An index to statistical data in non-governmental periodicals and reports, etc. It should be used in conjunction with the above cited *American Statistics Index.*

Statistical Sources: A Subject Guide to Data on Industrial, Business, Social, Educational, Financial, and Other Topics for the United States and Internationally. Jacqueline Wasserman O'Brien and Steven K. Wasserman, eds., 11th ed. (Detroit, Mich., 1987). The standard comprehensive guide for American statistical materials.

Abstracts, Handbooks and Yearbooks

America Votes: A Handbook of Contemporary American Election Statistics. (1956-). A biennial publication that covers presidential election statistics for the years from 1948. Publisher varies. For earlier years see the *Presidential Vote* and *They Voted for Roosevelt* (cited below).

"An Annotated Statistical Abstract of Communications Media in the United States." Dan Brown and Jennings Bryant, 259-302, in J.S. Salvaggio and Jennings Bryant, eds., *Media Use in the Information Age: Patterns of Adoption and Consumer Use* (Hillsdale, N.J., 1989).

Demographic Yearbook. (1949-). An annual publication of the United Nations Statistical Office.

Historical Statistics of the United States: Colonial Times to 1970. Bureau of Census, 2 vols. (Washington, 1975). A source intended to supplement *Statistical Abstract of the United States* (cited below). It describes itself as a "collecting" and "referring" source. Researchers will find excellent references to expanded detail of subject in the introduction to its various chapters.

The Presidential Vote. Edgar E. Robinson (Stanford, Calif., 1934). Covers the years 1896-1932. Election returns for subsequent years are covered in *They Voted for Roosevelt,* Edgar E. Robinson (Stanford, Calif., 1947). For subsequent presidential election statistics see *America Votes* (cited above).

Statistical Abstract of the United States (1879-). An annual publication considered the standard statistical summary of the United States.

Statistical Yearbook (1949-). An annual publication of the United Nations that continues the *Statistical Year-Book of the League of Nations* (1900-1945).

8. *Guides to Media Sources* (directories, indexes, and union lists)

(Union Lists are sources that contain bibliographical information and data about location.)

American Indian and Alaska Native Newspapers and Periodicals 1971-1985. Daniel F. Littlefield, Jr., and James W. Parins, eds. (Westport, Conn., 1986). This volume brings the work of the editors' two previous volumes up-to-date. The three volumes cover the subject from 1826-1985 and are part of the series Historical Guides to the World's Periodicals and Newspapers, published by Greenwood Press.

American Newspapers, 1821-1936: A Union List of Files Available in the United States and Canada. Winifred Gregory, ed. (Millwood, N.Y., 1937, repr. 1967). The standard source. It should be used in conjunction with *History and Bibliography of American Newspapers, 1690-1820.* Clarence S. Brigham, 2 vols. (Worcester, Mass., 1947, repr. 1976).

American Periodicals, 1741-1900: An Index to the Microfilm Collections. Jean Hoornstra and Turdy Heath (Ann Arbor, 1979).

Checklist of American 18th Century Newspapers in the Library of Congress. Library of Congress (Washington, 1936).

Chronological Table of American Newspapers, 1690-1820: Being a Tabular Guide to Holdings of Newspapers Published in America Through the Year 1820. Edward Connery Lathem (Worcester, Mass., 1972).

Editor and Publisher International Yearbook (1920-). Lists newspapers.

Gale Directory of Publications (formerly the *Ayer Directory of Publications*) (1869-). This is the basic directory for publications in the United States, Canada, and Puerto Rico. Its title has changed over the years, but it has traditionally been associated with the name of its founder, N. W. Ayer.

History and Bibliography of American Newspapers, 1690-1820.
Clarence S. Brigham, 2 vols. (Worcester, Mass., 1947). Another
work, *Additions and Corrections to History and Bibliography of
American Newspapers, 1690-1820,* appeared in the *Proceedings of
the American Antiquarian Society,* April 1961; and the entire source
is continued in *American Newspapers, 1821-1936: A Union List of
Files Available in the United States and Canada,* cited previously.

*National Union Catalog: 1973-1977, Films and Other Materials
for Projection.* Library of Congress, 7 vols. (Totawa, N.J., 1978). In
1953 *Films* became a separate publication among the Library of
Congress catalogs. This is the most recent of those separately published catalogs. The title and publisher of previous volumes vary.
The Library attempts to catalog all films, filmstrips, and slide-sets
produced in the United States and Canada that have an educational
value.

*Native American Periodicals and Newspapers 1828-1982: A
Bibliography, Publishing Records, and Holdings.* James P. Danky,
ed., and Maureen E. Hady, comp. (Westport, Conn., 1984). The volume identifies and locates 1,164 publications by and about American Indians.

*Newspaper Indexes: A Location and Subject Guide for Re-
searchers.* Anita C. Milner, 3 vols. (Metuchen, N.J., 1977, 1979,
1982).

Newspaper Press Directory and Advertisers' Guide (1846-).
One of the two standard British directories. *Willing's Press Guide*
(1874-) is the other.

Newspapers in Microform: United States, 1948-1983. Library of
Congress, 2 vols. (Washington, 1984). Identifies locations by repository of newspapers published in this country available in microform.

Newspapers on Microfilm, 6th ed. George A. Schwegmann, Jr.,
comp. (Washington, 1967). Succeeded by *Newspapers in Microform*
(cited previously).

"Preliminary Guide to Indexed Newspapers in the United
States, 1850-1900." Herbert O. Brayer (*Mississippi Valley Historical Review,* 1946).

*Union List of Serials in Libraries of the United States and
Canada.* Edna B. Titus, ed., 3rd ed., 5 vols. (New York, 1965).

United States Newspaper Program National Union List. Compiled by the Online Computer Library Center (OCLC), Inc., 8 vol.,
2nd ed. (Dublin, Ohio, 1987). This list, which is also available in
microfiche, is a compilation based on the results to date of the United
States Newspaper Program (USNP). Supported by the Organization
of American Historians, the Library of Congress, the Council on

Library Resources, and the National Endowment for the Humanities, the USNP is a cooperative effort by librarians, archivists, and historians to organize extant copies of newspapers in this country and its Trust Territories for purposes of research. Its work involves identifying existing newspapers, identifying newspaper holdings, and preserving through microfilming those papers deemed valuable for research. The USNP's work began in the mid-1970s. It is far from complete at this point, but in the future it will come to replace some of the standard newspaper sources mentioned above (e.g., *American Newspapers, 1821-1936*). The present union list is derived from an on-line database.

Writer's Market. Writer's Digest Books (Cincinnati, 1929-). Contains listings of magazines.

Comment. A number of published state and local listings of newspapers exist. See "Guides to Newspapers" in *Handbook for Research in American History* (previously cited), pp. 56-60. For those in your library, consult the reference librarian.

9. Sources for Government Publications and Documents (directories, indexes, guides and catalogs)

Catalog of the Public Documents of Congress and of all Departments of the Government of the United States for the Period, March 4, 1893, to December 31, 1940. U.S. Superintendent of Documents, 45 vols. (Washington, 1896-1945). The last set in a sequence of sources that indexed United States government publications back to the Continental Congress. The previous titles in the sequence were *A Descriptive Catalogue of the Government Publications of the United States, September 5, 1774 - March 4, 1881,* Benjamin Perley Poore, comp. (Washington, 1885) and *Comprehensive Index to the Publications of the United States Government 1881-1893,* John Griffith Ames, comp. 2 vols. (Washington, 1905). This series of sources has been replaced by the *Monthly Catalog of United States Government Publications* (cited below).

CIS/Index (the Congressional Information Service's Index to Publications of the United States Congress) (1970-). Issued monthly, this is the best index to Congressional documents, and by using this index one can order a complete microfiche copy of a document from the CIS if it is not available in the library.

Guide to U.S. Government Publications. John L. Andriot, ed., 2 vols. (McLean, Va., 1980). A documents index.

Index to U.S. Government Periodicals (1970-). Covers nearly 200 government published periodicals.

Introduction to United States Public Documents. Joe Morehead,

3nd. ed. (Littleton, Colo., 1983). An account of the location and use of public documents, mainly contemporary ones.

Monthly Catalog of the United States Government Publications. U.S. Superintendent of Documents. (Washington, 1895-). Title varies. Since 1940 this has been the standard index for government documents.

United States Government Publications. Rae Elizabeth Rips, 3rd. rev. ed. (New York, 1949). A revision of Anne Morris Boyd's standard compilation of publications up to the post-World War II period.

Comment. Many university libraries today have microfilm catalog indexes to U.S. government documents such as the Bradart Corporation's *Federal Government Publication Catalog,* but thus far they only offer ten years' searching. Also, there are a number of checklists, catalogs, indexes, and breviates to particular government publications as well as a variety of general guides. Researchers should become familiar with those available in their libraries; and, particularly for published historical documents, they should check the Card Catalog under the subject headings "Documentary History," "Documents of," "Documents on," etc. In this section we have considered some of the standard sources for government publications and documents. For an expanded treatment, researchers might wish to consult Thomas Mann's *A Guide to Library Research* (cited previously), chap. 12, and Helen J. Poulton's *The Historian's Handbook: A Descriptive Guide to Reference Works* (cited previously), chap. 1.

10. *Guides to Archival and Manuscript Materials and to Special Libraries and Special Collections.*

Archival and Manuscript Sources

American Literary Manuscripts: A Checklist of Holdings in Academic, Historical, and Public Libraries, Museums, and Author's Homes in the United States. J. Albert Robbins, ed., 2nd ed. (Athens, Ga., 1977).

Directory of Archives and Manuscript Repositories in the United States. National Historical Publications and Records Commission (Washington, 1978). Should be used in conjunction with *A Guide to Archives and Manuscripts in the United States and National Union Catalog of Manuscripts Collection* (cited later).

A Directory of Broadcast Archives. Donald G. Godfrey, comp. (Washington, 1983). Covers the U.K. and Canada as well as the United States.

A Guide to Archives and Manuscripts in the United States.
Philip M. Hamer, ed. (New Haven, 1961). For years this was the
standard work in the field. It remains a useful and much consulted
source.

*Guide to the Archives of the Government of the Confederate
States of America.* Henry Putney Beers (Washington, 1968).

Guide to the Hoover Institution Archives. Charles G. Palm and
Dale Reed (Stanford, Calif., 1980). A guide to materials in the
Hoover Institute on War, Revolution, and Peace. This major repository of historical materials since the late nineteenth century contains numerous items and collections of interest to communication
historians (e.g., on censorship, propaganda, public opinion, and
twentieth-century wars).

A Guide to Manuscripts in the Presidential Libraries. Dennis
A. Barton, et. al. (College Park, Md., 1985).

A Guide to Sources in American Journalism History. Lucy
Caswell, coordinator (Greenwood Press, forthcoming). Sponsored
by the American Journalism Historians Association, this volume
will offer a comprehensive list of sources regarding print and electronic news media throughout American history.

Guide to the National Archives of the United States. National
Archives and Records Service (Washington, 1974).

Handbook: The Center for Research Libraries (Chicago, 1987).
An inventory published by the Center describing its holdings. They
include various newspapers, periodicals, press summaries, clip-
ping files, radio broadcasts and scripts, and microforms of a variety of "underground press" titles.

*The National Inventory of Documentary Sources in the United
States.* Chadwyck-Healey, Inc., 4 parts: Part 1, *Federal Records;*
part 2, *Manuscripts Division, Library of Congress;* part 3, *State
Archives, Libraries and Historical Societies;* part 4, *Academic Libraries and Other Repositories* (Alexandria, Va., 1983-). A microfiche source that promises to be a major new publishing program.
It reports the location of collections and describes the material
available within them.

National Union Catalog of Manuscript Collections. Library of
Congress (Ann Arbor, 1962-). A standard and continuing source
first issued in 1962. The present issue of the NUCMC is the 21st in the
series that has published descriptions of about 52,320 collections
from 1,268 repositories.

North American Film and Video Directory. Olga S. Weber
(New York, 1976). Lists film archives but fails to describe their
holdings.

Comment. The Research Libraries Information Network (cited

previously) maintains a database assessing the research collections of each member. Also, beyond the basic guides listed here, there are numerous ones published for specific state, local, and private repositories. For a useful partial listing of those available, see *Handbook for Research in American History* (cited previously), pp. 48-51.

Directories for Special Libraries and Special Collections

(The term "Special Libraries" means libraries with a special focus and purpose such as the Library of the American Newspaper Publishers Association Foundation in Washington, D.C., or libraries devoted to particular studies such as film or journalism libraries at various universities.)

Directory of Newspaper Libraries in the United States and Canada. Grace D. Parch, ed. (New York, 1976).
Newspaper Libraries in the U.S. and Canada: An SLA Directory. Elizabeth L. Anderson, ed., 2nd ed. (New York, 1980). This volume supersedes the *Directory of Newspaper Libraries in the U.S. and Canada* mentioned previously.
Research Libraries and Collections in the United Kingdom: A Selective Inventory and Guide. Stephen Roberts, et. el. (Hamden, Conn., 1978).
Subject Collections: A Guide to Special Book Collections and Subject Emphasis as Reported by University, College, Public, and Special Libraries in the United States and Canada. Lee Ash, ed., 6th ed., 2 vols. (New York, 1985).
Subject Directory of Special Libraries. Brigitte T. Darnay, ed., 9th ed., 5 vols. (Detroit, 1985).

11. *Indexes to Miscellaneous Historical Materials*

Biography and Genealogy Master Index, 1981-1985: A Consolidated Index to More Than 3,200,000 Biographical Sketches. Miranda C. Herbert and Barbara McNeil, eds., rev., 2nd ed., 8 vols. (Detroit, 1980). A consolidated index to biographical indexes and directories, etc., with supplements in 1983 and 1985.
Biography Index (1946-). A guide to obituaries, letters, collections, diaries, etc., appearing in over 2,000 periodicals.
Directory of Oral History Programs in the United States. Produced by the Microfilming Corporation of America (Sanford, N.C., 1982).
Dissertations in History 1970-June 1980. Warren F. Kuell (Santa Barbara, Calif., 1985). An index by author and subject

covering all universities that award doctoral degrees in history. It supplements two previous volumes by the same author: *Dissertations in History: An Index to Dissertations Completed in History Departments of United States and Canadian Universities 1873-1960,* vol. 1 (Lexington, 1965) and *Dissertations Completed in History Departments of United States and Canadian Universities 1961-June 1970,* vol. 2 (Lexington, 1972).

Journalist Biographies Master Index. Alan E. Abrams, ed. (Detroit, 1979). Includes about 90,000 references to historical and comtemporary journalists appearing in approximately 200 biographical directories and other such sources.

Microform Research Collections: A Guide. Suzanne Cates Dodson, 2nd ed. (Westport, Conn., 1984).

Oral History: A Reference Guide and Annotated Bibliography. Patricia Pate Havlice (Jefferson City, N.C., 1985). An up-to-date source representing an improvement over other ones in the field.

The Oral History Collection of Columbia University. Elizabeth B. Mason and Louis M. Starr, eds. (New York, 1979). A catalog specifying the nearly 800 memoirs of the Columbia collection available in microform.

Oral History Collections. Alan M. Mechler and Ruth Mc-Mullin (New York, 1975). International in scope and containing a subject index.

Comment: Newspaper indexes. There are a number of published indexes to newspapers. (See *Newspaper Indexes,* previously cited above in "Directories and Union Lists: Communication Sources.") Particular mention should be made of the index for the New York *Times* because it is the major American paper of record. The index goes back to 1851 although its coverage is more complete after 1905 when it became an annually published index. Today a number of major newspaper indexes are available on-line.

Mass Communication Sources

Various types of original sources are available to communication historians. Since historians often deal with the content of the mass media, they should know how to find items such as newspaper and magazine files and broadcast transcripts and tapes. There are a vast number of collections of such material, many more than we can list here, and of indexes to the material. M. Gilbert Dunn and Douglas W. Cooper's *Journalism Monograph,* No. 74, "A Guide to Mass Communication Sources" (November 1981), mentioned earlier, will prove invaluable in the historian's search for indexes and media files. Indexes to the media and their contents are available in most good university research libraries.

For American newspaper holdings no library surpasses the Library of Congress. The American Antiquarian Society's collection of early American newspapers is the largest for that period, including some 2,000 newspapers published betweened 1690 and 1820 in most states east of the Mississippi River and in Louisiana, Arkansas, Texas, and Missouri. They are reproduced in a set of 70,000 microcards. The set is available in many libraries. The Wisconsin State Historical Society and Harvard University libraries also have substantial national collections. State, regional, and special newspaper collections can be found in various libraries. A number of state projects are now being conducted to identify all newspapers ever published in each state and to locate extant files of the newspapers. *Newspapers on Microfilm* (1967) and *Newspapers in Microform* (1984), both of which were discussed earlier in this chapter, catalog all American newspapers that are available in microform.

Once the researcher locates a newspaper, considerable effort remains to locate content relevant to the topic under study. Fortunately, indexes to the contents of a number of papers are available. Unfortunately, most have begun only recently and therefore do not include early newspaper issues. Indexing of the *Wall Street Journal,* for example, began in 1959 and of the *Christian Science Monitor* in 1960. The contents of some newspapers, however, have been indexed for long periods. The best known and most used index is that of the New York *Times,* dating from 1851. Thomas W. Jodziewicz's *Birth of America: the Year in Review, 1763-1783: A Chronological Guide and Index to the Contemporary Colonial Press* indexes fifty-two newspapers. Indexes are available in most libraries or through the inter-library loan system in either print or microprint. The historian should bear in mind, however, that most newspapers have not been indexed and research in their pages will require considerable time searching for particular types of material.

The same thing that has been said about newspapers applies to other mass communication sources. Material is available in abundance, but the historian must know how to find it. A number of guides will help. Most university libraries hold large collections of bound volumes of magazines which offer a wealth of material. Indexes of magazine content may be found in such references as *American Periodicals, 1741-1900; an Index to the Microfilm Collections* (1979), *Poole's Index to Periodical Literature, 1802-81* (1891), *Nineteenth Century Reader's Guide to Periodical Literature, 1890-1899, with Supplementary Indexing, 1900-1922* (1944), *The Reader's*

Guide to Periodical Literature (1900-), *Popular Periodicals Index* (1973-), and a number of other publications and services. In advertising history, both newspapers and magazines include thousands of advertisements which may serve as the raw material for study. Pamphlets, likewise, may be found in various libraries and collections. The researcher will find valuable such bibliographical sources as Charles Evans, comp., *American Bibliography: A Chronological Dictionary of All Books, Pamphlets and Periodicals Printed in the United States of America (1639-1800)* (a fourteen-volume work published between 1903 and 1959) and Bernard Bailyn's *Pamphlets of the American Revolution* (1956).

Finding historical material on film, radio, and television is more difficult. Much of the content of broadcasting never was recorded, and the high costs of recording and using broadcast material discourage preservation. Many silent films were photographed on combustible nitrate stock -- and entire archival collections have exploded, with the loss of numerous films. There have been efforts to transfer motion pictures to other types of film stock, but they come too little and too late, and much material has been lost permanently. Thus archives and library holdings for broadcasting and film are not as large as for print. Copyright regulations also have discouraged the duplication of material. The high costs of storing recordings sometimes have led to decisions by their owners to destroy them.

Despite the problems, substantial amounts of programming material may be found. Union lists provide guides to locating programs. Among the more thorough are *History in Sound: A Descriptive Listing of the KIRO-CBS Collection of the World War II Years and After* (1963), Alex McNeil's *Total Television: A Comprehensive Guide to Programming from 1948-1980* (1980), and Tim Brooks and Earle Marsh's *The Complete Directory of Prime Time Network Television, 1946-Present* (1979). Similar guides to motion picture films are also available. Some indexing to individual programs has been done, but it is not as voluminous as indexing for the print media. Vanderbilt University's Television News Archive has published *Television News Index and Abstracts* since 1972 covering evening news broadcasts on the national networks. Since 1975 the Microfilming Corporation of America has published *CBS News Indexing*. As the permanent value of broadcast programming has gained heightened recognition in the last few years, such services have increased, and today broadcast and film historians have at their disposal a considerable store of guides.

In addition to the media content that may be found in files, a number of sources of primary material are available. Anthologies of journalistic writing, editorial cartoons, newspaper front pages, magazine art, photographs, advertisements, and various other items have been published in large numbers. Works such as Louis Snyder and Richard Morris' *A Treasury of Great Reporting* (1962) and Allan Nevins' *Newspaper Press Opinion, Washington to Coolidge* (1928), for example, contain numerous articles as they originally appeared in newspapers. Most anthologies contain works in one genre (such as editorial writing) or works by a single author or publication. The historian also may find useful material in such works as journalists' and advertising executives' autobiographies and memoirs. They contain many personal recollections and much historical material based on first-hand observations. Trade journals such as *Editor and Publisher* (1901-), *Advertising Age* (1947-), and *Broadcasting* (1931-) also offer many articles written by historical figures in the mass media and other material based on primary research.

Computerized Bibliographic Systems

As one can see, the gathering of bibliographic materials is long and time consuming. In this day when they are becoming commonplace, might not computers be substituted for a manual search? At present the question must be answered with equivocation.

First of all, let us define our terms. In our brief discussion of this point, we shall use the term *database* to mean systematically collected and prepared information stored in a manner that facilitates searching and retrieval. *Database vendors* will be used to refer to companies that deal with the development and sale of timesharing systems, which allow many users to connect to computers housing databases. In some cases a database vendor also produces its own databases. Among the most used timesharing systems are (a) Bibliographic Retrieval Service (BRS AND BRS/After Dark), (b) DIALOG, (c) System Development Corporation Search Service (S.D.C.), and (d) Mead Data Central. It is the custom of universities to acquire the services of several but not all of these commercial database vendors. With the purchase of extra equipment, it is also possible for researchers who have their own microcomputers to connect to various database or timesharing systems. In any case, vendors charge fees as well as database royalties for telecommunication and computer time. The fees vary, but individuals can expect to pay somewhere in the neighborhood of $20 (at the time of this writing) for a bibliographic search on a fairly well-defined subject. Institutional rates can be less, and some libraries will subsidize a portion of the charges for an individual search.

Computerized searches, then, are possible. Moreover, the

reasons to use them appear compelling. They offer speed and convenience and might produce information difficult to find in a manual search. They can scan interdisciplinary sources and even locate institutions where there is cluster of activity on a given subject. Since researchers in one discipline are not always familiar with the research and sources in another, the computer can bridge that gap by providing cross-disciplinary access to activity and sources. Some important items for communication historians already are on database for recent years. They include *Historical Abstracts, America: History and Life, Dissertation Abstracts,* and indexes to the New York *Times,* the *Wall Street Journal,* and the Washington *Post* as well as several News Services. Indeed, services such as Mead Data Central's NEXIS service offer full text printouts of such materials rather than a simple citation.

There are, however, mitigating arguments to consider. Recent periodical literature and dissertations are fairly well covered as are recent books and documents. Such information will be of increasing value to historians with the passing of years. Unfortunately, at present the various databases have quite limited coverage of older books and unpublished materials. For instance, in the case of *Dissertation Abstracts,* the full text of the abstracts is available only for recent years, not for the full extent of the file. Beyond that, some of the databases most useful to historians are among the most difficult to use, and various databases are structured in different ways.

A computerized bibliographic search is of questionable value if done without adequate preparation. Only a well-delineated topic would be feasible to search, and, as we have seen, narrowing down a topic can take time and experimentation. Consequently, a good deal of manual preparation normally is necessary before one is ready to conduct a computerized search. Time spent in preparing for a compterized search will be time well spent. The preparation can be a positive experience even if the search is not run. Preparing for a search sometimes helps one to identify major statements relating to a topic. It can also hone skills used in manual work with the bibliographic sources. Such skills will serve one well in the everyday work of research. Students wishing to orient themselves to computerized bibliographic searches and to search strategies might consult W.H. Henry, et. al., *Online Searching: An Introduction* (1980) for an introductory overview.

All things considered, it seems advisable at this point to recommend that one not rely too much on a computerized search. It would appear to be most useful at the present as a method to use along with a manual search in an effort to determine the location of recently published materials on a well-defined topic. Because of the constantly changing nature of the information available on databases and sometimes because of the difficulty encountered in retrieving it, it is also recommended that researchers consult the appropriate librarian or information specialists at their institutions. As is so often the case, the best results will probably come as a result of the collaboration of the researcher and the librarian.

The Historical Researcher and Bibliography

Although there is no single total bibliographic tool for historians, the bibliographic apparatus available to them is vast. As we have seen, it is as diverse as it is extensive. To a considerable degree, one's success in producing worthwhile history depends on mastering bibliographic sources. They can provide the necessary direction to the multitude of materials that provide the foundation for historical inquiry. Beginning researchers should become familiar with the essential bibliographic sources in their university libraries and employ them to make their own working bibliographies comprehensive and up to date.

Young scholars today will encounter a bibliographic revolution in their lifetime. As a number of citations listed in this chapter prove, it has begun already. If it were possible for the young historians today to go back in time a mere twenty or twenty-five years, they would appreciate how striking the bibliographic expansion has been for historical studies in recent years. The computer, of course, has been responsible for some of this expansion, but not for all. Technology of many types has enlarged the potential of bibliography, and for that potential to be realized the historian and the bibliographer must work together. No one, however, doubts that as a consequence of technical advances influencing bibliography the historian's mastery of available primary and secondary materials will grow too.

What will be the result of it all? It seems reasonable to suggest that with all of the benefits that the bibliographic revolution can and will bring, historians will continue to work with scarcity amid abundance. They will, consequently, be forced to contemplate once again the limitations of historical knowledge, vast though it may be, and vaster yet though it may become.

6

Historical Sources
and Their Evaluation

Historical research involves materials and a critical method for their evaluation. Allan Nevins once said that "history was not born -- it could not be born -- until both these elements came into existence."[1] This chapter deals with both the types of evidence that historians use and the rules employed in evaluating them. Various types of historical evidence can be found in numerous places -- in an attic, a cemetery, a courthouse, as well as in a museum, a library, or an archives. Whatever reflects human activity in the past can be part of the historical record. The evidence historians study is much vaster than laymen realize. Even if it is fragmented and incomplete, which it is, the record of past events and episodes is massive, but without it there can be no history deserving of the name.

Communication historians will encounter sources extensive in quantity and varied in scope. It is no exaggeration to speak of the burden of abundance of their sources. Yet, acquaintance with that abundance is both sobering and exciting -- sobering because it forces respect for evidence and exciting because it is so suggestive for inquiry. As we have seen, the writing of communication history involves not only knowledge of the media at some point in the past but also an understanding of the general history of the life and thought of that time. The sources for communication history reflect those twin concerns. Accordingly, for purposes of illustration, we

---

[1]Allan Nevins, *The Gateway to History,* new rev. ed. (Garden City, New York: Doubleday & Company, Inc., 1962), 66.

shall discuss evidence both in terms of traditional historical types and in terms of those particular to the media themselves. But first, it is necessary to consider two basic categories of historical evidence, those designated "primary" and "secondary."

Primary and Secondary Sources

Primary sources are the raw materials of history. They are contemporaneous records, or records in close proximity to some past occurrence. Or they might be original documents. Secondary sources, on the other hand, rest on primary sources, and they are not contemporaneous with the subject under study. The record books entitled "Publishers of the U.S. Laws, 1820-70" found in the National Archives contain State Department appointments of various newspapers and their proprietors who were designated to publish the laws. The records of appointments are hand written and represent a primary source of State Department newspaper patronage. Culver H. Smith's book, *The Press, Politics, and Patronage: The American Government's Use of Newspapers 1789-1875 (1977)*, which uses those records as a source, is a secondary source. The priority historians give to primary records can be seen by studying the arrangement of bibliographies in scholarly works. Contemporaneous records, documents, and manuscript collections are placed first to underscore the depth and legitimacy of the research undertaken.

The fact that communication historians have based their writing too much on secondary sources has been one of its traditional weaknesses. In historical research, a basic maxim is that the scholar must ground the study on primary sources. In no other way can one gain a first-hand understanding of his or her subject. In communication history research, there has been altogether too much reliance on secondary sources, that is, on other historians rather than on the historical subjects themselves. Anytime a footnote refers to a secondary source -- especially to such general survey works as Eric Barnouw's series on broadcast history or to textbooks such as those by Frank Luther Mott and Edwin Emery -- it automatically raises a red flag. Such works are, themselves, to a large extent compilations of material produced by other historians rather than original research into primary sources. If the scholar cites Emery's *The Press and America*, for example, as a source, he actually is crediting Emery -- whose work is based almost solely on secondary sources -- for material Emery probably took from some other historian. The use of Emery as a source therefore automatically raises questions about the quality and thoroughness of the scholar's research. It shows that, at the least, the author is not adequately acquainted with the historical literature on the subject.

Despite the fact that using secondary sources for material is an elementary error, many communication historians persist in relying on them. Those historians who refuse to give up their reliance on secondary sources should at least do one thing: use the original secondary source. That is, they should find the first historian who provided the material. They should not use Emery if Kobre had the same material, not Kobre if Mott had it, not Mott if Alfred Lee did, not Lee if Bleyer did, not Bleyer if James Lee did, not Lee if Hudson did, not Hudson if Joseph Buckingham did, and not Buckingham if Isaiah Thomas did. The point in this list of authors of survey history books is that it is not unlikely that material Emery included might actually have been used first by Thomas and picked up by each succeeding historian. The person who would be a communication historian must become familiar with the basic literature on the field. Reading those survey histories should be one of the first things a student does. By doing so, one can at least avoid the misconception that a recent survey history is the best source on the subject. Yet, acquainting oneself with those books provides only a perfunctory beginning for historical knowledge. Whenever a historian selects a topic for study, he or she must read all the works that have been written on that topic. One will thus avoid the novice's error of ascribing to Emery or Mott the authority for material on a topic which they treat only cursorily and from secondary sources.

The error of using secondary sources is so serious in communication history that it deserves one final observation. Sometimes an historical work cites another historical work as its source. The student using the former should check its citation. Frequently, one will find that the citation is incorrect, that, for example, the page referred to is the wrong one. In other instances, one will find that the work cited actually used an earlier work as the source of the material. The student should continue checking the citations until the original source (or the secondary source first using the material) is located.

The distinction between primary and secondary sources is more involved than one might think. Consider the case of a personal record. An immediately recorded, eyewitnessed account of an event and a direct written command are examples of pure primary records. Yet, the primary status of a personal record is often not that clear. Is a letter or a diary entry that describes, let us say, an accident a primary source? The answer depends on the physical proximity of the recorder to the accident, the extent of time between the accident and the composition of the written record, and the object of the historian's research. If someone who was in close proximity to the accident observed it and recorded his or her impressions about it immediately, we would classify that record as primary. But suppose the witness did not write about it for several days or even for several weeks? The point at which we would say that it is no longer a contemporaneous record would be a matter of interpretation. Reporters and correspondents may produce pure primary records when they cover events, and, if the records survive in their original form, historians would classify them as such. But suppose the original recordings have been destroyed and all we have to consider is a published account. Is that primary? Suppose a reporter did not witness the accident and based his report on the testimony of people who did. Would the report be a primary record? Or imagine that the only record remaining of that accident was a diary comment recorded some hours after it occurred or an account of a conversation about it several days later. Would such records be primary? Most historians would accept the above examples as worthy of "primary" classification, particularly if they represented the best evidence remaining of the accident. To say that they only recognize an eyewitnessed account immediately recorded as primary is misleading. In practice, they deal with degrees to which a record is primary. They tend to use a flexible definition of "primary" and extend it to include evidence recorded in "nearness" to an event, and they allow reasonable judgment to guide them in determining the time and space requirements needed to establish "nearness."

There is still the matter of object to consider in determining primary evidence. Imagine that the accident referred to in the previous paragraph is mentioned in a letter written months after it occurred. That letter may be of only tangential importance if the historian's object were to describe the accident. On the other hand, it would be of great value and considered as primary evidence if the object were to probe into the thought of the person who wrote the letter. The object of the investigation makes a difference. A newspaper editorial, for instance, can be considered either as primary or secondary evidence depending on use. If the object of the study is the writer's opinion, an editorial would be primary. Moreover, a clearly defined secondary source in one instance might become a primary source in another. A published work by a nineteenth-century historian or journalist that would be identified as secondary in most cases might become primary in a study about American thought.

Now consider the case of public documents. These records involve yet additional classification problems. Legal and judicial statutes and reports, constitutions, treaties, and other public records are usually considered primary. In many respects, the label fits. Yet, here, too, there are a number of circumstances to contemplate. All public reports, for instance, are not contemporaneous. Some are produced well after the event. Some lack completeness. Treaties between states are public documents, but some have been known to contain secret clauses. Or consider records of proceedings of meetings. If they are unaltered, stenographic records, they are of great value. Nevertheless, sometimes they are modified for publication. Not everything recorded in the *Congressional Record*, for example, was spoken on the floor of Congress whose proceedings it records. Public documents, then, may or may not be primary, and, even if they are, there are questions regarding completeness and integrity of evidence to ask about them. In fact, all historical records must be scrutinized. Even primary sources, as valuable as they can be, may be inaccurate or biased.

Evaluation of Written Records

Written records are the best known traditional historical records, although there are and always have been other types of sources available to the historian. If you understand the principles of evaluation for written records, you can apply the standards to other types of sources as well. Two types of criticism, *external* and *internal*, characterize this process of evaluation. *External criticism* involves establishing the authenticity of a particular record; *internal criticism* involves matters of credibility and understanding of content. Explanation of record evaluation and the various questions that one can ask of multiple types of written records can be lengthy and detailed. The following discussion of external and internal criticism is intended as an introduction to the subject. All historians could add to it according to the nature and complexity of their own studies.

The purpose of *external criticism* is to determine whether a record is genuine. A number of means, some entailing the work of specialists, can be employed in the task. In the main, external criticism involves collation, identification, and textual verification.

Collation. This is simply the process of comparing various texts. Within the bounds of what is possible and practical, collation with an original record should be made.

Identification. In cases where the name of the author or other data identifying a record is missing, all possible effort must be made to attribute the record to its proper author and to fix it in its correct time. Ghostwritten speeches need to be attributed to their authors. Writers using pseudonyms need to be identified for a record to be considered authentic.

Textual Verification. To verify the genuineness of a record, let us say a letter to a newspaper, one might examine the spelling of words, the use of language, or the particular quirks of punctuation observable in the letter. It might be compared to other authentic letters by the same author. Does this particular letter reflect the normal opinions and ideas of the author, and, if not, are there reasons to explain the departure? In some cases questionable terms or erroneous references to chronological setting might raise doubts about the item. Sometimes authenticity can be decided with certainty while at other times that is not possible. Regardless of outcome, the process is one of weighing probabilities. The following examples will illustrate the process. The student also should note that these examples indicate that thorough and painstaking research is required in history.

In 1901 the New York *Sun* published a classic editorial entitled "The Oldest Living Graduate." Yet, owing to the *Sun's* practice of writer anonymity, the author of the editorial is unknown. Anonymous authorship frequently confronts the communication historian. Newspapers, especially, have published uncounted millions of unsigned articles. Anonymity presents a difficult problem to the historian studying any topic involving authorship by a particular individual. Sometimes, however, by industrious and detailed research, the historian is able to uncover authorship or at least to make an informed guess. As an illustration, let's look at the question of who wrote "The Oldest Living Graduate."

The clues to answering the question are slim. Stylistic analysis is made difficult by the fact of the *Sun's* policy of anonymity. Since the authorship of editorials never was made known, samples of a writer's editorials cannot be selected to compare with the "OLG" style. The exception is the famous editorial "Is There a Santa Claus?" by Francis Church, the authorship of which the *Sun* revealed upon that writer's death. The "Santa Claus" editorial provides, however, too little evidence to prove that Church also wrote "OLG," and it reveals nothing of the style of any other *Sun* writer.

Stylistic evidence is provided best by the authors of several histories of the *Sun*, the most helpful of which is *Memoirs of an Editor* by Edward P. Mitchell. He served for half a century on the *Sun* staff beginning in 1875. As a member of the editorial staff until 1903 and then as editor in chief, he knew individual editorial writers well. During his tenure, the editorial staff included more than a score of writers. Most, however, can be rejected as authors of "OLG" because their specialties were in styles and topics other than the human-interest approach of "OLG" -- writers such as Frank Simonds, the military historian, and Henry B. Stanton, a specialist on political affairs.

Based on Mitchell's and other historians' descriptions of styles, the most likely authors were Church, Mitchell himself, William O. Bartlett, Edward M. Kingsbury, Fitz Henry Warren, and Charles Dana, the *Sun's* editor. A check of biographical material reveals, however, that Warren died in 1878, Bartlett in 1881, and Dana in 1897 -- all before "OLG" was published. Each of the remaining three wrote with a style which would make possible the authorship of "OLG." Mitchell believed that the range of newspaper subjects should extend beyond hard news and major events, and in style he placed a premium on bright and enjoyable writing. His editorials focused primarily, however, on politics, thus leaving Church and Kingsbury as more probable authors of "OLG." Their writing styles and subject matter, as described by Mitchell, were similar, both resembling that found in the "OLG" editorial. Based on stylistic characteristics alone, an answer thus cannot be given on whether the author was Kingsbury or Church, or even Mitchell.

Other details of the editorial may, however, provide clues. The editorial mentions three colleges: Yale, two of whose graduates are named; Bowdoin; and Harvard, with two alumni named. The fifth paragraph names five individuals (Hooker Haynes, Brattle Holyoke, Bill Trumbull, a bishop Byles, and a senator Dwight) without reference to their alma mater. Should it be possible to identify their school, the information might provide another clue. A search of *The National Cyclopedia of American Biography* reveals no listing, however, for any of the five; and Congressional records indicate that no one named Dwight served in the United States Senate in the term before or after 1901, the year in which "OLG" was written. On such evidence, it appears that all five individuals may have been fictitious. But George Bancroft, named in the sixth paragraph, was the American historian. He was a Harvard graduate.

Based on the references to the three colleges, it seems reasonable to assume that the "OLG" author may have been a graduate of Bowdoin, Yale, or Harvard. A check of biographical references determines that while Church graduated from Columbia in 1859, Kingsbury graduated from Harvard in 1875 and Mitchell from Bowdoin in 1871. Such may be only coincidence and certainly is not solid evidence that either Kingsbury or Mitchell was the author.

The Bancroft paragraph indicates, however, that the author heard Bancroft speak to a Harvard freshman sixty years after his graduation. Bancroft had graduated in 1817. Thus, the year in which the episode occurred must have been around 1877, give or take a couple of years, assuming that the author of the editorial, writing in a casual style, was not attempting to be precise. It is not at all unlikely that the actual date could have been two years earlier, 1875, the year of Kingsbury's graduation. From such piecing together of assorted facts, then, we finally can arrive at the conclusion that the author of the "OLG" editorial probably was Kingsbury. Such effort may seem large in proportion with the simple fact it yields, but it must be done continually by the communication historian, who deals with anonymous authorship on a daily basis.

Remember also that forgeries and invented records exist. Any historian who can recall how *The Times* (London) published those forged letters of the great Irish leader Charles Stewart Parnell in the 1880s, thus impairing its own reputation and prosperity for the next twenty years, should have little difficulty in remaining on the alert for dishonest records. Curtis D. MacDougall includes almost 200 falsified newspaper accounts in his book *Hoaxes* (1940). Dishonest records do exist.

To demonstrate let us consider how one historian, Jerald S. Auerbach, has called into question the authenticity of one of the best known conversations between an American president and an editor. He probed into the matter in a way that would have pleased any detective worthy of the name. The principals in the alleged conversation were President Woodrow Wilson and Frank Cobb, the editor of the New York *World*, one of Wilson's favorite newspapers. Cobb was a confidant of the President and a frequent visitor to the White House. For years historians have referred to a particular conversation between the President and the editor that was supposed to have occurred on April 2, 1917, at one o'clock in the morning. At that time, as the story goes, Wilson was preparing to deliver his war message to Congress and expressed many of his forebodings about American intervention to the *World's* editor. He told Cobb about his apprehensions regarding how the war would unleash a spirit of illiberalism among Americans that would be destructive of the things they most valued. In his predictions regarding the meaning of the war, he declared that Germany would be beaten and that there would be a "dictated peace." Wilson's predictions, all of which came true, sound more like the words of one who had already experienced the future than those of one discussing it.

Auerbach's investigation into this alleged conversation went beyond textual examination. He noted that it first appeared in John Heaton's *Cobb of The World*, published in 1924. At that time, the conversation could no longer be validated. Both Cobb and Wilson had died. Then Auerbach discovered that Heaton had not heard of the conversation from Cobb at all. Rather he learned of it from two of Cobb's colleagues, Maxwell Anderson and Laurence Stallings, who collaborated on the antiwar drama *What Price Glory?* also produced in 1924. From them Heaton learned what Cobb was supposed to have said about a conversation with Wilson seven years after it occurred. It was "hearsay evidence twice removed," as Auerbach said. Thus the rules of evidence led him to suggest that Wilson "never spoke the words so frequently attributed to him."[2] There is reason to believe, as Auerbach also suggested, that rather than a record of the President's words, the reported conversation expressed the outrage against war that Anderson and Stallings articulated in the postwar years.

Let us consider now the matter of *internal criticism*. It deals with interpreting a record rather than establishing its authenticity. It involves two basic tasks: establishing the credibility of the author and understanding the content.

Credibility. This task touches the real expertise of the historian. To establish credibility of a personal record or a public document, one must have a command of historical contexts and a correct perception of the people or agencies who produced them. Ability and willingness to tell the truth are twin concerns of record evaluation in this instance. Historians have a number of questions regarding someone's ability to report the truth: (a) How near was this person to the event in terms of time and space? (b) How available was evidence to this person? (For instance, what was the evidence upon which correspondents based their news reports from Stalin's Russia?) (c) How competent was this person to understand the event? Competency might involve training, experience, class and cultural differences, or even physical fitness. Regarding willingness to express the truth, historians have the basic proposition of intent of composition to clarify. Was the purpose of someone or some agency in producing a record to describe, to interpret, to condemn, to praise, to promote, to propagandize, to publicize, or to persuade? Perhaps it was to offer a truthful explanation.

Understanding of Content. Here again the historian's command of context is crucial. One must understand a record to use it, and there is much in historical records that must be clarified for understanding to occur. Records may be complicated by archaic, colloquial, and technical language. They might contain political, diplomatic, journalistic, or military terminology. Perhaps they include references to titles, ranks, and various terms of social, political, military, or economic gradation. Moreover, some words change in meanings from time to time (e.g., "imperialism," "gay," "correspondent," "printer," "broadcast," etc.); some vary in meaning according to how they are used and to the person using them (e.g., "freedom of the press," "democracy," "revolution," "protest," etc.). Sometimes words have a more restricted meaning

---

[2]Jerold S. Auerbach, "Woodrow Wilson's 'Prediction' to Frank Cobb: Words Historians Should Doubt Ever Got Spoken," *Journal of American History* 54 (December 1967): 611.

than they literally imply (e.g., "freedom," "self-determination," "social order," "discipline," etc.). In all such cases, the real meaning of the words used in the record must be grasped. In essence, the historian must understand as far as is possible what the contents mean. That task involves an ability to use the techniques of textual elucidation plus open-mindedness, imagination, and common sense.

Understanding content, however, goes beyond comprehension of language and expression. It also deals with asking the fundamental question: What type of evidence is contained in this record? What type of information does the record relate? Perhaps it is hearsay; perhaps it is inferential; perhaps it is circumstantial; perhaps it is direct (i.e., a direct proof of fact or a direct reference to something perceived by one of a person's five senses). That basic question, however, does not stand alone. It should be accompanied by several others such as what does this record leave unsaid and how does this item relate to other pieces of evidence. Diplomatic records and newspaper reports from foreign correspondents, for instance, should be studied in sequence. That is also true of most news coverage and interpretation of prolonged events. Internal criticism is a fascinating and involved process, and students may wish to sharpen their understanding of its many elements by consulting a volume on legal evidence. Should that be the case, either G.D. Noke's *An Introduction to Evidence* (1967) or Sir Rupert Cross's *Evidence* (1974) might be recommended.

Types of Sources

The sources of history may be of several types. Any categorization of historical sources reflects, however, one's own perceptions of usage and involves some matters of choice. For the purpose of discussion in this case, we shall place the sources into eight basic categories: (a) original written records, (b) published personal records, (c) published official documents, (d) secondary written sources, (e) statistical sources, (f) oral sources, (g) pictorial sources, and (h) physical remains. Communication historians, like legal and military historians, explore and exploit certain types of sources with particular interest. Accordingly, we shall separate these communication sources from the rest and consider them in the next section of this chapter.

Original Written Records. Into this category fall a wide variety of original sources as they exist in their unpublished state. Many will never be published. Found in libraries, archives, and other repositories, and sometimes kept by individuals, these are the sources that constitute much of the historian's richest raw material. Whether or not particular items found in these sources are primary evidence in regard to the subject of the inquiry remains for the historian to decide. Some of this material, of course, finds its way into published collections, and they are useful. Nevertheless, whenever possible the historian wishes to consult records in their complete and original form. By studying records in their preserved original state, it is possible to see individual items in relation to surrounding remaining records. An original collection of personal papers, for instance, can reveal many nuances of understanding about its author as a real person.

Let us consider collections of personal papers as a type of an original written source. A mosaic of items capable of adding a life-giving dimension to historical study can be found in a well-compiled collection of original personal papers. For instance, in sizable manuscript collections such as the William Allen White Papers or the Josephius Daniels Papers, which are both located at the Library of Congress, one will encounter the most complete original source records available for the study of these figures. In collections such as these, one will find personal correspondence of all sorts (i.e., routine, general, and special), communiques of various kinds, memoranda, reports, and a variety of records (e.g., of observation, of conversation, etc.). There, too, one might find original manuscript versions of published speeches, books, dramas, or journalistic writing, as well as manuscript copies of such items never published. Large collections, and some smaller ones too, can contain a great variety of personal records: diaries, journals, notebooks, datebooks, appointment books, itineraries, and address books. Some of the most revealing material found in a manuscript collection is of a miscellaneous variety: family records, financial statements, scrapbooks, picture albums, clippings, and assorted memorabilia. There is good reason why manuscript collections of original personal papers are among the most valued holdings of major libraries, but personal paper collections, small and large, also can be found in many repositories such as special libraries, historical societies, and archives. Some remain in the possession of individual families.

The type of original material that can be found in archives deserves particular attention. In an earlier chapter we explained the basic difference between a library and an archives. The difference can seem blurred. As mentioned earlier, some personal papers can be found in archives. When that is the case, the logic that explains their inclusion in a particular archives is the fact of their "collective significance" to the focus of that archives or to a special collection in it. Archival records, of course, include much more than personal manuscript items. They are the repositories of materials pertaining to some type of organized activity and of basic local and national records. In fact, by considering that an archives might be local, state, national, international, organizational, or specialized, it is possible to imagine the vast array of records they contain. The National Archives in Washington preserves the basic records of national government and those of government agencies, commissions, and departments as well as the records of the courts, the censuses, etc. Its holdings are monumental as are those of many other national archives. On the other hand, an archives of a single organization, or those of a particular newspaper, are confined in scope to records pertaining to their own activity. Even they can be far more extensive than the layman might think. Archival records, then, heterogeneous as they are by their nature, are prime original written sources. They are preserved in a manner that allows them to retain the attributes of their first creation.

Mention should be made at this point of local government records. Since there are about 81,000 units of local government in the United States, the extent of records produced by the routine of their work tests the imagination. In content they range from records of birth, death, marriage, and divorce to ones regarding matters of property and taxation. Storage is a problem in preserving them. Some are kept in local archives, but most remain in courthouses, townhalls, or the office of their origin. Using such records can also be a problem. Researchers may find themselves intruding into the daily work of municipal record keepers. To achieve the best results in research and to enhance the chances of a cordial reception, researchers should study beforehand the various guides available for the object of their inquiries. They should be as prepared as possible before making a visit. That can be translated into a basic rule of research: Always be prepared and, whenever possible, use the records in their complete and original form. One should be prepared to visit manuscript libraries, archives, and other places where records are kept. Only the most specified and retrievable data (e.g., a birth certificate) should be requested by mail. Such requests should be specific, well defined, and addressed to the appropriate office.

Published Personal Records. Often the correspondence, journals, or writings of an important figure will appear in published form. They are, of course, valuable historical records, but not quite as valuable as they are in their original form. Moreover, the historian must consider why such records are published. Did an author keep a diary intended for publication; and, if that is the case, what is its value as a historical record? Was it edited for publication? Perhaps it is of little value; perhaps it is significant. To diaries published by their keepers, one must apply the rules of evidence as he or she must for any personal record intended for publication. Speeches, public debates, major addresses, and autobiographical and memoir literature are all made or produced with a public audience in mind. Whether or not they are accurate in what they describe or are distortions of truth or apologetic exercises remains for the historian to decide. Nevertheless, even if they are deemed untrustworthy as one type of evidence, let us say as descriptive evidence of particular happenings or verbatim evidence of conversation, they may be valuable as another type. Such records, for instance, may reveal a great deal about one's personality, values, and perceptions of life. Moreover, what a person remembers years later, even if clouded by the passing of time, is of significance in any attempt to understand that person and can be informative also about historical time.

Published personal records edited by someone other than their author, valuable though they are, can entail problems of usage, too. There are principles to follow in scholarly editing, and knowledge of them will help the historian evaluate the worth of a particular edited selection of personal papers. For a full explanation one might wish to consult the appropriate section in Savoie Lottinville's *The Rhetoric of History* (1976). Suffice to mention here, no substantive changes should be made in the original record, and its attributes of creation should be retained as much as possible. The criteria used for selection of material should be explained. Most editors of published personal records select items from the original source to include rather than reproducing the full original record. Many published personal records reflect the editors' excellent discernment and perception of the value of sources. This is the case in Trevor Wilson's *The Political Diaries of C.P. Scott 1911-1928* (1970). Scott, the respected editor of the Manchester *Guardian*, kept extensive diaries and other written records. In editing Scott's political diaries, Wilson used about half of the diaries and appropriate related excerpts from correspondence. "Another editor, " he admitted, "would have selected rather differently."[3] Helpful as Wilson's selections are, the historian cannot help wanting to know about the rest.

Published Official Documents. Here is a source of obvious importance, but it is one that also needs evaluation. In this case, we are using the term document to mean an official record authorized by some institution or agency. The records may be the official documents of a government, church, business, institution, or organization, and they may include legal and judicial documents,

---

[3]Trevor Wilson, ed., *The Political Diaries of C.P. Scott 1911-1928* (Ithaca, N.Y.: Cornell University Press, 1970), 12.

proceedings of organizations and legislative bodies as well as reports, records, and questionnaires that have been published. A legal published document such as a constitution or a judicial ruling or a law usually would be considered as an unimpeachable record. Such documents can be verified by the original document. Yet there remains much about those documents to evaluate. Their authenticity may be proven, but it is a more difficult thing to grasp their meaning.

Here we turn to the principles of internal criticism. Since 1791 the American people have had the Bill of Rights as one of their fundamental legal principles. The authenticity of that document and of the constitution itself is not a matter of question, but the matter of the meaning of such documents has been the subject of debate since the earliest years of this republic. A court ruling is a clear pronouncement, but the judicial opinion standing behind it is a matter of interpretation. A law is a clear statement, a binding rule of action for a community; but, as we are reminded by such an obvious example as that of the Alien and Sedition Acts, a social philosophy exists behind laws. When dealing with such documents, historians want to know not only what a particular one says and whether it can be trusted as a genuine version of the original; they want to know a good deal about the "why" that lies behind the document itself and the "what" that connects it to a social historical context. Why were the Alien and Sedition Acts passed? What do they tell us about American society of the 1790s? What do they fail to tell us? Or, to skip to the twentieth century, why did Congress adopt the Radio Act of 1927 and what do we need to know about the concept of freedom and responsibility in the 1920s to comprehend the meaning of that law? To comprehend even the best known statutes one must be able to grasp their meaning in terms of time and setting, in terms of the traditions, conditions, and personalities responsible for their presence in history.

Published government documents tend to have a hallowed quality about them. Original documents are even more impressive, but it is the published version that most people see. Students of history must avoid falling into the common trap of accepting authorized government documents, original or published, as valid evidence. They should ponder the "how" and "why" of their composition. As an exercise in understanding government documents as historical evidence, students should take the time to read the documents produced by the various belligerent powers to justify their involvement in World War I. By itself, the case of each country seems convincing, but when viewed collectively each of those cases is far less persuasive. Only by the use of wide knowledge of historical circumstances and by determined effort to be fair and balanced in judgment of evidence, can one reach conclusions about which country or countries may have been responsible for the war. Yet, think about how much of subsequent history rests upon assumptions regarding responsibility for that conflict -- either the way it began or the way it ended.

Government documents are important evidence, but their meaning must be understood in terms of the circumstances and intent of publication. Many government documents, like documents pertaining to other organizations, are published with the honest intent of making information available to the public. Indeed, it would be hard to imagine scholarly work proceeding without such publications. There are two considerations to bear in mind when using them: (a) be aware of the criteria used in selecting them for publication (usually found in the introduction to the first and perhaps following volumes of a set), and (b) particularly in documentary histories (usually single-volume compilations), observe if the document is reduced from its original form. If reduced for publication, such a version of the document would fail to conform to the rule of best evidence.

Secondary Written Sources. Secondary sources, as we have seen, are those based upon primary sources and removed in time from the subjects they describe. They compose a varied category of sources, including (a) pamphlet and periodical literature, (b) major historical studies and monographs, (c) biographies, (d) current affairs literature, (e) official histories, and (f) imaginative literature.

These sources have a definite place in historical research, and that fact should not be forgotten in the historian's effort to employ original sources in a study. The bibliographic searching related to historical inquiry produces a rich yield of secondary literature. It should be studied and used; in fact, one would be remiss if he or she failed to use this category of literature. Even imaginative literature has its place in historical research. It can tell us a great deal about the time or age in which it was written and can provide a sense of color and atmosphere that can enhance historical understanding. Thus a novel written in the 1950s about World War II might be a valuable source to use in understanding the mind of the 1950s. Sometimes a novelist can capture the essence of a particular moment or event in history or perhaps the life of an institution. There was, for instance, a good deal of truth about journalism in *Deadlines* (1922) and *Josslyn* (1924), those two novels by Henry Justin Smith, which in their day were considered classic portrayals of the newspaperman's life that Smith knew so well.

Most of the secondary literature the historian will use, of course, will be factual. It might be consulted for general information, for the primary evidence it contains, or for the interpretation it has to offer. It should not, however, be used as a source of primary evidence if that evidence is available itself for investigation. If it has to be put to that use, remember that it is evidence selected by another person and perhaps for a purpose other than your own. Regarding interpretations, naturally you want to know what authorities have said on subjects of their expertise. Moreover, secondary literature can be studied for ideas, for new questions to ask in an inquiry, and to see how others have handled particular topics. Journalists, moreover, are often called contemporary historians, and through the years they have been some of the most frequent contributors to that variety of secondary literature called current affairs literature. It can be used for attitudes and impressions and sometimes as a type of early history of an event. Secondary literature in its many varieties is a valued body of information for the historian, but remember that although the work of other writers can be used to help you understand your subject, your inquiry into that subject must be your own.

Communication historians should remember also that the quality of much of the writing in their field has been mediocre. Allan Nevins and others have confirmed that fact.[4] Too many biographies of journalists have been sentimental and impressionistic portrayals; and too many histories of newspapers have been written, to quote Nevins, "with an eye to pious commemoration or profitable promotion."[5] One has only to think of a fine biography such as W.A. Swanberg's *Citizen Hearst* (1961) or Nevins' institutional history *The Evening Post: A Century of Journalism* (1922) to know that there have been exceptions to that statement. Yet it holds as a generalization. Therefore, of all historians, communication historians should adhere to the rules for evaluating secondary literature as a source. Consider a book's author whenever possible. Appraise the volume's tone and quality and whether or not it manifests the attributes of good scholarly writing. If it is a work of current affairs, try to determine if its subject receives reasonable and full treatment and if the opinions expressed are well supported or, if they are not, if they are statements reflecting whim, emotion, or bias.

Statistical Sources. Earlier in this book we underscored the importance of statistical studies in our discussion on quantification in history. For the sake of perspective, recall that the fascination with figures predated the appearance of the computer. It comes as no

---

[4]Nevins, "American Journalism and Its Historical Treatment," *Journalism Quarterly* 36 (1959): 411-23, 521.

[5]Ibid., 413.

surprise that the emergence and growth of computer technology with its capacity for data processing have increased interest in statistics as historical sources. Those sources hold a great potential for many topics in history. They open up new possibilities for the study of local history, for the study of everyday life (as opposed to the history of elites), and for institutional studies. Indeed, political, economic, and social history are all filled with subjects that have statistical characteristics. The growth of data archives such as the Inter-university Consortium for Political Research indicates that the potentiality for using such sources as historical evidence will continue to expand.

Like all historical sources, statistics must be evaluated before they can be accepted as convincing evidence. Where do statistics originate, and can they be trusted? If they come already gathered for the historian, perhaps in a census, they might be less than accurate. The first British census of 1801 was a far less certain record than ones gathered fifty years later. Newspaper circulation figures of a century ago may not be accurate. Perhaps they were padded for purposes of circulation or to attract advertising. Or suppose that the figures the historian wishes to use have to be extrapolated from surviving records. Those records may or may not be trustworthy, and even if the original records of the data attempted to present it according to the dictates of honesty, the person who did the tabulation may not have had the expertise to implement that intention. How well trained were people charged with the collection of data a century or two ago?

It is often claimed that historians make qualitative statements that have quantitative implications (e.g., "many people," "few people"). Such quantitative inferences, indeed, can be sharpened by the careful use of statistics in many cases. But the reverse is also true: Quantitative references can have qualitative inferences. It is one thing to use numbers to show that middle-class voters performed in one way or another in a given election; it is quite another matter to define who were the middle-class voters and to have one historian's definition accepted by other historians. A similar problem of selection might appear in statistical delineation of any group in society. Historians often are interested in using statistics to trace a trend over some period of time. The work involves variables of time, place, and circumstance regarding the figures used. The same is true of comparative examples in their inquiries. There are many variables involved in such comparisons when they are statistical. What constitutes an adequate salary for a reporter in one decade might be inadequate in another, or the amount of profit necessary to make a newspaper prosperous at one time or place might be different from that required at another time and place. We can conclude that the validity of historical statistics involves evaluation of their reliability and selection as well as tests of their suitability for use as sources of comparison or representation. Finally, once they have been verified as usable sources, statistics still have to be explained. That returns us to qualitative techniques.

Oral Sources. As historical sources, these records can be subdivided into (a) oral tradition and (b) sources of oral history. *Oral tradition* refers to verbal testimony transmitted from one generation to another. Used by social anthropologists before it attracted the attention of historians, it is a study that deals with interpreting the types and means of transmission of verbal traditions. In the study of literature and industrial societies oral tradition may include riddles, childhood rhymes, legends, folklore, and proverbs. It is, moreover, a source of great significance for reconstructing the history of preliterate societies, and it has risen as an historical methodology as a result of the emerging interest in the history of pre-colonial African societies in the 1960s. Jan Vansina's *Oral Tradition: A Study in Historical Methodology* (1961) is the most significant explanation of the many procedures involved in this methodology, and anyone interested in applying oral tradition in practice should consult that book.

John Tosh, British historian and African specialist, has pointed out, however, that there are major problems of distortion connected with accepting oral traditions as accurate. The discussion of this matter in his *The Pursuit of History* (1984) should be used to balance Vansina's. At least, one must consider the possibility that an oral tradition may have been modified or remolded over time and that it may be used today with a particular effect or audience in mind. For instance, it now seems apparent, according to Tosh, that stories were invented in Gambia for Alex Haley, the American writer who went there in 1966 in search of information about his slave ancestor, Kunta Kinte. Later he incorporated that information into his best-seller *Roots*.[6] Oral tradition, then, represents a significant and fascinating historical source, but, as is always the case, one that should be used with utmost care.

The term *oral history* refers to the creation of a somewhat different source than that known as oral tradition. Oral history is a less than perfect term that refers to the historical recovery of the remembered but unrecorded past. It is as old as history itself. Herodotus used it as did a number of medieval and modern historians. Only with the prevalence gained by the written record as an

---

[6]John Tosh, *The Pursuit of History: Aims, Methods and New Directions in the Study of Modern History* (London: Longman, 1984), 185-86.

historical source in the late nineteenth century did it fall out of fashion. Interest in oral sources grew sharply in the 1960s among historians as they concentrated more than before on the history of ordinary people, workers, and even the inarticulate struggling poor. Many recent historians working on traditional subjects also have used it with great success (e.g., T. Harry Williams in his biography of Huey Long and Gordon W. Prange in *At Dawn We Slept*). The use of oral evidence has become a major new historical trend as proven by the establishment of the Oral History Collection at Columbia University and the more recent British Oral Archive of Political and Administrative History at the London School of Economics. Oral sources, however, do not of themselves constitute history. They must be used by a discerning historian and in conjunction with other sources. The documents of oral history may be legend, folklore, ballads, interviews, taped conversations, or recordings -- any spoken record useful to history. In some cases (such as legend and folklore) the distinction between oral history and oral traditions is somewhat blurred. Oral history, however, usually refers to the use of oral sources in a literate society. Its main tool is the retrospective interview.

Many communication historians no doubt are familiar with the practice of interviewing. Those who are not may wish to consider the strategies of historical interviewing in James Hoopes' *Oral History: An Introduction For Students* (1979). Suffice to mention here that the historical interview involves three stages: (a) preparation, (b) the interview itself, and (c) subsequent reconstruction. The first involves background study and selection of and approach to an interviewee; the second deals with strategies for conducting the interview. In the last stage, an interview must be transcribed and its validity verified by the interviewer. After that the interview becomes an authentic oral record to be tested by all of the means of internal criticism.

Pictorial Sources. Like spoken records, those classified as "pictorial" can provide a corrective to an elitist bias in history. Posters and films, after all, were made with popular appeal in mind. Old photographs are the valued possessions of ordinary people as well as the rich and powerful. Such visual records are, in fact, the exclusive preserve of no particular class or group in society. They are simply revealing sources for the study of modern history. Because of their interest in photojournalism and films of record (e.g., newsfilm, newsreels, documentaries, etc.), communication historians may be more alert than other historians to these visual records as historical sources.

The term *pictorial*, however, includes materials beyond photographic and film sources. It encompasses the greater and lesser works of art in their many graphic forms. To be used as historical sources, all types of pictorial records must first be evaluated. The simplest photograph should be studied for traces of its intent and incidental substance as well as for its main subject. When dealing with the work of a well-known photographer, that person should be studied. What was his purpose? His approach? Did he have a particular class or cultural interest that his work reflected? Before any extensive use of photographic sources, the researcher should become familiar with the works of historians such as Beaumont Newhall, and before employing serious or popular examples of art in his study he should consult the writings of a reputable art historian. In both cases, such authorities can sharpen one's perception of these sources both in terms of content and intent.

The growth of film archives attests to the qualification of the film as a major source for twentieth-century history. Here we shall refer mainly to fictional films. What can they tell us about past reality? To answer that question the historian must consider a film from three perspectives: production, content, and audience.

Critique of evidence is involved in consideration of each of these three perspectives. Regarding production, the reasons and restrictions accompanying a film's appearance must be analyzed. Did Frank Capra produce *Mr. Smith Goes to Washington, It's a Wonderful Life,* and other films of that genre because he wanted to create "the American dream" or in response to its existence? At various times and places have either official or unofficial censorship or the needs of propaganda influenced the production of certain types of films? Perhaps it is possible to make a topical grouping of films. That could be suggestive about what was produced and what failed to be produced. Regarding content, historians are interested in how films reveal popular attitudes and cultural values and in how they transmit messages. Analysis of film audiences is the hardest area of film evaluation to penetrate. Nevertheless, in terms of using the film as an historical source, it is important to know about the distribution of a film, the number and type of theaters showing it, and audience attendance and reception. That information requires a great deal of digging, and, unfortunately, all records of such things have not been kept and those kept are difficult to find. We can conclude by noting that for films to be used effectively as an historical source, they must be used in a systematic way. Those who wish to use the film as an historical source may wish to consult Paul Smith's *The Historian and the Film* (1976) for a useful elaboration of the subject.

Physical Remains. This category is a somewhat arbitrary one by design. It includes the remaining objects created by people. Although they might in some cases be inscribed (e.g., coins, cemetery markers, various types of engravings, etc.), they display characteristics of things apart from the records of the written or spoken word. Some were made with no intention of preservation in mind (such as a tool); other objects were constructed to stand for something in a particular society and to endure (e.g., a public building). The category includes relics, mementos, and an array of things used by people in work and leisure as well as buildings, vehicles of transportation, and the instruments of technology (such as printing presses and radio receiving sets). Some may be artistic objects. Although these physical remains may be crucial to the study of medieval, ancient, and primitive history, they remain, with the exception of a few areas of interest, supplementary to the pursuit of modern history.

Yet, in their own way, they are valuable to the modern historian. How does one acquirê a foothold on the past? The answer, of course, depends on the person, but a contact with the past can be acquired by contemplating those physical objects that remain for us to see. Have you ever visited an historic home or building, strolled the streets of a ghost town, walked through an old newspaper office, sat in an antiquated railway car, found an old coin, or studied some inscribed artifact of the past? If you have, you no doubt expanded your imagination and perhaps your curiosity about the past and about how men and women lived in some previous time. That is one of the benefits that you can derive from these physical objects. They can also inform you about past styles, fashions, and inventiveness. Perhaps they can offer explanation for puzzling references to items you have encountered in your other sources. In the case of a newspaper, these objects inform us about matters of production, design, and distribution. Or consider architecture. It can tell us something about how a previous society used space and reveals important aspects of the society's creative nature.

Some of these silent remains of the past exist in today's society. Museums, of course, have rescued many specimens of objects out of the past that otherwise would have been lost or perhaps not appreciated. No one who has ever browsed through basic museum directories such as *The Directory of World Museums* (1981), or in the case of the United States and Canada, *The Official Museum Directory* (1976), can question how rich and ranging a resource museums offer to enhance understanding. Grasping the full meaning of these remaining objects carries us into the domain of specialized studies (e.g., epigraphy, heraldry, numismatics, etc.). The more you can introduce yourself to the fundamentals of these related studies as they pertain to your inquiry, the more you will perceive in the objects you view or may wish to view.

Using Mass Communication Sources

Historical sources in mass communication are more abundant than one at first may realize. They include not only the material researchers most often think of first -- old newspaper and magazine files -- but personal papers, broadcasting archives, pamphlets, business records, trade journals, and a multitude of other original sources. Even the familiar sources such as newspaper files are available in greater numbers than researchers often think. References to many of the sources are included in Chapter 5 of this book. Historians must acquaint themselves with those and various other references. They also must keep in mind that historical research must be conducted in primary sources and that the array of primary sources they use must be as broad as possible. In evaluating those primary sources, they also must apply a number of tests to assure that they properly understand the information that the sources yield. All the criteria already discussed in this chapter apply to evaluating mass communication sources, but particular points bear emphasizing.

Most historical work in mass communication probably requires research into media content and other published matter. The historian, however, should be aware of a number of limitations and of proper standards in using such material. Rarely is public material by itself adequate for conducting historical study. A study of newspaper news stories, for example, may allow the historian to determine nothing more than the news content of a newspaper. Study of television commercial content may reveal nothing of historical significance beyond a superficial description of the content. Historians should be aware of the limitations of popular methods such as content analysis, as discussed in Chapter 3, which offer only one dimension of the picture necessary in historical study. Published or broadcast materials are necessary but, except for very limited projects, inadequate by themselves as research sources. Historians must consider all possible sources that will help them answer the questions they have posed for study. Office memos, corporate papers, and private correspondence, for example, always should be examined when available.

In fact, communication historians' interests carry them beyond the content of a given report or series of reports. They want to know, for instance, about news accounts. Were they controlled by some type of authority or shaped by particular circumstances, either of origin or transmission? They need to probe behind the public report itself and into matters of motive and context. They also want to know about circumstances (e.g., censorship, propaganda, etc.) that might have a bearing on a given account such as a news story.

The fact that published material is public forces another limitation on its use by the historian. A cardinal rule of evaluating historical material is that the smaller the intended audience for it, the more reliable the material is. Conversely, the larger the intended audience, the less reliable it is. That rule should warn the historian not to assume that published or broadcast statements necessarily reveal the innermost beliefs of their writers. A private diary, for example, would be better evidence, probably revealing more accurately a writer's attitude or motivation than does a newspaper article. The latter might be intended to put the best public light on the writer's motives. The historian must continually keep in mind the purpose the author had in putting down any particular thought in writing or uttering it on the airwaves.

Other problems in dealing with published material confront the historian. One is distinguishing between opinion and news. Opinion often has masqueraded as news in the media. From colonial times through much of the nineteenth century, newspaper editors made little attempt to distinguish their opinions from news. They frequently interspersed their views with their news accounts. Although the passage of time and changes in newspaper practices lessened the use of news columns for statements of opinion, even today few observers would argue that news is completely objective. It is not true that every news item that has appeared in a newspaper accurately described events. Historians usually consider a reporter a reliable source. Contemporary studies show, however, that even today's reporters, most of whom are better trained than their predecessors, make errors of fact or explanation in a large percentage of their stories. News accounts also often are based on second-hand information rather than a reporter's eyewitness observation. Many providers of information are not trained observers. The historian should keep such factors in mind when examining news reports and should not necessarily accept statements of fact as face value. One should take all possible steps to verify any statements that play a substantive part in one's study. Examining various reports of the same events is one way to do that. The suggestions for determining reliability that the journalism historian Frank Luther Mott made years ago still are useful for historians today to know. He spelled out a number of tests that communication historians may and should use before they accept material as fact simply because it appeared in print.[7]

---

[7]Frank Luther Mott, "Evidence of Reliability in Newspapers and Periodicals in Historical Studies," *Journalism Quarterly* 21 (1944): 304-10.

The historian also should be careful to avoid attributing all material that appears in any medium to its owner, editor, manager, or any other staff member. Communication historians, regrettably, frequently have been guilty of taking statements from a newspaper and attributing them directly to the editor or to the editor's influence and direction. It is not necessarily true, however, that an editor had the responsibility, even indirectly, for everything that appeared in his newspaper. An editor normally did exercise some oversight over editorials; but even so, the historian must be wary of assuming that all editorials mirrored an editor's opinions. The problem Horace Greeley had with the views of some of his correspondents, staff members, and co-owners of the New York *Tribune* which his newspaper published should alert the historian to the danger of assuming that any editor agreed with everything his newspaper printed. The historian must have good reason to attribute authorship before doing so. Marked files of publications and other internal and external evidence should be examined studiously, as discussed earlier in this chapter.

Then there is the personal factor to consider in evaluation of sources. As we indicated earlier in the discussion of internal criticism, this factor is frequently involved. That is surely the case in much of communication history. Let us suppose, for instance, that we are trying to appraise the effectiveness of Edward R. Murrow's *See It Now* series, which was so heralded a television news effort in the 1950s, during TV's "Golden Age." Suppose the object of the investigation is to attempt to determine why *See It Now,* despite being ably presented, well-financed, and technically innovative, failed to achieve a wide following. By 1958, under the burden of its own falling ratings, it left the air. Why the poor ratings?

To answer the question one can turn to a number of written and visual records about the series itself. One can study the content and format of the series plus a number of records about its production. Such records are vital, but they are not sufficient to satisfy the object of the inquiry. Whatever else is of importance in the study, there is Murrow himself to consider. Was his style too serious, too political, or too controversial? Was there something about the atmosphere of urgency that he was able to create or about his "doomsday voice" that failed to attract large audiences in the optimistic 1950s? Had Murrow's rhetorical style become dated? How can we explain the penetrating seriousness that he continued to personify? Perhaps his style was the product of his experiences in the 1930s and 1940s and was shaped by occurrences of global consequence -- the collapse of European democracies and the rise of fascism. The public records of the program and the various records relating to its production would not inform us sufficiently about such a proposition. Yet they are essential ones in the inquiry, and they will provide indispensable additions to it. Communication historians, therefore, mush probe deeply into private personal records in order to discover evidence about the motive or actions that lie behind the public record to give the latter its full meaning.

At least when examining the produced works of journalists, communication historians want to know many things about those people. What were they about as journalists? What were their professional values? Did they have personal commitments that influenced their work? If so, what were they and how did they influence the work? Just as it is difficult to examine a work of literature without knowledge of the author, so it is difficult to analyze a record of mass communication without knowledge of the person or people responsible for it. If communication historians wish their work to reflect the highest standards of historical scholarship, they must seek and study sources both public and private, and they must contemplate and interpret the interaction that exists between the two.

Historians interested in conducting research into broadcast and film material confront a number of particular difficulties. For example, determining authenticity of these materials can be perplexing. When dealing with film, the historian should be aware of several problems. A print of a film may not be complete; that is, it may have been altered for various reasons. In many instances, a variety of copies were made. Frequently the original version as approved by the film's director has been altered, shortened, for example, perhaps to fit a two-hour television slot. Most films made for the wide theater screen that are reproduced on videotape for television have been altered in shape to fit the proportions of the TV screen. Therefore, part of the image on each frame has been eliminated. (To avoid that problem, some directors, such as Woody Allen, have stipulated that their films must retain the original frame proportions if reproduced on videotape.) Verifying the original hues of some color films is virtually impossible. The color dyes that were used in Eastmancolor film in the 1950s have faded, and even computerized technology used today cannot restore the original colors. The historian also should be aware of the recent projects to add color to motion pictures originally filmed in black and white; such colorized versions alter the original material and therefore cannot be considered authentic. It also is difficult to measure the original technical quality of silent films because they have been reproduced on different film material and shown on different types of equipment (including projectors that run the film at a different speed than the original equipment did.)

A number of other factors must be of particular concern to the historian doing research in film or any other type of performed work. A historian must be careful about ascribing "authorship" for a film. For years, the accepted thinking was that a film's director was its "author." Today, the assumption generally is that films have multiple authorship. They are the result of the ideas and input not only of the director, but of screenwriters, set directors, photographers, and others. The historian also must recognize that sometimes a film had multiple directorship -- with a second director called in, for example, to handle one special scene -- without all directors being named in the film credits. The historian also should consider the question of whether a script or a transcription of a film (or a broadcast) accurately reflects the actual performed work. Scripts and transcriptions cannot capture fully the performance, and historians wishing to study the performed work should use whenever possible the actual film, broadcast, or recording for study.

Because so many films have been lost and so many broadcasts and performances were never recorded, the historian also must be suspect about whether the work that survives truly and fully represents the subject under study. Some early motion picture studios, for example, preserved their material, while others did not. The historian therefore must be cautious in treating material as if it is indicative of the total.

The case of newsreels presents problems of another sort. These productions appeared to resemble news reporting normally associated with the printed media. Did they? Did they present reality or an illusion of reality? Did they convey an accurate representation of events to the viewing audience? Newsreel coverage of the Yalta Conference of 1945, for instance, tended to present an image of harmony suggestive of Allied cooperation near the end of World War II. It contained little substantive analysis of the meeting of the "Big Three," Churchill, Roosevelt, and Stalin. Yet decisions reached there shaped the future of Europe and had other far-reaching effects. Are such newsreels valid records of historical events? What do they tell one about the news media? Raymond Fielding's study, *The American Newsreel 1911-1967* (1972), helps to answer those questions. It also alerts one to the fact that, despite the air of confidence the newsreels radiated and the tone of certainty that characterized their commentary, they contained enough personality impersonation, faked content, and manipulation of news to make their validity questionable.

To communication historians, however, they are valuable records of one form of twentieth-century news that countless numbers of theater audiences viewed. In using these records, the historian must scrutinize their content carefully and compare it to other known and more reliable records of the time. Moreover, in using these films as sources, one would want to know about the circumstances and restrictions that accompanied their production and distribution as well as the purposes they were intended to serve.

While the limitations on evaluating historical material can be frustrating, the historian must remember the key attitude with which it must be approached: caution. The historical record, because so much of what happened in the past went unrecorded and is lost forever, never can be complete. Caution and recognition of the limitations, however, will assist the historian in treating the material that survives judiciously and insightfully. That treatment, rather than total record, is the standard expected in historical study.

7

Explanation in History

When historians practice their craft, they normally perform a number of overlapping tasks. They gather and evaluate information and consider ways to explain it. They might begin to compose preliminary drafts of the written product at an early stage of the investigation. There is no better way to stimulate thought about a subject. For the sake of illustrating the component elements involved in history, it is again necessary to make a somewhat artificial division of the process. What happens in historical inquiry after one gathers and evaluates all the germane evidence about a topic? At that juncture it is necessary to confront a mass of collected material and to decide how to explain it, or, to be more precise, to explain that part of the material that bears importance to the subject of the inquiry.

Clarification of Purpose

The task involves understanding of subject, for the subject must be comprehended fully before it can be deemed ready for formal presentation. In some respects, this comprehension entails clarification of purpose. From the start of the project one has had ideas about the subject and why and how the investigation of it should proceed. At some early point in the inquiry, one delineated the topic under study and probably used a working hypothesis as a tool to lend purpose and direction to the study. Consequently, the matter of clarifying purpose has been interwoven with the investigation throughout its course. Now, however, it must be refined into final form before the writing of the narrative can occur. Definition of purpose of inquiry, of course, varies from person to person and from topic to topic. For example, Donald H. Stewart examined copies of 550 papers for a twelve-year period for his study, *The Opposition Press of the Federalist Period.* For what purpose? Many things could be derived from such a mass of material. In this case Stewart decided to use a descriptive approach to his subject and to delineate the "chief measures of attack and defense, of the rhetoric and reason employed, of the way Republican editors reacted to both favorable and unfavorable quirks of fate, and of which appeals were most widely used."[1] His purpose was to enhance understanding of the era by describing both the emotional and logical type of argument that Republican opposition editors used to create a rising tide of feeling against the Federalists.

Consider another case, that of Stephen Koss and his biography of A.G. Gardiner, one of the best known British Liberal publicists of the first quarter of this century. Why should Gardiner's biography be written? Perhaps because he wrote no autobiography or perhaps because he was one of the most influential of British editors during a time historians tend to perceive as probably the last "golden era" of newspaper editors in England. Reason enough, it would seem. However, if Gardiner had failed to produce an autobiography, he had published, aside from his regular journalistic writing, a number of books, essays, and pamphlets. Therefore, he had expressed himself on most of the subjects that would command historical attention, and the record of that expression existed for any historian to study. Koss' problem in deciding why this biography was necessary, in determining the purpose of the study, was made more difficult by the fact that Gardiner was himself no stranger to the craft of biography. He had several biographies to his credit. In fact, he was quite aware of the limitations of biography and once warned that "there are few more agreeable forms of impertinence than to sit in judgment upon other people." Gardiner knew that biography could never be a substitute for someone speaking for himself and that it could never reach a subject's deepest feelings. But he also had said that biography could achieve things that autobiography could not. It could, for instance, transcend the life of its immediate subject by placing that person in the context of historical events. Thus Gardiner believed that biography could be informative about the values of men and about how men interact with the events of their day. By producing such studies, he claimed biographies performed "a

---

[1]Donald H. Stewart, *The Opposition Press of the Federalist Period* (Albany: State University of New York Press, 1969), X.

conspicuous public service."[2]

Koss' biography reflects Gardiner's thoughts on the subject. It is a well-tooled professional biography that is informative about the Liberal politics of Gardiner's day and also about the workings of the press and the social and intellectual currents of British life at that time. Just when he reached his decision about how to treat his subject in this instance, Koss did not say. Perhaps it occurred early in his work; perhaps it grew as his knowledge of his subject matured. Regardless, at the point of contact with constructing the final version of the biography, Koss understood the particular nature of his study. His purpose in writing was clear, and that fact is present throughout his well-defined study of this major journalist.

Understanding the purpose behind an investigation is but one element in the refinement of thinking about an inquiry that has to occur for it to proceed. In fact, refinement of thinking about a topic involves a number of considerations and activities. As was the case in clarifying the purpose of a study, these elements of thought and design may have been present from the beginning of the inquiry, but they must be honed into precise form before the construction of the final narrative can be attempted. They include matters of interpretation, causation, and theory.

Interpretation in History

An interpretive element permeates all history. One begins research by selecting a particular topic to investigate. Why? As research proceeds, one refines the purpose of the inquiry. That is an interpretive act. One attempts to answer certain questions based on evidence discovered. Why those and not others? One evaluates evidence. That involves constant interpretation. Since all the material gathered cannot be used, some will be kept and some discarded. Again, that involves interpretation. We all hold values about life and society, and we know how different individual values can be. Individual as well as social and cultural values shape historical thought. The merest consideration of current politics and public debate affords proof enough of that proposition. People unfamiliar with the study of history are apt to say, "historians say this" or "history proves this." The only thing such statements prove is the historical naiveté of the unbaptized. Historical explanations once advanced are not facts frozen in eternal correctness. They are interpretations based on interpretations. Nowhere is this more evident than in the

---

[2]Quoted in Stephen Koss, *Fleet Street Radical: A.G. Gardiner and the "Daily News"* (Hamden, Conn.: Archon Books, 1973), 1-2.

way in which historians attempt to treat facts and handle generalization.

History involves the interpretation of facts. That statement is more complex than it seems. When historians discuss the interpretation of facts, they do not have in mind uncontroversial or conventional data about the past. Many things that happened in the past can be validated notwithstanding the possibilities of human error or deliberate falsification. They can be proven beyond reasonable doubt, and, indeed, they constitute much of our knowledge about the past. Dwight Eisenhower was born on October 14, 1890, in Denison, Texas. Article II, section 4 of the United States Constitution provides for the removal of a president from office by means of impeachment and conviction for "Treason, Bribery, or other high Crimes and Misdemeanors." On August 15, 1896, William Allen White published an editorial, "What's the Matter with Kansas?" These are all, of course, easily demonstrable statements. In their discussion of facts historians have another type of fact in mind -- facts with extended meanings. We shall call these "historical facts." They may be a human action, an event, an idea, a social condition -- anything of historical significance that existed in the past.

These facts, as E.H. Carr explained in his classic statement, *What Is History?*, cannot stand alone.[3] For instance, in 1896 Alfred Harmsworth inaugurated the *Daily Mail*. An immediate success as a half-penny newspaper, it became the core publication in his expanding press empire. He became, as Lord Northcliffe, Britain's, and probably the world's greatest press baron, and the *Daily Mail* became Britain's most prosperous popular newspaper. Other papers and proprietors copied it; none could match it. Lord Salisbury's often quoted comment that it was a paper "written by office-boys for office-boys" was mere fiction -- as erroneous as the idea that it was a cheap paper for cheap minds. In general, the *Daily Mail* contained trustworthy news, well-written features, and attractive human interest stories, plus advertisements in abundance. Northcliffe supervised it from a distance. He insisted it be clean and respectable as well as interesting; and, as it matured, he tried to increase its quality.

Nevertheless, the mere mention of Harmsworth's launching the *Daily Mail* in 1896 is a fact with an idea always attached to it. The paper is commonly known from its inception as the vanguard of irresponsible sensationalism in the British press. There were, of

---

[3]Edward Hallett Carr, *What Is History?* (New York: Alfred A. Knopf, 1965), 15.

course, many examples of sensationalism in the British press before this time, and during his lifetime Northcliffe despaired of the "yellow journalism" then popular in the United States, the journalistic style his critics claimed he copied.

The extended fact in this case goes beyond the simple fact that Harmsworth launched the *Daily Mail* when and where he did, and includes ideas about how he changed the British press and influenced society. Accordingly, this extended fact deals with Harmsworth's ambition, power, and personality as well as his philosophy of journalism and his genius at implementing it. All of these matters are subjects of controversy. They were when Northcliffe was alive, and they remain so today. Consequently, they must be explained. Such explanation or interpretation gives meaning to the basic fact (i.e., Harmsworth started the *Daily Mail* in 1896). Consequently, one can say, "historical facts," facts with extended meanings, do not speak for themselves. Historians interpret them.

Ideas, as we can see, frequently attach themselves to facts. Consider the example of the tabloid newspapers that appeared in the United States in the 1920s. What were they? In terms of basic fact, they were small newspapers, about one half the size of a standard paper. But the mention of tabloid journalism conjures up certain images or ideas, not particularly inspiring ones. Most often the idea of disreputable journalism springs to mind in connection with the tabloids of the 1920s. To understand the development of this variety of journalism as an historical fact, historians have many questions to ask about it. When did it first appear? Why did it appear and flourish at that time and place? Why did it have mass appeal? Why did "respectable" journalists hold it in disdain? Did it perform any social function? Did it represent a natural or abnormal development in journalism? Historians, of course, are not of one mind when responding to those questions, though they do not dispute the presence and growth of tabloid newspapers in the 1920s. It is the ideas attached to the basic fact that occasion disagreement -- an act of interpretation.

Nowhere is the interpretive element in history more pronounced than in the efforts historians make to generalize about their material. In the first chapter of this book, we spoke of history as present thought about particular things of the past. It should now be obvious that these particular things might be large past occurrences. They may be a war, a revolution, or a movement. Or they may be a single human action. The range is great. It bears repeating that the concern for the particular is one of the distinguishing characteristics of history. But individual things, as we have seen in our discussion of historical facts, do not exist alone.

Consequently, historians not only attempt to understand a

particular thing but also to comprehend it in its relationship to other things. The process involves, as G.R. Elton explained, understanding how the pieces of a phenomenon fit together. "Meaningful interconnections in the particular, illuminating generalization beyond the particular -- these are the marks that distinguish the inspired and inspiring historian from the hack," he said.[4] In relating a particular historical phenomenon to other associated ones, historians employ a variety of methodological techniques. They may use content analysis, or literary analysis, or perhaps a comparative approach. Frequently, they search their information for ideas to serve as bridges of explanation. Even those historians who speak with candor about how they shuffle and reshuffle their notes in search of an idea, in fact, describe a process of hunting for connections.[5] The goal is to understand relationships and patterns within and among historical phenomena. Every stage of the process (i.e., establishing the meaning of an historical fact, discovering its relationship with other facts, or perceiving a broad generalization or pattern to describe it) involves interpretation.

A consideration of these forms of interpretation delivers us to the core of historical reconstruction. Interpretation in history, however, is easy to mismanage. Since we know that it is influenced by selection, imperfect evidence, and the values of the interpreter and that it can be imperfectly expressed, the suggestion of possible mismanagement does not surprise us. Successful management of interpretation depends on five types of control. The first concerns evidence. It must be controlled by mastering the various methods used in evaluating sources. Beyond that, the evidence must be selected by the use of some logical criteria for selection. This is basically a task of finding the evidence that is germane to the subject and of adjusting one's "working hypothesis" to fit it. It bears repeating at this point that a "working hypothesis" must be broad enough in design to accommodate all the evidence, including that which can be called "contrary evidence."

The second control relates to context. Knowledge of the context of an historical topic is one of the hallmarks of history, and it carries one beyond the evidence that directly relates to the topic. John Tosh stated what most historians know when he wrote, "Questions of historical explanation cannot...be resolved solely by reference to

---

[4]Elton, *The Practice of History,* 98.

[5]See comments by Robert W. Palmer and John William Ward in L.P. Curtis, Jr., ed., *The Historian's Workshop* (New York: Alfred A. Knopf, 1970), 175 and 312.

evidence. Historians are also guided by their intuitive sense of what was possible in a given historical context, by their reading of human nature, and by claims of intellectual coherence."[6] They need, then, perspective, imagination, and a sense of historical time. How much? Enough to inform them about how the various influences on their topics developed, enough to allow them to understand the social, economic, political, and cultural realities that gave meaning to society at the time under consideration, and enough to allow them to grasp what it was like to live at that time.

The third control relates to the status of historical writing on the topic. As we have mentioned before, the researcher must take into account the opinion of others who possess a significant knowledge about the topic. The historiographical element is essential, since historical writing changes over time. In a sense, a topic acquires a historical life of its own. Historical interpretation of a particular topic might expand or change as new information is discovered or new preferences exercised. Or it might evolve in accordance with changing social outlook. The researcher must know about the main currents of this changing historical commentary on the subject and be able to respond to it when necessary.

The fourth control deals with constructing generalizations. They should not be impaired by simplistic reduction or by overexpansion, or by careless language. There is an art to generalizing in historical writing. General statements should be related to textual details and to specific examples. They must rest on evidence -- or on a sound expansion of the meaning of that evidence. The reverse is also true. Specific material must be related to generalization to give writing focus, force, and direction. The interaction between the two, between the specific and the general, is an ongoing manifestation of the interplay that exists between the historian and his or her material.

The final control concerns the need to develop a particular type of self-discipline. Opinion and judgment pervade all history. Bias can take many forms and needs to be controlled. It may be an unrestrained preference, a prejudice, or an unexamined opinion. It may be a manifestation of a too enthusiastic commitment to a communication theory, a philosophy, a nation, an ideology, or a political system. It might be uncontrolled class, cultural, or occupational attachment. The best controls for bias are self-awareness and recognition of an objective standard. Regarding the former, it is important to develop an awareness of self -- of your own values, commitments, and preferences. Then, for your history to have the integrity

---

[6]Tosh, *The Pursuit of History,* 117.

it deserves, you must attempt to transcend your own time and circumstances and to assume the status of an honest referee between past and present. Subjectivity there will be in history, but there also can be a recognition of an objective standard. It is a plausible corrective for bias.

Explaining Causation

Discussion of causation is an old element in history. It is also subjected to much abuse. In particular, people unfamiliar with the nature of history tend to reduce historical causation to levels of argument (or persuasion, conviction, or hunch) that have little lasting consequence. Think of the number of people in our own present society who claim to know what caused the Cold War or the American intervention in Vietnam. Causation, in fact, is one of the main features of the way in which teachers present history. Consider the number of topics encountered in most surveys of United States communication history such as the causes of Yellow Journalism, the growth of the media as big business, etc. Beyond such obvious examples of concentration on causation, it can be added that causal statements frequently appear in historical narration. All of this is proof that historians as well as their audiences are as interested in the "why" as much as in the "who" and the "what" of history. That interest may be a reflection of the influence of science on modern life, or it may be an indication of belief in the idea that people are free agents in life. Perhaps it is a manifestation of man's timeless curiosity. Regardless, it exists.

The matter of handling causation involves major problems. It is much more complex than many people, even beginning researchers, might suppose. Ascertaining causes in history is a precarious matter. For instance, what caused the New Journalism that became so important in England and the United States at the end of the nineteenth century? Perhaps the Pulitzers and Harmsworths caused it. Or, if they had never lived, perhaps other people like them might have appeared to do what they did. On the other hand, the New Journalism may have resulted from conditions of the time. Perhaps it occurred as the result of the "chance" convergence of many factors at that particular time. It is clear that problems of historical causation involve consideration of the full scope of possible explanations.

They also deal with an understanding of the relationship between causes and results. Do causes produce results in history? Did high literacy rates and newspaper reading help bring about the American Revolution? In many respects, few causes appear as "causes" until the results that people attach to them occur. The concept of causal effect can be a problem for the historian. "No historical cause ever must have a given known effect, namely, the historical event to be explained," claimed G.R. Elton. "The best that historians can say is that it did have that effect."[7] The distinction he made must be grasped to understand the nature of historical causation, which differs from causal explanations advanced in the physical sciences and to lesser extent in the social and behavioral sciences. Scientists sometimes posit that certain causes must produce certain results. It would be more accurate to describe the relationship between historical cause and result as one in which causes produced effects and consequences.

The problem of causation is complicated further by the understandable tendency to want to make distinctions between causes. Are some causes "immediate" and others "antecedent," and, if they are, can they be separated? The idea, for example, that the American colonial press was a vehicle for the spread of the revolutionary idea in the decade or so before the start of the American Revolutionary War is usually accepted as true. Very well, what made that press, or a particular part of it, a revolutionary weapon? What caused it to be what it was? Does the work of revolutionary publicists explain that cause or should one search more deeply and widely? Perhaps the explanation lies beyond the seemingly immediate cause of publicists mobilizing the printed word to achieve revolutionary goals. An indispensable part of the explanation might lie in the gradual growth of a revolutionary mentality, or perhaps it was a by-product of the development of the press in the American colonies. In fact, there probably were many causes that explain the presence of the revolutionary press at that time. Some causes appeared later than others, while some were concurrent. How far back should one go in pursuit of causes? How immediate to the revolution should we attempt to be in our explanation, and how much should we deal with antecedent causes? Could the immediate causes have occurred without the antecedent ones; and when, where, and why did the latter make their appearance? Furthermore, once these decisions are made, should one then affix weights to the various designated causes?

A number of historians claim that the distinctions between "paramount" and "contributory" causes are artificial. Jacques Barzun and Henry F. Graff warn that making exact distinctions leads to "self-stultification."[8] Some historians believe it is useful

---

[7]Elton, *Political History,* 141.

[8]Barzun and Graff, 189.

to discuss various causes of an event separately in order to explain them. This does not mean, however, that they are making a substantive distinction between them. Some causes may be incidental to an event, and common sense impels one to dismiss these from serious discussion in a causal explanation. But full and adequate explanation must be given of all the causes that can be discovered to have had a meaningful relationship to the event.

Can quantitative and qualitative distinctions be made between these causes? Most historians doubt that such measurements can be made and, therefore, avoid assigning priority to any one cause or to an order of causes. Discussion of historical causation depends on available evidence and on the judgment of the historian. Neither is sufficient to produce certainty.

In resolving these problems -- and let us admit that no one can ever resolve them with complete satisfaction -- there are a number of considerations to keep in mind. For instance, unlike natural causes, historical causes exist in time and are conditioned by it. They are products of things created by people -- institutions, opinions, interests, and other manifestations of their existence. Consequently, we return once again to the matter of context. In this instance, mind and conscience must be searched for answers to the questions: Does one know enough about the times under consideration and the forces acting upon them to probe into the causation of an event? Has one achieved sufficient detachment from present assumptions and presuppositions to allow that event and those people involved in it the benefit of being understood on their own grounds?

None of the recognized principles that historians employ when dealing with causation are devoid of the personal element. In many cases, for instance, causal explanations can run beyond what the evidence tells us. Inferences must be made. It is at this point that the historian's intuition, which is something different than a hunch or guess, comes into play. The historian's intuition involves advancing reasonable conjecture rather than poorly informed speculation. It involves making statements, suggesting elements of explanation, governed by a grasp of probability that, in turn, reflects available evidence plus wide knowledge of the subject. Or consider the historian's rejection of single causation. Since there is no single cause for all occasions and since a number of causes can be associated with any important event, historians deal with multiple causation. Interrelationships and interactions among them often can be explained only by the historian's intuition. Understanding too that the causes of important events and institutional changes can never be known in full, we can appreciate that there is no room in historical causal explanation for dogmatic thinking. Such causal discussion must have a certain degree of tentativeness, one that allows the debate about causes to remain open.

Finally, consider the matter of evidence. No one expects to encounter causal explanations that are not grounded in evidence. Surely, ones that can be refuted by evidence would be deemed unsatisfactory. But it is the historian who selects the evidence and attaches a causal significance to it, though not to all of it. Human actions, moreover, are reported by word and deed, but the two may not tell the same thing. Motive may be blurred. Furthermore, even the most informed historian must allow for the imperfect nature of historical evidence. Whether we approach historical causal explanations with contextual knowledge, intuitive judgment, multiple causation, or evidence in mind, it is clear that the historian's professional competency is crucial in the equation.

Theory and Historical Explanation

When some scholars speak of "theory," they have a specific concept in mind. Theory, however, has shadings of meaning and should be defined as it is used. For many social scientists, theory is an element in the conceptual (or theoretical) framework that characterizes their explanations. In that case a theory might be advanced to support an idea. Sometimes theory may refer to conjecture or to a scientifically accepted general principle or body of principles. In general a theory might be considered as a device to organize and classify knowledge. Thus a historical hypothesis might be considered a theory.

The place of theory in history is a matter of continuing debate. There are theories in history and theories of history. Some historians reject completely the use of theory in their inquiries. They believe that it improperly superimposes a structure on the human actions of the past and that it impairs the singularity of the people and events they are studying. Moreover, they see theory as a detriment to their own type of rigorous generalization that proceeds from the bottom up. Others treat theories as useful devices that can provide a means for describing, and possibly for understanding, human behavior. They might also use a theory to provide intelligible connections between related human actions. Of course, historians, like other scholars, theorize all the time about problems in their inquiries. The term theory, however, usually means something more specific than theorizing in general. It is used to connote the application of a certain, coherent, structured explanation for a particular problem. One may speak, for instance, of a theory of social mobility, or of economic growth, or of social behavior, or of communication effects, etc.

Historians commonly use theories in history in a number of ways. Some casually adopt them from one of the social sciences. Some treat them as they would handle any interpretation, as an idea to be used or discounted. In *The Generation of 1914,* for instance, Robert Wohl studied generational theories and found "that no available model of generations was flexible enough to encompass the baffling variety of ways in which the term generation of 1914 and its synonyms had been used in the discourse of early twentieth-century Europe." In the end he decided to "abandon theoretical and lexicographical consistency as standards and try to find out what people living in the early twentieth century meant by 'the generation of 1914.'"[9] His book is a superb example of an historian who refused to subordinate his evidence to theory.

Peter Gay, however, in *The Education of the Senses,* aimed "to integrate psychoanalysis with history." He claimed his intention was not to write psychohistory but rather "history informed by psychoanalysis." "...The ways of psychoanalysis, its theories and its techniques," he maintained, might "build the very bridge between individual and collective experience that most historians, deeply uneasy with the Freudian dispensation, have persisted in treating as problematic."[10] By using that approach, he was able to overturn a number of stereotyped ideas about Victorian sexual attitudes and behavior.

When most historians use theory, they do so by applying it to their study of a particular situation. Some work with theory in an explicit manner; others do not. But if you start with the idea that a simple hypothesis is a theory, then it is clear that theory, whether used in an implicit or explicit way, is part of historical inquiry.[11] Some historians make the distinction between "small scale theory," theory applied to specific problems, and "grand theory," a theory of a more general type such as Frederick Jackson Turner's frontier thesis or the agenda-setting theory of the mass media. The latter might be part of an historian's knowledge before he or she begins a

---

[9]Robert Wohl, *The Generation of 1914* (Cambridge, Mass.: Harvard University Press, 1979), 2.

[10]Peter Gay, *The Bourgeois Experience: Victoria to Freud, Vol. 1: Education of the Senses* (New York: Oxford University Press, 1984), 8 and 16.

[11]Some historians such as Lester Stephens prefer to make a distinction between a theory and a hypothesis and see the former as broader than the latter (Stephens, *Probing the Past,* 33). Some others choose to consider a hypothesis as a type of theory. See, for example, Tosh, *The Pursuit of History,* 115; and James West Davidson and Mark Hamilton Lytle, *After The Fact: The Art of Historical Detection,* 2nd ed. (New York: Alfred A. Knopf, 1986), 86.

particular inquiry.[12] Regardless, it is difficult to deny the presence of theory in history.

Theories of history also have attracted some historians. Since ancient times, numerous scholars have been fascinated by the idea that there is a force that determines history and establishes a pattern for human events. Because they ponder the question of the ultimate historical reality, they might be better called philosophers of history. They are the grand systematizers of history; they detect regularities and correlations in and among human actions. Some of their established patterns are cyclical in nature, others linear, but, since they impose a systematic meaning on history and explain that meaning by a pattern they believe all history follows, their type of metaphysical conceptualization of history is deterministic. They are interested in discovering the laws behind history. Karl Marx, Oswald Spengler, and Arnold Toynbee are among the better known philosophers of history in recent generations. A more common type of determinism is that associated with the word "progress." The Whig interpretation of history, which has had numerous proponents in the English-speaking world, is a classic example of using the idea of progress to interpret history. Historians who accept this interpretation view human events as a record of upward progress, and their ideas have influenced a great deal of historical perception. The various interpretations of communication history, as discussed in Chapter 2 of this book, are based on underlying assumptions about the fundamental causes behind history.

The majority of historians remain unconvinced by deterministic explanations of history. They are dubious about the existence of single causes and laws of history. Determinism, they believe, is a form of reductionism that forces historians to be too selective, even manipulative, in choosing supporting evidence and leads them to organize that evidence in a manner that fails to correspond to the great diversity of human reality. They have serious doubts about the idea that the key to man's experience lies in a mechanistic force that is beyond his control. By making other causal factors a manifestation of that force, they contend, determinists impose an inevitability on history that is not there.

Nevertheless, most historians find deterministic conceptualization of history and the grand patterns suggested by a Toynbee or a Marx to be of value. Theories can stimulate thought about history and can suggest possible explanations for particular chapters of history. One does not have to be a Marxist, for instance, to recognize

---

[12]Davidson and Lytle, ibid.

that his philosophy of history can help one to understand the nature of capitalism. Or, to carry the example of capitalism a bit further, communication historians might well find substantial assistance in Marx's ideas if they wish to inquire into the relationship between business and the press.

It can be reasoned that historians in general use theory in some way in their studies. For the most part, however, they use it in a different way than many social scientists who shape their studies according to a strict theoretical framework as defined by their various disciplines. Simply stated, theory does not play the role in historical inquiry that it does in the social sciences. Historians use theories in a more elastic manner than social scientists. In most cases, they employ theory as they would use any interpretation, as an explanation to be adapted, developed, or rejected. The philosophers of history excepted, their focus is on men and women in the past who lived in endless variety and on the way they interacted with the forces that influenced their times.

How Much Research is "Enough"?

Concrete research is the foundation of good history. But how much research must be done? There is no simple answer to the question of when one should stop an investigation and begin work on a final draft of an essay. All researchers must make that decision for themselves. The following list of questions may help in reaching that decision.

1. Are you satisfied with your evidence both in terms of scope and depth? Is it sufficiently exhaustive?

2. Have you studied your evidence in terms of its validity and potential meaning?

3. Have you sharply defined the purpose of your inquiry?

4. Have you tested your explanations against your own best critical thought, including tracing through possible alternative explanations?

5. Do you understand the people involved in your subject, and have you reached a stage of understanding where little that they do comes as a surprise?

6. Do you feel that you understand the historical context of your subject and the various geographical, economic, religious, social, cultural, and political forces that shaped it?

7. Do you feel that you have asked the right questions about your subject? Are they ones that carry you beneath the surface of your evidence?

8. Do you feel informed about the edge of knowledge of your

subject -- about what other scholars have said about it?

9. Do you feel competent to make judgments about questions, large and small, that are germane to your inquiry?

10. Have you given serious thought to the nature of history, and does your inquiry conform to the principles of the discipline?

These questions deserve your careful attention because the writing of the final draft of your essay will depend on the clarity, depth, and continuity of your thought about the subject.

Writing

To say that the narrative element is important to history is like observing that numbers are important to arithmetic. The beginning researcher, however, needs to contemplate the meaning of that statement in its fullness. While it is true that any advice on historical writing is bound to displease some practitioners of the craft, the topic cannot be avoided. In the following discussion, we shall concentrate on those general elements that are most germane to historical writing.

The Historical Narrative

The object of historical research is communication that normally takes the form of a composition. It may be a book-length composition or one of shorter variety. For most beginning researchers, it will be a seminar paper. When should writing begin? It would be misleading to suggest that it occurs only at the end of a research project. To the contrary, it should begin as early as possible, not only because it is an incentive to precise and serious thought about the subject but also because it is the surest means for discovering gaps and dead-ends in the material collected. The final composition must be a polished version. Aside from incorporating all pertinent evidence and the previously discussed elements of historical thinking, it also must manifest the qualities that characterize the historical narrative. Composition is perhaps the most difficult task involved in historical inquiry -- and the most satisfying.

History, as we have seen, differs from the social sciences,

which are modeled on the natural sciences, in a number of ways. Consideration of composition underscores that difference, which is, as we also know, not absolute. No one would deny that a strong analytical as well as a narrative element characterizes history, but without the narrative element history becomes something other than history. Moreover, many of the methodological techniques associated with newer areas of interest such as historical demography are, as Barbara Tuchman said, "methods of research, not of communication."[1] History communicates through narrative, which is perhaps its greatest cognitive instrument.

The historical narrative, a mixture of explanation based on evidence and intuitive reasoning, is one of the oldest forms of investigation that have characterized the study of humankind. History's commitment to narrative is as old as Western civilization, and many historians including Allan Nevins, a journalism historian who was outspoken on the subject, have believed that, since the time of Herodotus, history has been at its greatest when considered a type of literature rather than a branch of science.[2] In fact, many of the founders of history as it emerged and grew in the modern world were concerned with its literary qualities. Both Voltaire and Gibbon even entertained thoughts of making history the modern successor of the epic.[3] Surely there was an epic character to a number of the great nineteenth-century masters of the craft such as Jules Michelet, Thomas Macaulay, and Francis Parkman.

While it is true that a scientific school emerged among historians in the late nineteenth century and succeeded in placing a great stress on research and critical method in the discipline as it was coming into its own as a separate field of inquiry, interest in the narrative was never lost. It remains to this day an esteemed and irreplaceable quality of history.

The historical narrative has much in common with the fictional narrative. Both are stories about events and people, both strive to create a perceptive and lasting impression of life, and both involve essentially a chronological arrangement. The similarity is

---

[1]Barbara W. Tuchman, *Practicing History: Selected Essays by Barbara W. Tuchman* (New York: Alfred A. Knopf, 1981), 63.

[2]Ray Allen Billington, comp., *Allan Nevins On History* (New York: Charles Scribner's Sons, 1975), 202.

[3]Lionel Gossman, "History and Literature: Reproduction or Signification," in Robert H. Canary and Henry Kozicki, eds., *The Writing of History: Literary Form and Historical Understanding* (Madison: University of Wisconsin Press, 1978), 13-14.

not surprising since history was a branch of literature until about 200 years ago and since both history and literature are custodians of the literary tradition. To write history, one must give serious thought to the narrative element and its implementation. The social sciences in general cannot make those claims.

If this stress on narrative has been a distinguishing quality of history, it also has created problems. At times it has encouraged too great an emphasis on portraying individuals in history and too little on conditions affecting them, or too much stress on political history and too little on social. Moreover, as the pull of sciences grew in modern society, a number of scholars came to question history's commitment to narrative. History lacked analysis, precision, and objectivity and was too subjective, they charged. There was a degree of truth in those criticisms, depending on what history and whose history one has in mind, for there are flaws enough to be found in historical writing over the years. That hardly makes history different from any other major form of scholarship. The charges of the critics, however, frequently reflected the wishes of some scholars that history become more scientific, that it become a social science. That being the case, it should be remembered that the historical narrative always has contained an analytical element and, whether at times flawed or not, that it has as much soundness to its credit as any other field of study.

It also is worth remembering that the historical past, as its records show, is an imperfect object to study and that the results of such a study must bear the imperfection that its evidence imposes. History attempts to capture parts of the ever-expanding and diverse mosaic of the past in fullness and truthfulness. Its object is not certainty. Therefore, it is possible to agree with Jacques Barzun when he explained the "futility of trying to make history say something positive in answer to system and method....In the end multiplicity defeats regularity and no one can turn from the record or the history feeling that 'now he knows.'"[4] The historical narrative, which remains the most widespread form of historical writing, has its limitations. They cannot be dismissed. Indeed, recognition of them explains why its major generalizations are seldom unqualified.

Of the problems integral to historical writing, none is more pervasive than that of the tension between the analytical and narrative elements in its construction. The analytical element, of course, has grown during the last hundred years. Are the ramifications of this growth detrimental, or even fatal, to history? G.R. Elton

---

[4]Jacques Barzun, *Clio and the Doctors: Psycho-History, Quanto-History* (Chicago: University of Chicago Press, 1974), 123.

provided a point worth considering about that question. "The essential demand of all historical material," he wrote, "is that it be used to recreate life, which is movement. The whole difficulty of historical reconstruction and writing lies in this fundamental truth about history: it contains a multiple situation forever on the move."[5]

The analytical element poses a twofold problem in historical writing. First, it is difficult to accommodate it to the intrinsic movement in history to which Elton referred, and, second, there is the danger that it will fragment narrative -- perhaps destroy it.

The problem of tension between these two elements in history is an old one that reflects the nineteenth-century conflict between scientific and literary history. Most historians, however, consider the problem as one of integration rather than conflict. Arthur M. Schlesinger, Jr., wrote that historical writing "should integrate narrative and analysis in a web rendered seamless by literary art."[6] Although it is possible to wonder if that web can ever become seamless, the goal of integration of analysis and narrative is laudable. It respects artistry, the concern for truth and evidence, and the demand for full and intelligible explanation that is in history.

Despite its flexible format, the historical narrative has identifiable characteristics. Since it goes beyond simple narration and involves analysis, questioning, and generalization, it is, before all else, an interpretive narrative. It is also concerned with movement and with historical time. It has a beginning and an end and in between a unified development that is, to varying degrees, chronological.

Consequently, the historical narrative has a structure. For most historians that structure is not based on theory, which, as Louis O. Mink explained, "makes possible the explanation of an occurrence only by explaining it in such a way that the description is logically related to a systematic set of generalizations or laws."[7] Rather than impose that type of theoretical structure on their writing, historians structure it to fit the particularity of their subject and their own grasp of it. The way they perceive the subject and mold it into an intelligible and truthful whole gives the historical narrative its unity. In the process, at least to some degree, they must indulge in

---

[5]Elton, *Political History,* 160.

[6]Carol Bondhus Fitzgerald, "Toward a Bibliography of the Writings of Arthur M. Schlesinger, Jr.: 1935-June 1984," with a Foreward by Arthur Schlesinger, Jr., *American History: A Bibliographic Review* 1 (1985): 37.

[7]Louis O. Mink, "Narrative Form As a Cognitive Instrument," in Canary and Kozicki, eds. *The Writing of History,* 131-32.

pattern-making. Pattern in this case refers to the effort to see logical ways in which evidence fits together rather than to an over-arching systematic explanation. For instance, Stephen Koss' *The Rise and Fall of the Political Press in Britain* (2 vols., 1981/1984), one of the most important contributions to recent communication history, is a superb example of a work by an historian who discovered the necessary pattern to make his abundant material comprehensible to his readers.

This concern for readers is another characteristic of the historical narrative. The audience is an imperative factor for historians to consider. History should be directed to a wide audience that might be described as generally educated. To reach that audience historical writing should possess order, lucidity, and crispness. That means it should be free of jargon, that overused technical terminology characteristic of specialized activity. History's language must allow it to communicate to the general, educated audience.

Far from being a mechanical creation, historical writing involves personal choices and preferences of many sorts. Style is among the foremost of these. By simple definition, one can describe style as the manner, tone, or character of discourse. On one level, it depends on the use of words and phrases -- on their selection, pairing, and rhythm -- and on the connotations they convey. On another level, style reflects a writer's sense of proportion and his or her literary ability to create a mood. In either case, style reveals the creative spirit behind the composition. As a personal element in writing, style is, as Edward Gibbon once wrote, "the image of character."[8] Although style in historical writing can be as varied as the writers themselves, it should reflect the basic attributes associated with this form of inquiry. At its best it also has literary grace. Accordingly, the stress on style can be considered as another evidence of the importance of the narrative element in historical composition.

Unity of Composition

It is easy enough to understand that historical writing should have coherent unity. That principle, however, is easier to state than to achieve. A composition must have thematic unity. A narrative must be structured around one central idea, or theme. Without it, the work falls apart. If the composition is no more than a collection of

---

[8]Dero A. Saunders, ed., *Autobiography of Edward Gibbon* (New York: Meridian Books, 1967), 27.

historical data and details, or if it is an unintegrated assortment of pieces of information, it works poorly. It must do more than pull together a group of facts, quotations, dates, places, names, and details of how the historian conducted the research. All of its parts must work together as a unified whole knit around the central theme. To achieve unity, the historian must consider the question of organization of material. To what degree should it be topical and to what degree should it be chronological? Too much of either could destroy the historical narrative. The former represents a horizontal expansion of subject that can destroy movement, and, if one uses a strict multitopical approach, it can be repetitious beyond the limits of a reader's patience. On the other hand, excessive use of chronology would reduce narrative to a simple listing based on order of occurrence. Some mixture of the topical and the chronological is needed, and it must be capable of covering the evidence and unifying it into a coherent whole. There are other factors to consider in establishing continuity. Where does the narrative start and why there? Once you provide logical answers for those questions, then there is the matter of sustaining continuity.

There are a number of literary and rhetorical devices to assist one in that task, but sustained continuity is mainly the result of an historian's imagination. Only that imagination informed by evidence can reconstruct from the remaining record of the past the life that once was part of it. The process is one of providing a natural coherence for diverse evidence that can be found to explain your subject.

One other matter regarding unity deserves mentioning, in particular, for the consideration of communication historians whose scholarly backgrounds are varied. It will deliver us again to differences between history and the social sciences. In this case, the difference is one of form. Historians attempt to reconstruct some segment of life in their presentations and in their explanations try to provide a coherent unity true to that life. From start to finish their compositions are built around the reality of life that is their subject, and they tend to have continuous flow. Social scientists, to the contrary, tend to structure their compositions as though they were parts of a scientific problem. They divide them according to the perceived parts of that type of problem. Consider the following headings that one might encounter in a composition in one of the social sciences:

Introduction
Prior Published Research on the Topic
Hypothesis
Method
Discussion of findings
Conclusion

Such a division, of course, might have been made for pedagogical purposes. Nevertheless, it exemplifies the social science approach to a problem and sometimes appears in a modified form in historical papers presented at conferences of communication educators. Composition so divided bears obvious comparison with the arrangement associated with writing in the natural sciences.

Such an arrangement might serve the compositional needs of the social sciences, but it does not lend itself to the prerequisites of historical writing. It lacks narrative flow and, indeed, destroys the integration characteristic of historical composition. Its methodological divisions impose a systematic form of explanation on its subject. While it is true that an historical composition has an introduction, a body or main text, and a conclusion, it is also true that it reflects individual design and has little or no textual delineation by separate heading. When divisions of some form are used in historical writing, they indicate a change of focus in the ongoing narrative. They do not reflect parts of a scientific problem. Historical narrative is the art of communicating to a general audience what you know, what you do not know, and what the readers expect to discover about a particular subject. It is a type of discussion that explains as it proceeds.

Two problems of style and structure have come to plague much writing in communication history in recent years. Some historians imitate the structure of soft-science articles appearing in such journals as *Journalism Quarterly* and fill their manuscripts with tedious descriptions of their research methods and lengthy listings of their numerical findings. Those problems are the marks of researchers unfamiliar with historical methods, those who rely too exclusively on behavioral and social science methods that theorists and researchers have tried to adopt in communication "science." Soft-science methods are, however, while sometimes useful, inadequate by themselves for historical research. Historical method has a long and solid tradition. Historians using it properly face no compulsion to provide ponderously minute descriptions of precisely where and how they got their material. The quality of the research should be obvious from the narrative, the sources, and the soundness of historians' reasoning. Researchers who emphasize their methods tend to be the ones who also list in excruciating detail the findings of those methods. They pile percentage upon percentage and number upon number. When finished, their manuscripts sometimes have twenty pages of technique and numbers, and a half page of not quite meaningful narrative and discussion. In historical study, as in other research, the researcher should remember that techniques are important primarily because they are ways to discover something. Findings are important because of the understanding they can help provide. In historical writing, the emphasis should be on the discoveries and on understanding.

Constructing an Effective Historical Composition

Historians are no exception to the rule that writers must pay attention to numerous practical aspects of composition. Although it is beyond the scope of this book to review all the elements of writing, it can be recommended that beginning researchers follow the old dictum: study the language. Make a habit of reviewing syntax and vocabulary. Though written many years ago, *The Elements of Style* by William Strunk, Jr., remains a fine source to consult for guidance about constructing effective language. Beginning researchers might wish to consider that classic brief introduction to plain English or some other selection of the same genre along with Savoie Lottinville's more recent *The Rhetoric of History*.[9] Regardless, effective use of the language is a requirement of good history, and the following four aspects of scholarly writing deserve the attention of anyone who undertakes to write history for the first time.

1. *Clarity and Continuity.* These twin qualities of proficient historical narrative depend, of course, on one's command of the basic mechanics of writing. Beyond that, they stem from three requirements of composition: plain words, effective sentences, and well-formed paragraphs.

Consider *plain words.* They need not be bland. Indeed, they can be eloquent. But they must be intelligible to the wide audience historians hope to reach. The key lies in selecting the word most capable of conveying the precise meaning you have in mind. A well-chosen word connotes sharp meaning and can eliminate awkward phrasing. Be precise about what you want to say, find the appropriate word that expresses it, and eliminate careless language. Study the meanings of words; be curious about language; and make a habit of reaching for the dictionary.

Intended meaning can be obscured by sentences and sentence pattern as well as by faulty word selection. *Sentences* provide a connecting function, establish rhythm of expression, and give structure to the relationship between words. They coordinate, subordinate, and emphasize ideas. Effective sentence structure depends on

---

[9]William Strunk, Jr., *The Elements of Style,* rev. ed., with revisions and Introduction by E.B. White (New York, Macmillian Company, 1979); Savoie Lottinville, *The Rhetoric of History* (Norman: University of Oklahoma Press, 1976).

correct syntax, perception of logical relationships, placement of words, and stylistic preferences. If reflects the literary artistry of the writer as much as any other component of writing. Therefore, study each sentence you write, and rewrite it until you are convinced that it gives graceful expression to the idea that you wish it to convey.

Well-constructed paragraphs, the third requirement needed to establish clarity and continuity, are hallmarks of all effective writing. They are, of course, units, not mere collections of sentences; and as such they must be visualized and developed. Unlike paragraphs in journalistic writing, they are not simply typographic blocks. In almost all cases, a common theme permeates a paragraph and integrates the sentences within it. Those sentences should not only convey information but also interact with one another. Most paragraphs have a well-defined topic sentence that receives early and prominent display. By stating the subject of a paragraph, a topic sentence gives it focus and directs the reader to the sentences that follow. As the remainder of the paragraph unfolds, various transitional devices can be employed to smooth connections and sharpen movement. Thus a paragraph acquires internal clarity and continuity.

It is also necessary for a paragraph to have external continuity, a sequential relationship with the paragraphs preceding and following it. The way in which the paragraph relates to the whole composition helps to build its external continuity as does a writer's conscious effort to make the topic of one paragraph a continuation in some way of the subject and narrative flow of the preceding one. This sense of continuation may result either from creating a natural chronological or topical transition from one paragraph to another or from the use of a number of transitional devices. Regarding the latter method, the writer might refer to a word or idea at the end of the previous paragraph, or repeat a word from it, or perhaps use a transitional expression. In such instances, the transitional or connecting language usually appears at the beginning of the following paragraph. Paragraphs, like words and sentences, are rhetorical supports that sustain the structure of composition, and there is no substitute for the care a writer should take in constructing them.

2. *Introduction and Conclusion.* Since book-length compositions with their prefaces, introductions, and various types of concluding chapters allow more flexibility in handling these elements, we consider here an article-length composition. Moreover, we are using the terms introduction and conclusion to refer to the beginning and ending of the composition rather than to separate parts. The first page of a short composition is indeed, as several authorities on historical writing suggest, one of the "supreme tests of the art

of composition."[10]   That being the case, opening lines assume particular significance. Consider these two. William E. Smith wrote the first; Charles Levermore, the second.

> "Send it to Bla-ar!" exclaimed President Andrew Jackson when he and his friends were puzzled with a baffling problem.[11]

> The mechanical evolution of the modern newspaper is due chiefly to the steam-engine and the telegraph, but the evolution of the modern journalistic spirit is due chiefly to an aggressive democracy.[12]

Both historians, as these examples show, understood the requirements of effective openings. As an initial sentence, neither could fail to capture one's imagination. They illustrate the first rule for opening lines: they must engage the reader's interest. They must also suggest the central idea of the composition. First lines cannot be duds. They connect the reader with the subject and set the narrative in motion. They must, therefore, encourage the reader to continue. The way is thus open for the remaining part of the initial paragraph and perhaps one or several following ones to establish the setting and purpose of the composition. That, in turn, should be done in a natural manner that complements the narrative. Concentrate on beginnings; it is easy to err in constructing them. They should bear the same precision of thought and sense of narrative flow that characterize the body of the composition.

The final paragraph or paragraphs of the compositions should contain your concluding thoughts about the subject rather than a summary of material covered. Summaries are unnecessary. In forming concluding comments for a composition, it can be helpful to keep in mind the definition of a conclusion as "reasoned judgment." Accordingly, one can expect to find meaningful reflections about the subject in concluding comments. Care should be taken not to allow conclusions to over-run either the evidence presented or the limits of logical reflection based upon that evidence.

3. *Footnotes and Quotations.*   Nothing more characterizes

---

[10]Barzun and Graff, *The Modern Researcher*, 288.

[11]William E. Smith, "Francis P. Blair, Pen-Executive of Andrew Jackson," *Mississippi Valley Historical Review* 17 (March 1931), 543.

[12]Charles H. Levermore, "The Rise of Metropolitan Journalism, 1800-1840," *American Historical Review* 6 (April 1901): 446.

scholarly writing than the presence of footnotes and quotations. Both are used for specific purposes. Footnotes may be either of a citation or supplementary type. Sometimes the two types are combined. Citation (or reference) footnotes supply the necessary reference for both direct and indirect quotations, paraphrased material, statistical data, material taken from a specific source, references to distinct ideas and interpretations not your own, and essential facts that are not part of general knowledge. They acknowledge sources used and validate the composition. If it is necessary to quote from a passage itself quoted in a secondary source, cite it as such. The footnote reference should contain the identity and location of the quotation plus a citation of the secondary source in which you found it. Usually, "as cited in" or some similar phrase follows the reference to the quotation and introduces the secondary source that contains it. There is no need to cite references for general knowledge, such as information readily found in encyclopedias or, in a routine manner, in a variety of secondary sources. Nor is it necessary to cite conventional facts or well-known remarks.

Supplementary footnotes elaborate matters of record referred to in the text. You can also use them to comment on a point introduced in the composition, perhaps a controversial point, and to reflect on the commentary of another historian on a particular question. Employ them in a judicious manner and keep them brief. They should not become repositories for all other knowledge about material covered in the text.

Quotations, like footnotes, should be used with care. They might be utilized to illustrate a point, to provide a sample of your evidence, to increase the forcefulness of your argument, to give life to a character in the narrative, or to confront readers with a particular point of record or with someone's original language. Barzun and Graff, who make a habit of offering sage advice on historical writing, suggest the following as the first principle of the art of quotations: "Quotations are illustrations, not proofs. The proof of what you say is the whole body of facts and ideas to which you refer, that is, to which you point. From time to time you give a sample of this evidence to clinch your argument or to avail yourself of a characteristic or felicitous utterance."[13] That principle merits particular attention, for it is frequently misunderstood. When using quotations in historical writing, (a) try to integrate them into your own narrative, (b) keep them short, (c) keep their use to a minimum, (d) keep them in the context of their original meaning, (e) consult an original source for a quotation whenever possible, (f) introduce

---

[13]Barzun and Graff, *The Modern Researcher*, 339.

quotations (e.g., H.V.Kaltenborn commented...), (g) comment on uncustomary language and ideas involved in the quotation, and (h) avoid quoting from textbooks or general reference sources unless the quoted words are themselves the subject you wish to examine.

4. *Revision of Composition.* Good writing evolves in stages, one of which is that of revision. "The best history is the product of revision almost as much as it is of vision," wrote Arthur M. Schlesinger, Jr.[14] His comment elicits the consent of anyone who has ever attempted to write a serious piece of history. Early drafts of compositions afford one the opportunity to experiment with language, arrangement, and explanation. Revision provides the opportunity to refine all matters of composition from syntax to interpretation.

At this stage of writing, careless language should be purged from the narrative as well as all contractions, archaic words, and examples of tautology. Weed out any pedantic or euphemistic expressions that slipped into the composition. Remember too that history should be written in the past tense and in the active voice. Although it is permissible to take some liberty with the latter, minimize using passive verbs. Excessive use of the passive voice can hinder effective writing by blurring subjects in sentence constructions. It caters to indirect and imprecise expression. Consequently, be conscious of the use you make of it and employ it only when reflection convinces you of its propriety. Examine the composition for matters of connection, continuity, and clarity. Revision gives you the chance to sharpen language, to smooth transitions, to tone up or down the particular phrases, and to make any modification that might be in order when the individual parts of the composition are viewed in the perspective of the full draft.

Revision also should go beyond matters of syntax and rhetoric and include substantive considerations. In terms of explanations, does the composition say, in its various parts and in whole, what you intended for it to say? Can you prove by a convincing amount of evidence or by reasonable argument what you have stated in writing? Does it conform to the dictates of common sense? Revision, we can conclude, is valuable beyond question in the construction of composition. It is a creative and imaginative act in the art of writing.

---

[14]Schlesinger, Forward to Fitzgerald's "Toward a Bibliography of the Writings of Arthur M. Schlesinger, Jr.," 37.

Checklist for Proofreading

After completing the final copy of the composition, there is still one more exercise to perform. You are responsible for everything in the composition from correctness of fact to correctness of language. This means you also assume responsibility for any typing mistakes that appear in the final version of the composition. Consequently, a careful proofreading of your work is a necessary final act of composition to rid it of mechanical mistakes. The following list enumerates items that always merit checking.

Accuracy of quotations
Agreement of verb tense
Capitalization (capitalize names of deities, races of mankind, historical periods, etc.)
Clear antecedents for pronouns
Footnotes (be sure there is a textual citation for every footnote and an entry in the bibliography for every footnote source)
Formation of plural nouns
Hyphenated words and phrases (check for proper and consistent usage)
Pagination (check for order and omissions)
Subject-verb agreement
Titles of offices
Titles of sources

Proofreading your own writing necessitates a great deal of concentration and patience. It can be done in several ways, of which a line by line ruler check is one. Regardless of the time and effort it requires, it can make a difference in the appearance and quality of your work.

9

Presentation and Publication

Historians have a duty to share their findings with others. They do not study for self-gratification alone. Even though the knowledge historians gain in their search for the past may be satisfying in itself, the true historian has an obligation to contribute that knowledge to others. The biblical declaration that "you are the light of the world" applies in a modern sense to historians. They may not hide their light under a basket. The necessity of sharing knowledge goes beyond the cliché "publish or perish" known to untenured professors. Only by publication or public presentation can historians fulfill their role of keeping alive knowledge of the past and expanding the understanding of present and future generations.

But few historians think of publication as only a duty. Most relish the thought. To see one's work presented to the public is one of the things that dreams are made of; to know one's cogent ideas and explanations are read by other members of the history profession, a delight devoutly to be wished. How dreary would be the profession if historians thought of presentation and publication only as obligations. There would be little joy then, little brightness, only the drudgery of working in the mines. While the true historian glows with excitement over each nugget discovered during research, few can put out of mind the anticipation of seeing those nuggets displayed.

Perhaps it is that anticipation -- combined with the fear of failure for professors whose jobs, tenure, and salary frequently depend on publication -- that makes the attempt to have a paper accepted for conference presentation or an article or book for publication a cause for anxiety. All types of worries run through the mind: Where should I submit my article? What if it's rejected? Why haven't I heard from the publisher yet? Do I dare open this letter from the publisher? These worries are natural, and the historian must accept the fact that they come with the profession. But the worries never should be a cause for not attempting publication or presentation. No historian, no writer of any sort, ever published anything without trying. The first attempt, moreover, is always the most difficult. There are keys to writing publishable history. Familiarity with the topic, adequate research, and competent composition are the main ones, but to these should be added one other: experience. The more one attempts to publish, the more experience one gains. Experience improves the likelihood of publication, and success in publication can encourage additional attempts.

How should one proceed in pursuit of that goal? With a focus on the practical aspects of getting historical works accepted for presentation and publication, the following advice is not intended as a lofty discussion of historical ideas and practices. Rather, it is offered as a body of pragmatic suggestions which deal with the basic subject of turning historical writings into print. Much of the chapter is intended to aid the student or professor who has never published or made a conference presentation; some of it will benefit historians who wish to expand their production. It covers various topics ranging from the basic practices of locating a paper competition to preparing a journal manuscript to finding a book publisher.

Conference Presentations

It is easier to have a paper accepted for presentation at a conference than to have an article accepted for publication. Consequently, historians sometimes let their research and writing quality slip when preparing a submission for a paper competition. Such a practice should be avoided. Ease of acceptance should not reduce the rigor of historical study. Once an historian accepts slipshod work, subsequent shoddiness becomes more readily acceptable. No matter what the final form of public display -- whether it is a book, a journal article, or a conference paper -- the historian should be satisfied with no less than the best historical work possible.

Conferences, conventions, and symposia abound for the presentation of papers on communication history. Some are national; many more are regional. A small number are devoted solely to communication history; most accept papers on communication history along with papers on other topics. Some are listed at the end of this chapter as an indication of the number and variety of conferences offering outlets for work in communication history. Since dates and locations for most conferences change from year to year, the historian considering submitting a paper should check with the sponsoring organization for details on the conference and competition. Addresses of scholarly, academic, and historical organizations are listed in the *Directory of Associations,* which can be found in the reference section of most good libraries.

The only national conference dealing solely with communication history is that of the American Journalism Historians Association. The AJHA holds its annual conventions during the early part of October at various cities. The deadline for the paper submission normally is in the spring. Research papers are selected on a competitive basis. Since the AJHA's process for accepting papers is typical for others that use a competitive procedure, familiarity with its details will provide the historian with an awareness of such competitions in general. Papers submitted to the AJHA should not exceed twenty-five pages. A paper must be accompanied by a one-page abstract and a cover page including the paper's title, the author's name and address, and the author's institutional affiliation (that is, faculty position or student status, department, university, or office). On the first page of the manuscript, only the title should appear. Omitting the author's name is designed to assure anonymity in the evaluation process so that judges' decisions are not influenced by the name or position of the author. The AJHA competition requires that papers not be submitted simultaneously to other competitions. That restriction is intended to eliminate the possibility that an author might send the same paper to two competitions at the same time, requiring a duplication of judging effort. Not all conference papers are accepted on the basis of competition. Some history conferences proceed along other lines and simply ask for proposals. On the other hand, some ask for papers long in advance of the conference.

Some principles of the mechanics of preparing a paper for submission apply almost universally. Papers should be typed double-spaced, and the manuscript should be as clean and neat as possible (containing no strike-overs or handwritten corrections, for example). They should be well researched, themes should be readily apparent, the writing should be readable, and conclusions should flow naturally from the evidence. Normally, multiple copies should be submitted. (Details on specific requirements should be obtained from the sponsoring organization.) Papers, unfolded, should be mailed in a large manila envelope. A self-addressed envelope or postcard should be included if the author wants to be assured of being notified that the addressee received the paper.

Each AJHA submission is "blind" judged by two readers. Blind judging assures that paper evaluators do not know who the authors are. Each judge completes an evaluation form on each paper and gives a brief statement of the basis for the evaluation. Decisions on papers, along with judges' comments, normally are given to authors approximately one month after the submission deadline.

One advantage to authors that the AJHA competition has over most other competitions is that the three best papers are accepted for publication in the AJHA's quarterly journal, *American Journalism*.

Among the other conferences that hold competitions specifically for papers in communication history are the national convention of the Association for Education in Journalism and Mass Communication, the AEJMC Southeastern Regional Colloquium in Newspapers, History, and Law, the Midwest Journalism History Conference, the East Coast Regional Journalism Historians Conference, and the West Coast Regional Journalism Historians Conference.

Journal Articles

Outlets for articles on communication history are more numerous than many historians realize. Along with several journals that deal exclusively with communication history, scores of scholarly journals publish articles on the subject. Among those devoted solely to communication history are *American Journalism, Journal of Advertising History* (a British journal which publishes articles not only on British history but also on international topics), *Journal of Newspaper and Periodical History* (London), *Victorian Periodicals Review,* and *Journalism History.* Other journals in the various fields of communication -- such as the *Journal of Broadcasting and Electronic Media, Journalism Quarterly, Journal of Advertising, Journal of Communication,* and *Journalism Monographs* -- publish historical articles, while numerous historical journals outside those fields publish articles on communication. A list of representative journals which publish studies on communication history is provided at the end of this chapter.

Journals vary in their requirements, and authors should familiarize themselves with any journal to which they plan to submit an article. *Media History Digest,* for example, although publishing well-researched articles, attempts to appeal to a popular readership and, as one illustration of its editorial approach, omits footnotes, while *American Journalism* accepts only articles based on well-documented research in primary sources.

In preparing a manuscript, the author should adhere to scholarly standards and neat, professional practices. Some journals require their own, unique stylistic usages and citation formats. Manuscripts prepared specifically for those journals should abide by their guidelines. For whatever journal the historian is writing, however, the guiding principle is that manuscripts should be consistent with normal, acceptable scholarly practices. Footnotes, no matter what the format used, should be consistent, providing the information necessary to show the reader clearly the source of the information, so that any reader who should wish to do so can find the source. While some journals have their own rules, normally stylistic usage should adhere to that of a standard guide such as the University of Chicago Press' *A Manual of Style* or *The MLA Style Sheet* of the Modern Language Association. An essential point to be remembered by the author who might have been trained in the writing style of advertising, broadcasting, journalism, or some other communication field is that historical articles must follow the mechanical requirements of normal English usage and style rather than the peculiar styles of professional fields in communication. No article submitted to a scholarly journal, for example, should use Associated Press style.

Here are some practices that normally should be followed:

*On the title page, include the author's name and address along with the study's title.

*At the beginning of the first content page of the manuscript, only the title should appear, with the author's name omitted.

*Type all material double-spaced, including footnotes and legends for illustrations and diagrams. Quotations also should be double-spaced, including long quoted passages. The latter should be set off from the text by indenting them five spaces from the left-hand margin. Do not use quotation marks around long quoted passages that are set off from the text.

*Use only a good grade of 81/2 X 11-inch white typing paper; avoid onion-skin or some other type of erasable paper.

*Type on only one side of the paper.

*Leave margins around the page at least one-inch wide.

*Do not hyphenate words at the end of lines.

*Number pages consecutively, with the title of the study or distinctive word or phrase from the title appearing at the top of each page.

*Type footnotes on a separate page or pages at the end of the manuscript, rather than at the bottom of the content pages. Number them consecutively throughout the manuscript (and in book-length manuscripts consecutively throughout each chapter). They should be indicated in the text by Arabic numbers, raised slightly above the line. If they occur at the end of sentences or at any other punctuation point, they are placed outside all marks of punctuation.

*Multiple copies of the manuscript are required by most journals. Be sure that photocopies are legible.

What happens to a manuscript once its author has mailed it? Although hundreds of journals exist, what goes on in the inner sanctum of a journal's editorial office is, to many authors, mysterious. What historian has not wondered how those forces work that hold supernatural power over publication decisions? Not all journals operate in the same fashion, but several standard practices are followed by most. A look at how one journal, *American Journalism,* functions may serve to illustrate the general principles.

For every manuscript, the editor of *American Journalism* chooses three readers from the journal's Editorial Board, which is composed of about one hundred communication historians. The selection of readers is based on their areas of specialization, assuring that all three readers possess expertise in the topic covered by the manuscript. Along with a copy of the manuscript (with any clue to authorship removed), each reader receives a rating sheet covering various aspects of its research, topical significance, and presentation and an open form for the reader to make a written critique. Readers are encouraged to make comments which the author may use to improve the manuscript or which indicate clearly why a manuscript is rejected. All readers are required to recommend either publication or rejection and are encouraged to return their evaluations promptly. The normal length of time for all three evaluations to be returned to the editorial office varies from two to six weeks. (Authors should be aware, however, that many journals take six months or longer to complete the evaluation process.) When a reader is tardy, the editor writes him or her a request for an immediate evaluation. (Some readers stick manuscripts in piles of "things to do next week," and not all editors of journals energetically encourage readers to complete reviews. An author who has not received a decision within a reasonable time should not be reluctant to inquire of an editor about the status of the evaluation process.)

Rarely does *American Journalism* accept a manuscript in the original form submitted by the author. If no reader or only one reader recommends acceptance, the editor automatically rejects the manuscript. If two or three readers recommend acceptance, the author normally is asked to revise the manuscript in accord with the readers' suggestions. The editor and associate editors evaluate the revised manuscript and then make a decision on publication. Four decisions can be made: (a) the manuscript is rejected, (b) the manuscript is rejected with a recommendation that the author revise it taking into consideration the comments of editors and resubmit it, (c) the manuscript is tentatively accepted pending satisfactory revision, or (d) the manuscript is accepted without changes but with recommendations for revisions. In all four instances, comments of readers and editors are given to authors, with the intent being to make unpublishable manuscripts acceptable for publication upon revision or to improve acceptable manuscripts before publication.

American Journalism accepts one in ten submissions, making its acceptance rate one of the smallest in the field of communication. The normal acceptance rate for most communication journals is about one in three, although it is lower for some and higher for others. Some journals, primarily historical ones such as the *Journal of American History,* accept fewer than ten per cent of submissions. The more demanding journals frequently have multitiered reviewing procedures in which manuscripts recommended for acceptance by readers are then evaluated by a top-echelon editorial board. At the other end of the spectrum are a few journals which claim to be refereed but which occasionally accept manuscripts without sending them through their normal evaluation process.

Book Publishing

Papers and articles can be satisfying, but for many historians they are not enough. Books are the goal. They allow the historian to develop an idea more fully, they normally are more prestigious than articles, and some even make money. But how does one publish a book in communication history?

There are no sure-fire schemes for publication, but a number of practices will increase the possibilities. Along with conducting solid historical scholarship -- knowledge of the topic, exhaustive research, competent writing -- would-be authors should be familiar with various procedures in book publishing. Here is a checklist, but by no means exhaustive encyclopedia, of pertinent points.

*Be knowledgeable about the scholarly field. Is the idea large enough to be made into a book? What other books have been published? Is the proposed book a significant addition to the field? Would other historians be interested in the book?

*Determine which publishers, if any, might be interested in the book. Which firms have published books on communication history? Before querying the first publisher, compile a list of all potential publishers. Since most proposals are rejected by a number of publishers, knowing that there are others that might be interested can help the author from becoming dejected.

*Consider whether a market exists for the book. The minimum number of potential sales before a publisher will accept a book may vary from publisher to publisher, from about 1,000 to 7,000. Although some historians may feel that pure historical study cannot consider salability, it is incumbent for the would-be author to recognize that most firms are in book publishing as a business. Even nonprofit university presses must break even.

*Write a polished, complete, but concise query. It should state clearly the following items: (a) the book's theme, (b) the topics to be covered and special features, (c) the projected word length, (d) the perceived audience (other historians, libraries, university classes, and so forth), (e) competing books and the proposed book's advantages, and (f) the author's credentials (academic position, education, and related publications, for example). Enclose an annotated topical, chapter outline of the book. While much of the material -- the outline, for instance -- may be photocopied, the cover letter should be an original.

*Indicate whether the manuscript can be provided on a computer disk or a disk from an electronic editing system. Each year, a larger and larger percentage of manuscripts are provided on disk, reducing the publishers' production costs. For some proposals, the form in which the author can provide the manuscript can be a critical factor.

Responses from publishers take many forms. The most common is rejection. Although publishers rarely give a contract on the sole basis of the original query, some do if they are confident that a market for the book exists and that the author has the credentials and track record to assure a quality work. More commonly, publishers with a tentative interest in the proposal ask for sample chapters or the entire manuscript before committing themselves to a contract.

Scholarly Paper Conferences

Listed here are conferences representative of those that include papers on communication history. Details and arrangements may change from year to year, and the historian considering submitting a paper should get the most recent information from the sponsoring organization.

Agricultural History Society
American Antiquarian Society

American Historical Association
American Journalism Historians Association
American Military Institute
American Printing History Association
American Society of Church History
American Studies Association
Association for Education in Journalism and Mass Communication
AEJMC, Southeast Regional Colloquium
Association for the Study of Afro-American Life and History
Broadcast Education Association
Business History Conference
Duquesne History Forum
East Coast Regional Journalism Historians Conference
Economic History Association
Great Lakes History Conference
Mid-America Conference on History
Mid-Continental American Studies Association
Mid-West Journalism History Conference
Military History Symposium
Missouri Valley History Conference
New England Historical Association
New York Historical Society Conference
Northern Great Plains History Conference
Oral History Association
Organization of American Associations
Popular Culture Association
Social History Association
Society of Historians of the Early American Republic
Southern Historical Association
Southwest Symposium on Mass Communication
West Coast Regional Journalism Historians Conference
Western History Association

Journals Publishing Articles on Communication History

Following is a partial list of journals intended simply to illustrate those that publish articles on communication history. It includes not only journals specializing in communication history, but those also in general history, in various areas of communication study, in regional and state studies, and in related fields. Wm. David Sloan's *American Journalism History: An Annotated Bibliography* (1989) includes approximately 200 publications which have printed articles on the topic. The historian considering submitting a manuscript to one of them should study the journal to determine requirements. If a particular journal cannot be found in a nearby library, the historian should consult *Magazines for Libraries*   (Bill and Linda Sternberg Katz, eds.). It is a standard bibliographic source in most libraries, and it describes the bulk of the history journals currently in publication in this country.

American Bar Association Journal
American Heritage
American Historical Review
American History Illustrated
American Jewish History
American Journal of Economy and Sociology
American Journal of Legal History
American Journalism
American Political Science Review
American Quarterly
American West
Annals of the American Academy of Political Science
Arizona and the West
Business History Review
California History
Civil War History
Georgetown Law Review
Georgia Historical Review
Historian
Historical Journal of Film, Radio and Television
Huntington Library Quarterly
Indiana Magazine of History
Journal of Advertising
Journal of Advertising History
Journal of American Culture
Journal of American History
Journal of American Studies
Journal of Arizona History
Journal of Broadcasting and Electronic Media
Journal of Communication
Journal of Communication Inquiry
Journal of the Early Republic
Journal of Negro History
Journal of Newspaper and Periodical History
Journal of Politics
Journal of Popular Culture
Journal of Southern History
Journalism History

Journalism Monographs
Journalism Quarterly
Labor History
Maryland Historical Magazine
Mass Communication Review
Massachusetts Historical Society Collections
Media History Digest
Michigan Law Journal
Midwest Communications Research Journal
Missouri Historical Review
Negro History Bulletin
New England Quarterly
New Jersey History
New Mexico Historical Review
New York History
Newspaper Research Journal
North Carolina Historical Review
Ohio History
Pacific Historical Review
Papers of the Bibliographical Society of America
Pennsylvania Magazine of History and Biography
Political Quarterly
Politics
Public Opinion Quarterly
Public Telecommunications Review
Publications of the Colonial Society of Massachusetts
Review of Politics
Rhode Island History
Social Forces
South Atlantic Quarterly
Southern Historian
Southwestern Historical Quarterly
Syracuse Law Review
Tennessee Historical Quarterly
Vermont History
Victorian Periodicals Review
Virginia Magazine of History and Biography
William and Mary Quarterly

Bibliography

Historians will find available innumerable reference works, historical research manuals, and other works pertinent to their craft. Because of the volume of work, the following bibliography is necessarily abbreviated. It attempts to point the researcher to only the most useful writings. In instances where works are abundant, a decision has been made to include only the most recent ones and, with a few exceptions, only those of book length. For guidance in most general matters of historical study and for direction to additional guides and reference works, historians will find Jacques Barzun and Henry F. Graff's *The Modern Researcher* continually useful. Despite its general title, it emphasizes historical research. The works in the following bibliography comprise two broad categories: writings about historical study and research guides useful to the communication historian. The works cited in Chapter 5 of this manual also should be consulted for guidance in these areas.

The Study of History

Butterfield, Herbert. *The Origins of History*. New York: Basic Books, 1981 (reprint).

Carr, Edward Hallett. *What is History?* New York: Alfred A. Knopf, 1965.

Conkin, Paul K., and Roland N. Stromberg. *The Heritage and Challenge of History*. New York: Dodd Mead & Company, 1971.

Davidson, James West, and Mark Hamilton Lytle. *After the Fact: The Art of Historical Detection.* 2nd ed. New York: Alfred A. Knopf, 1986.

Elton, G.R. *The Practice of History.* New York: Thomas Y. Crowell, 1967.

Goldstein, Leon J. *Historical Knowing.* Austin: University of Texas Press, 1976.

Guinsburg, Thomas N., ed. *The Dimensions of History.* Chicago: Rand McNally, 1971.

Gustavson, Carl G. *The Mansion of History.* New York: McGraw-Hill Book Company, 1976.

Hexter, Jack H. *Doing History.* Bloomington: Indiana University Press, 1971.

Lewis, Bernard. *History Remembered, Recovered, Invented.* Princeton, N.J.: Princeton University Press, 1975.

Marwick, Arthur. *The Nature of History.* London: Macmillan, 1970.

Murphey, Murray G. *Our Knowledge of the Historical Past.* Indianapolis: Bobbs-Merrill, 1973.

Plumb, J.H. *The Death of the Past.* Middlesex, England: Penguin Books, 1973.

Smith, Page. *The Historian and History.* New York: Alfred A. Knopf, 1964.

Stephens, Lester D. *Probing the Past: A Guide to the Study and Teaching of History.* Boston: Allyn and Bacon, Inc., 1974.

Vaughn, Stephen. *The Vital Past: Writings on the Uses of History.* Athens: University of Georgia Press, 1985.

Conducting Historical Research

Aydelotte, William O., Allan G. Bogue, and Robert W. Fogel, eds. *The Dimensions of Quantitative Research in History.* Princeton, N.J.: Princeton University Press, 1972.

Barzun, Jacques. *Clio and the Doctors.* Chicago: University of Chicago Press, 1976.

Barzun, Jacques, and Henry F. Graff. *The Modern Researcher.* 4th ed. New York: Harcourt Brace Jovanovich, 1985.

Benson, Lee. *Toward the Scientific Study of History.* Philadelphia: Lippincott, 1972.

Block, Jack. *Understanding Historical Research: A Search for Truth.* Glen Rock, N.J.: Research Publications, 1971.

Cantor, N.F., and R.I. Schneider. *How To Study History.* Northbrook, Ill.: AHM Publishing Corp., 1970.

Clark, G. Kitson. *The Critical Historian*. New York: Basic Books, 1967.

Daniels, Robert V. *Studying History: How and Why*. 2nd ed. Englewood Cliffs, N.J.: Prentice-Hall, 1972.

Dollar, Charles M., and Richard J. Jensen. *Historian's Guide to Statistics: Quantitative Analysis and Historical Research*. New York: Holt, Rinehart and Winston, 1971.

Elton, G.R. *Political History: Principles and Practice*. New York: Basic Books, Inc., 1970.

Felt, Thomas E. *Researching, Writing, and Publishing Local History*. Nashville: American Association for State and Local History, 1981.

Fischer, David Hackett. *Historians' Fallacies: Toward a Logic of Historical Thought*. New York: Harper & Row, 1970.

Fling, Fred M. *Outline of Historical Method*. New York: B. Franklin, 1971.

Gottschalk, Louis. *Understanding History: A Primer of Historical Method*. 2nd ed. New York: Alfred A. Knopf, 1969.

Heller, Louis G. *Communicational Analysis and Methodology for Historians*. New York: New York University Press, 1971.

Hexter, Jack H. *The History Primer*. New York: Basic Books, 1971.

Hockett, Homer Carey. *The Critical Method in Historical Research and Writing*. Westport, Conn.: Greenwood Press, 1977 (reprint).

Isenberg, Michael T. *Puzzles of the Past: An Introduction to Thinking About History*. College Station: Texas A&M University Press, 1985.

Landes, David S., and Charles Tilley, eds. *History as Social Science*. Englewood Cliffs, N.J.: Prentice-Hall, 1971.

McClellan, Peter D. *Causal Explanation and Model Building in History, Economics, and the New Economic History*. Ithaca, N.Y.: Cornell University Press, 1975.

Mahoney, James. *Local History: A Guide for Research and Writing*. Washington: National Education Association, 1981.

Sanderlin, David. *Writing the History Paper: How to Select, Collect, Interpret, Organize, and Write Your Term Paper*. New York: Barron's Education Series, 1975.

Shafer, Robert J., et. al., eds. *A Guide to Historical Methods*. 3rd ed. Homewood, Ill.: Dorsey Press, 1980.

Stoffle, Carla J., and Simon Carter. *Materials and Methods for History Research*. New York: Libraryworks, 1979.

Taylor, Robert M. Jr., and Ralph J. Crandall., eds. *Generations and Change: Genealogical Perspectives in Social History*. Macon, Ga.: Mercer University Press, 1986.

Thompson, Paul. *Voice of the Past: Oral History.* New York: Oxford University Press, 1978.

Vansina, Jan. *Oral Tradition as History.* Madison: University of Wisconsin Press, 1985.

Winks, Robin W., ed. *The Historian as Detective: Essays on Evidence.* New York: Harper and Row, 1969.

Communication Research

Anderson, James A. *Communication Research: Issues and Methods.* New York: McGraw-Hill, 1987.

Anderson, Peter J. *Research Guide in Journalism.* Morristown, N.J.: General Learning Press, 1974.

Bowen, John W., and John A. Cartwright. *Communication Research Methods.* Glenview, Ill.: Scott Foresman, 1984.

Edelstein, Alex. *Comparative Communication Research.* Beverly Hills, Calif.: Sage, 1982.

Mander, Mary S. *Communications in Transition: Issues and Debates in Current Research.* New York: Praeger, 1983.

Murray, Michael. "Research in Broadcasting: An Overview of Major Resource Centers." *American Journalism* 1: 2 (Winter 1984): 77-80.

Rubin, Rebecca, Alan Rubin, and Linda Piele. *Communication Research Strategies and Sources.* Belmont, Calif.: Wadsworth, 1986.

Stempel, Guido H. III, and Bruce H. Westley, eds. *Research Methods in Mass Communication.* Englewood Cliffs, N.J.: Prentice-Hall, 1981.

Ward, Jean, and Kathleen Hansen. *Search Strategies in Mass Communication.* New York: Longman, 1987.

Research in Related Disciplines

Altick, Richard D. *The Art of Literary Research.* rev. ed. New York: Norton, 1975.

Bailey, Kenneth D. *Methods of Social Research.* 2nd ed. New York: Free Press, 1982.

Bell, C., and H. Newby, eds. *Doing Sociological Research.* London: George Allen and Unwin, 1977.

Bell, James Edward. *A Guide to Library Research in Psychology.* Dubuque, Iowa: Wm. C. Brown, 1971.

Best, John M., and James V. Kahn. *Research in Education.* 5th ed. Englewood Cliffs, N.J.: Prentice-Hall, 1986.

Bevill, Hugh Malcolm, Jr. *Audience Ratings: Radio, Television, Cable.* Hillsdale, N.J.: Lawrence Erlbaum Associates, 1988.

Bogdon, R. and S.J. Taylor. *Introduction to Qualitative Research Methods.* New York: John Wiley and Sons, 1975.

Bowen, Catharine Drinker. *Biography: The Craft and the Calling.* Boston: Little, Brown and Company, 1968.

Chadwick, B.A., H.M. Bahr, and S.L. Albrecht. *Social Science Research Methods.* Englewood Cliffs, N.J.: Prentice-Hall, 1984.

Cohen, Morris, ed. *How To Find the Law.* 7th ed. St. Paul, Minn.: West Publishing Co., 1976.

Cohen, Morris. *Legal Research in a Nutshell.* 3rd ed. St. Paul, Minn.: West Publishing Co., 1978.

De George, Richard T. *A Guide to Philosophical Bibliography and Research.* Englewood Cliffs, N.J.: Prentice-Hall, 1971.

Dominick, J.R., and J.E. Fletcher. *Broadcasting Research Methods.* Boston: Allyn and Bacon, 1985.

East, W. Gordon. *The Geography Behind History.* New York: W.W. Norton, 1965.

Garson, David G. *Handbook of Political Science Methods.* 2nd ed. Boston: Holbrook Press, 1976.

Gergen, Kenneth J., and Mary M. Gergen (eds.). *Historical Social Psychology.* Hillsdale, N.J.: Lawrence Erlbaum Associates, 1984.

Gore, Daniel. *Bibliography For Beginners.* 2nd ed. Englewood Cliffs, N.J.: Prentice-Hall, 1973.

Holt, Jensen A. *Geography: Its History and Concepts: A Student Guide.* Totowan, N.J.: Barnes Noble Books, 1982.

Kalvelage, Carl, and Morley Segal. *Research Guide in Political Science.* 2nd ed. Morristown, N.J.: General Learning, 1976.

Kee, Howard Clark. *Miracle in the Early Christian World: A Study in Sociohistorical Method.* New Haven, Conn.: Yale University Press, 1983.

Krathwohl, David R. *Social and Behavioral Research.* San Francisco: Jossey Bass, 1985.

Langness, L.L., and Gelya Frank. *Lives: An Anthropological Approach to Biography.* Novato, Calif.: Chandler Sharp, 1981.

Leedy, P.D. *How To Read Research and Understand It.* New York: Macmillan Publishing Co., 1981.

Leiter, Kenneth C. *Primer of Ethnomethodology.* New York: Oxford University Press, 1980.

Mann, Thomas. *A Guide to Library Research Methods.* New York: Oxford University Press, 1987.

Nisbet, Robert. *Sociology as an Art Form.* New York: Oxford University Press, 1976.

Pitt, David C. *Using Historical Sources in Anthropology and Sociology.* New York: Holt, Rinehart and Winston, 1971.

Rombauer, Marjorie D. *Legal Problem Solving: Analysis, Research and Writing.* 2nd ed. St. Paul, Minn.: West Publishing Co., 1973.

Rose, Gerry. *Deciphering Sociological Research.* London: Macmillan, 1982.

Samuels, Warren J., ed. *The Craft of the Historian of Economic Thought.* Greenwich, Conn.: JAI Press, 1983.

Sanders, Chauncey. *An Introduction to Research in English Literary History.* New York: Macmillan 1952.

Shively, W. Phillips. *The Craft of Political Research: A Primer.* Englewood Cliffs, N.J.: Prentice-Hall, 1974.

Simon, Julian L. *Basic Research Methods in Social Science.* New York: Random House, 1969.

Slaven, Robert E. *Research Methods in Education: A Practical Guide.* Englewood Cliffs, N.J.: Prentice-Hall, 1984.

Smith, Barbara Leigh, et al. *Political Research Methods: Foundations and Techniques.* Boston: Houghton Mifflin, 1974.

Stoffle, Carla J., and Simon Carter. *Materials and Methods for Political Science Research.* New York: Libraryworks, 1979.

Taylor, Steven J., and Robert Bogdon. *Introduction to Qualitative Research Methods: The Search for Meaning.* 2nd ed. New York: Wiley, 1984.

Tilly, Charles. *As Sociology Meets History.* New York: Academic Press, 1981.

Wiersma, William. *Research Methods in Education: An Introduction..* Boston: Allyn and Bacon, 1985.

Wilson, John F., and Thomas P. Slavens. *Research Guide to Religious Studies.* Chicago: American Library Association, 1982.

Communication History Research

Altschull, J. Herbert. "The Journalist and Instant History: An Example of the Jackal Syndrome." *Journalism Quarterly* 50 (1973): 389-96.

Bashin, Bryan Jay. "How TV Stations Are Trashing History." *Columbia Journalism Review* (May/June 1985): 51-54.

Beasley, Maurine, and Richard R. Harlow. "Oral History: Additional Tool for Journalism Historians." *Journalism History* 7 (1980): 38-39.

Boyce, D. G. "Public Opinion and Historians." *History, the Journal of the Historical Association* (June 1978): 214-28.

Covert, Cathy. "Some Thoughts on Research." *Journalism History* 1 (1974): 32-33.

Dahl, Folke. "On Quoting Newspapers: A Problem and a Solution." *Journalism Quarterly* 25 (1984): 331-38.

Dahl, Hans Frederick. "The Art of Writing Broadcast History." *Gazette* 24: 2 (1978): 130-37.

Endres, Kitty. "Oral History: Preserving a Multimedia Past." *Matrix* 65 (Spring 1980): 8-10.

Henry, Susan J. "Private Lives: An Added Dimension for Understanding Journalism History." *Journalism History* 6 (1979): 98-102.

Housman, Robert T. "Journalism Research in Relation to Regional History." *Journalism Quarterly* 13 (1936): 402-06.

Mott, Frank Luther. "Evidences of Reliability in Newspapers and Periodicals in Historical Studies." *Journalism Quarterly* 21 (1944): 304-10.

Rapport, Leonard. "Fakes and Facsimiles: Problems of Identification." *American Antiquarian* 42 (January 1979): 13-58.

Salmon, Lucy Maynard. *The Newspaper and the Historian.* New York: Oxford University Press, 1923.

Small, Melvin, ed. *Public Opinion and Historians: Interdisciplinary Perspectives.* Detroit: Wayne State University Press, 1970.

Smith, Mary Ann Yodelis. "The Method of History, " Chapter 16, pp. 305-19, in Stempel and Westley (cited above).

Smith, Paul. *The Historian and Film.* Cambridge: Cambridge University Press, 1976.

Taft, William H. *Newspapers as Tools for Historians.* Columbia, Mo.: Lucas Brothers, 1970.

Vacha, John E. "The Student Newspaper as a Historical Source." *Social Educaton* 43 (January 1979): 35-36.

Approaches to History

Barker, John. *The Superhistorians: Makers of Our Past.* New York: Charles Scribner's Sons, 1982.

Billington, Ray Allen, comp. *Allan Nevins on History.* New York: Scribner, 1975.

Burckhardt, Jacob. *Judgments on History and Historians.* Boston: Beacon Press, 1958.

Butterfield, Herbert. *Writings on Christianity and History.* New York: Oxford University Press, 1979 (reprint).

Butterfield, Herbert. *Man on His Past: The Study of the History of Historical Scholarship.* Boston: Beacon Press, 1960.

Butterfield, Herbert. *The Whig Interpretation of History.* New York: Scribners, 1951 (reprint).

Cartwright, William H., and Richard L. Watson, eds. *The Reinterpretation of American History and Culture.* Washington: National Council for the Social Studies, 1973.

Collingwood, R.G. *Essays in the Philosophy of History.* Austin: University of Texas Press, 1965.

Commager, Henry Steeele. *The Search for a Usable Past.* New York: Alfred A. Knopf, 1967.

Conkin, Paul K., and John Higham, eds. *New Directions in American Intellectual History.* Baltimore: Johns Hopkins University Press, 1979.

Cunliffe, Marcus, and Robin Winks. *Pastmasters: Some Essays on American Historians.* New York: Harper and Row, 1969.

Curtis, L.P., Jr., ed. *The Historian's Workshop: Original Essays by Sixteen Historians.* New York: Alfred A. Knopf, 1970.

Donovan, Timothy Paul. *Historical Thought in America: Postwar Patterns.* Norman: University of Oklahoma Press, 1973.

Fogel, Robert William, and G. R. Elton. *Which Road to the Past? Two Views of History.* New Haven: Yale University Press, 1983.

Gay, Peter. *A Loss of Mastery: Puritan Historians in Colonial America.* Berkeley: University of California Press, 1966.

Grob, Gerald N., and George Athan Billias. *Interpretations of American History: Patterns and Perspectives.* 2 vols. New York: Free Press, 1967.

Hexter, Jack H. *On Historians: Reappraisals of Some of the Makers of Modern History.* Cambridge, Mass.: Harvard University Press, 1979.

Higham, John. *The Reconstruction of American History.* London: Hutchinson University Press, 1963.

Higham, John. *Writing American History: Essays on Modern Scholarship.* Bloomington: University of Indiana Press, 1970.

Hofstadter, Richard. *The Progressive Historians: Turner, Beard, Parrington.* New York: Alfred A. Knopf, 1968.

Hughes, H. Stuart. *History As Art and As Science.* New York: Harper and Row, Publishers, 1964.

Kraus, Michael. *The Writing of American History.* Norman: University of Oklahoma Press, 1968.

Levin, David. *History as Romantic Art: Bancroft, Prescott, Motley, and Parkman,* New York: AMS, 1959.

Nevins, Allan. *The Gateway to History.* rev. ed. Garden City, N.Y.: Anchor Books, 1962.

Patrides, C.A. *The Grand Design of God: The Literary Form of the Christian View of History.* London: Routledge and Kegan Paul, 1972.

Seligman, Edwin R. *The Economic Interpretation of History.* 2nd ed. New York: Gordian, 1966.

Skotheim, Robert Allen, ed. *The Historian and the Climate of Opinion.* Reading, Mass.: Addison-Wesley, 1969.

Stern, Fritz, ed. *The Varieties of History: From Voltaire to the Present.* New York: Random House, 1973.

Thompson, James W., and Bernard J. Holm. *A History of Historical Writing,* 2 vols. Gloucester, Mass.: Peter Smith, 1967.

Tillinghast, Pardon E. *The Specious Past: Historians and Others.* Reading, Mass.: Addison-Wesley, 1972.

Tosh, John. *The Pursuit of History: Aims, Methods and New Directions in the Study of Modern History.* London: Longman, 1986.

Trevelyan, George Macaulay. *Clio, A Muse and Other Essays.* Folcroft, Pa.: Folcroft, 1973.

Vaughan, Alden T., and George A. Billias. *Perspectives on Early American History: Essays in Honor of Richard B. Morris.* New York: Harper and Row, 1973.

Von Mises, Ludwig. *Theory and History.* New Haven, Conn.: Yale University Press, 1957.

Wagner, Anthony. *Pedigree and Progress: Essays in the Genealogical Interpretation of History.* Chichester: Phillimore, 1976.

Walsh, William H. *An Introduction to Philosophy of History.* rev. ed. Atlantic Highlands, N.J.: Humanities Press, 1976.

Wise, Gene. *American Historical Explanations.* Homewood, Ill.: Dorsey, 1973.

Wish, Harvey. *American Historians.* New York: Oxford University Press, 1962.

Approaches to Communication History

(Comment: Little substantial work has been done on perspectives and interpretations in communication history. The student should be aware of the following articles while recognizing that some are based primarily on the historian's intuition rather than on substantive research.)

Atwood, Roy. "New Directions for Journalism Historiography." *Journal of Communication Inquiry* 4: 1 (1978): 3-14.

Beasley, Maurine. "A Conversation with Sidney Kobre." *Journalism History* 1 (1981): 18-24.

Carey, James. "The Problem of Journalism History." *Journalism History* 1 (1974): 3-5 and 27.

"A Conversation with Alfred McClung Lee, " *Journalism History* 4 (1977): 2-7.

"A Conversation with Edwin Emery." *Journalism History* 7 (1980): 20-23.

"A Conversation with Harold L. Nelson." *Journalism History* 6 (1979): 66-69.

Covert, Catherine L. "Journalism History and Women's Experience: A Problem in Conceptual Change." *Journalism History* 8 (1981): 2-6.

Dennis, Everett E., and Claude-Jean Bertrand. "Seldes at 90: They Don't Give Pulitzers for that Kind of Criticism." *Journalism History* 7 (1980): 81-86 and 120.

Emery, Michael. "A Conversation with Robert W. Desmond." *Journalism History* 11 (1984): 11-17.

Emery, Michael. "The Writing of American Journalism History." *Journalism History* 10 (1983): 38-43.

Erickson, John E. "One Approach to the Cultural History of Reporting." *Journalism History* 2 (1975): 40-41 and 43.

Garcia, Hazel. "'What a Buzzel is This...about Kentuck?' New Approaches and an Application." *Journalism History* 3 (1976): 11-15 and 19.

Gilbert, David A. "Eric W. Allen: Journalism Educator and Historian."*Journalism History* 2 (1975): 50-53.

Huntzicker, William. "Historians and the American Frontier Press." *American Journalism* 5 (1988): 28-47.

Hynes, Terry. "A Conversation with Leonard Levy." *Journalism History* 7 (1980): 96-103.

Jowett, Garth S. "Toward a History of Communication." *Journalism History* 2 (1975): 34-37.

Kahan, Robert S. "Historians: Our Critics, Craft and Mental Health." *Journalism History* 6 (1979): 70-72.

Kobre, Sidney. "The Sociological Approach in Journalism History." *Journalism Quarterly* 22 (1945): 12-22.

McKerns, Joseph P. "The Limits of Progressive History." *Journalism History* 4 (1977): 88-92.

Marzolf, Marion. "American Studies & Ideas for Media Historians?" *Journalism History* 5 (1978): 13-16.

Marzolf, Marion. "Operationalizing Carey -- An Approach to the Cultural History of Journalism." *Journalism History* 2 (1975): 42-43.

Nevins, Allan. "American Journalism and Its Historical Treatment." *Journalism Quarterly* 36 (1959): 411-22.

Nord, David Paul, and Harold L. Nelson. "The Logic of Historical Research," Chapter 15: 278-304, in Stempel and Westley (cited previously).

Park, Robert E. "The Natural History of the Newspaper," pp. 80-98 in Park, Ernest W. Burgess and Robert D. McKenzie, *The City*. Chicago: University of Chicago Press, 1925.

Schwarzlose, Richard A. "A Conversation with Frederick S. Siebert." *Journalism History* 5 (1978): 106-09 and 123.

Schwarzlose, Richard A. "First Things First: A Proposal." *Journalism History* 2 (1975): 38-39.

Sloan, Wm. David. "Examining the 'Dark Ages' Concept: The Federalist-Republican Press as a Model." *Journal of Communication Inquiry* 7 (1982): 105-19.

Sloan, Wm. David. "Historians and the American Press, 1900-1945: Working Profession or Big Business?" *American Journalism* 3 (1986): 150-62.

Sloan, Wm. David. "Historians and the Party Press: 130 Years of Scholarship." *Studies in Journalism and Mass Communication* 1 (1983): 27-32.

Sloan, Wm. David, and Thomas A. Schwatz. "Historians and Freedom of the Press, 1690-1801: Libertarian or Limited?" *American Journalism* 5 (1988): 159-78.

Stevens, John D., and Hazel Dicken Garcia. *Communication History*. Beverly Hills, Calif.: Sage, 1980.

Stevens, John D., and Donald L. Shaw. "Research Needs in Communications History." *Journalism Quarterly* 45 (1968): 547-49.

Taft, William H. "Let's Probe Your State's Newspaper History." *Journalism Educator*, 19: 4 (1964): 115-18.

Ward, Jean. "Interdisciplinary Research and Journalism Historians." *Journalism History* 5 (1978): cover and 17-19.

Weaver, David H. "Frank Luther Mott and the Future of Journalism History." *Journalism History* 2 (1975): 44-47.

Writing and Forms

Barzun, Jacques. *Simple and Direct: A Rhetoric for Writers*. New York: Harper and Row, 1975.

Canary, Robert H., and Henry Kozicki, eds. *The Writing of History: Literary Form and Historical Understanding*. Madison: University of Wisconsin Press, 1978.

The Chicago Manual of Style, 13th ed. Chicago: University of Chicago Press, 1982.

Follett, Wilson. *Modern American Usage*. New York: Hill and Wang, 1966.

Lottinville, Savoie. *The Rhetoric of History*. Norman: University of Oklahoma Press, 1976.

Modern Language Association of America. *The MLA Style Sheet*. 2nd ed. New York: MLA, 1973.

Sears, Donald A. *Harbrace Guide to the Library and the Research Paper*. 3rd ed. New York: Harcourt Brace Jovanovich, 1973.

Strunk, William, and E.B. White. *The Elements of Style*. 2nd ed. New York: Macmillan, 1973.

Turabian, Kate L. *A Manual of Writers of Term Papers, Theses, and Dissertations*. 5th ed. Chicago: University of Chicago Press, 1987.

Index of Subjects

Index of Names